MEDIATION IN FAMILY DISPUTES

Second Edition

For Simon, Adam and Sara
and my parents.

Mediation in Family Disputes

Principles of Practice

Second Edition

Marian Roberts

arena

Published by
Arena
Ashgate Publishing Limited
Gower House
Croft Road
Aldershot
Hants GU11 3HR
England

Ashgate Publishing Company
Old Post Road
Brookfield
Vermont 05036
USA

British Library Cataloguing in Publication Data
Roberts, Marian, 1943–
    Mediation in family disputes: principles of practice. –
    2nd ed.
    1. Family mediation – England 2. Domestic relations – England
    3. Divorce – Law and legislation – England 4. Family
    mediation – Wales 5. Domestic relations – Wales 6. Divorce –
    Law and legislation – Wales
    I. Title
    346.4'2'0166

ISBN 1 85742 318 6 Hardback
ISBN 1 85742 315 1 Paperback

Typeset in Palatino by Raven Typesetters, Chester and printed and bound in Great Britain by Hartnolls Ltd, Bodmin.

Contents

List of cases

Table of statutes

Preface

The most valuable knowledge about mediation is that gained from doing it. Each session is a fresh challenge so that, whatever one's accumulated experience and understanding, the task does not get easier. On the contrary, the difficulty of mediating well becomes more apparent. Therefore I want to say how much I owe to all the couples with whom I have worked and who have taught and continue to teach me so much. I would like to thank my colleagues at the South East London Family Conciliation Bureau for all that I have learned in working with them and in our many discussions and seminars. I have also gained much from my involvement in the training programme for mediators at the Jewish Family Mediation Service, where it became necessary for me to clarify and organize my ideas about principle and practice.

I should like especially to thank Gwynn Davis, whose idea it was that I should write this book. His research and writings over many years have illuminated thinking about family mediation. Our collaboration in research into consumers' experience of mediation has taught me much. I am indebted too to all our informants and in particular to those whose words appear in the Prologue and Epilogue. They bring home the wider themes, as well as the uniqueness of each predicament in which the mediator becomes involved.

Gwynn Davis, Tony Gerard and Fred Gibbons were kind enough to read the manuscript; I am grateful to them for the care they took in making many informed and valuable suggestions for its improvement. Of course, the views expressed in the book and all its limitations remain my own. I am grateful too to Susan Hunt who undertook the unenviable task of transcribing my handwritten first draft into immaculate typescript in record time.

Simon Roberts knows more about mediation than most. Without his encouragement and unstinting support at every level, I could not have managed. I dedicate this book to him.

Marian Roberts 1988

Preface to second edition

Since 1988, when the first edition of this book was published, there has been a transformation in the growth and status of family mediation in the UK. Then innovatory and on the margin of significance in relation to family dispute resolution, family mediation is now the officially recommended mainstream approach, embodied in statute, endorsed for public funding for the first time, and enthusiastically embraced by large numbers of eager potential practitioners, including many solicitors. This new centrality could leave both the public and the integrity of the mediation process vulnerable. That is why there needs to be vigilance – in relation to the essential ethical principles that distinguish mediation, and in relation to the emergent regulatory framework for the protection both of high standards and of the autonomy and independence of professional practice. In this way, there will be proper recognition that the value and effectiveness of mediation lies not only in the outcomes it produces, important though these are, but in how it produces them.

Having practised as a family mediator since 1981, and also having been actively involved through my work at National Family Mediation (NFM) in major professional developments over the past seven years, I am increasingly reminded of the heavy responsibility of mediators. We enter, as strangers – for however limited a period and however modest an objective – the most private, intimate, individual, complex and mysterious lives of others, at times of stress and upheaval. I find this work as demanding as it is satisfying, not only because one's own expectations of achievement grow higher, but also because, perhaps unexpectedly, instead of becoming toughened by exposure to the pain of family breakdown, one becomes increasingly moved.

My thanks go to all my colleagues at NFM and at the South-East London Family Mediation Bureau. I am especially grateful to Elizabeth Lawson QC, Chair of the Family Law Bar Association (and my erstwhile pupil master), who made meticulous amendments to Chapter 3 on the legal context, bringing me up to date and challenging my perspectives. Susan Hunt, to my huge relief and gratitude, resumed her role as careful transcriber of my hand-written script to disk.

Simon Roberts made indispensable suggestions for improvements throughout, and as ever, encouraged and sustained me.

Again, the views expressed in the book, any errors and all its limitations remain my own.

Marian Roberts
8 September 1996

Prologue

... I simply wanted some kind of reasonableness to operate, recognizing the marriage had ended but seeking to achieve, you know, an ending in a reasonable manner. *Non-resident father*

One needs a neutral Guardian Angel to step in – someone not legal, not family, who has no vested interest but is very aware of both sides. *Mother with residence*

We thought there should be something in between two people talking and a court hearing. We thought there must be something in between, surely ... we didn't want something as drastic as court ... when it gets as far as court it's taken out of your hands. So we felt that wasn't satisfactory ... but the two, one to one, wasn't working. So we needed something in between. *Father with residence*

Well, we weren't talking really. We were very hostile to each other then. And I think we needed somebody to act as intermediary, to break the ice and to get us talking. *Non-resident mother*

1   What is family mediation?

> The varieties of dispute settlement, and the socially sanctioned choices in any culture, communicate the ideals people cherish, their perceptions of themselves, and the quality of their relationships with others. They indicate whether people wish to avoid or encourage conflict, suppress it, or resolve it amicably. Ultimately the most basic values of society are revealed in its dispute-settlement procedures. (Jerold S. Auerbach, 1983, *Justice Without Law?*, pp.3–4)

The emergence in the UK of mediation as a recognized approach to settling family disputes following family breakdown has been, in many ways, a remarkable development. Its adoption involves a new and evolving application of an old method of settling quarrels, perhaps better suited than any other to the special characteristics of family disputes.

Mediation is also based on certain values which justify its use, both for the disputants and for those who choose to become mediators. These are summed up by comparison with the way people are treated under existing forms of intervention:

> It strikes me that if you have some kind of grading scale for your institutions, like courts, schools, and hospitals, as to which gave the participants the most adult setting, it might be interesting to see how different institutions rank. Are you told what to do or asked what you want to do? Are you made to wait or is your time valued? Are you allowed to know what is going on or are you kept in the dark? Are you powerful or powerless? Are decisions made for you or do you get to make the decisions? Are you treated as a human being or are those qualities not considered? One of the things that strikes me in mediation is that it comes out much higher on that scale than many of our institutions and I think that is why it works. (Davis, 1984, p.54).

This standard of 'adult behaviour' goes to the heart of mediation. Respect for the parties' capacity and authority to make their own decisions is paramount in mediation, as is respect for their perceptions and values. This is necessary if the mediator is to have proper regard for the right of the parties, whatever the difficulties, to be the architects of their own agreements, and if party competence and control, as the distinguishing characteristic of mediation, is to have any meaning. Norms of fairness, mutual respect and equity of exchange inform the expectations of adult behaviour that underlie the practice of mediation (Fuller, 1971; Rubin and Brown, 1975). Decision-making capacity is what defines this standard of adulthood, and is therefore what distinguishes mediation both from other forms of dispute-resolution (such as lawyer negotiation and adjudication) and from other forms of professional intervention (such as social work).

Until relatively recently, couples (married or cohabiting) had a limited choice of methods to sort out their differences in the wake of the dissolution of their relationship. They could negotiate together and make their own decisions on the vital and interrelated issues that confronted them on parting – issues relating to their children, their home, maintenance payments and divorce itself. Some couples, perhaps managing on their own or with the help of the local vicar, doctor, respected friend or family member, work out mutually satisfactory arrangements. Although no statistics are available, many couples do not manage to engage in face-to-face discussions, let alone discussion free from the tumult of anger, bullying and rowing. Perhaps in many cases, matters are just left unresolved – to the satisfaction of none of those involved, especially the children (Mitchell, 1985).

The solution in most cases has been for each partner to consult a lawyer, and for the two lawyers to negotiate on their clients' behalf, reach agreement if possible or, if not, hand over to a judge the responsibility of making decisions. The judge then makes an order, which is imposed on the parties, on the basis of the facts before him/her.

Therefore, for couples unable to reach agreement on their own, the only alternative was to transfer responsibility for negotiating and decision-making to third parties – lawyers and/or judges. Then another choice became available. The establishment in 1978 of the first services of family mediation in the UK gave separating and divorcing couples who were unable or unwilling to manage entirely on their own, yet who did not wish to relinquish responsibility for making their own decisions, the opportunity to meet together on neutral territory, and with the help of a third party – the mediator – work out and agree their own arrangements by means of a negotiating process structured to achieve this. The crucial point was that the parties themselves retained authority and responsibility for reaching and making their own decisions.

So mediation emerged to fill a space hitherto unoccupied, which none of the existing services – welfare, advisory or therapeutic on the one hand, or lawyers and the courts on the other – could, by their nature, have filled.

Mediatory intervention neither can nor should seek to substitute for these other services. Mediation generally presupposes that the parties have obtained separate legal advice. Being properly informed about legal rights is vitally important if people are to negotiate fairly. Counselling or therapeutic help may also enable a party to engage more effectively in negotiation, by alleviating incapacitating emotional stress. Mediation must be distinguished clearly from these other forms of intervention, which offer quite different kinds of help.

The development in the late 1970s of mediation in the sphere of family disputes (as well as in the field of community and neighbourhood quarrels) in the UK, and a decade earlier in the USA, represents the modern discovery of a mode of dispute-resolution that has a long-established anthropological and historical heritage (Roberts, 1979; Rwezaura, 1984; Acland, 1995). With this legacy of cross-cultural practice experience (the 'second oldest profession', according to Kolb, 1985, p.1!) and large and distinguished body of knowledge, mediation has been readily adaptable to the specific conditions of joint decision-making in the context of family breakdown. Practitioners in this field can learn a great deal about mediation and how it works from the writings of those who have studied it firsthand and come to understand its processes and the role of the mediator on the basis of their empirical observations (for example, Gulliver, 1979).

Handbooks for family mediators have been in short supply, and until recently, those that existed were North American (Coogler, 1978; Haynes, 1981a; Lemmon, 1985; Saposnek, 1983). While these contain many valuable insights for the practising mediator, they have been of limited use in the UK. In the first place, the US focus was primarily on the resolution of property and financial disputes (for example, Coogler, 1978; Haynes, 1981a), while the British concern was primarily, though not exclusively, disputes involving children. Secondly, where the focus was on children, the authors had grafted mediation on to their practice of family therapy, and their approach to mediation therefore reflected this professional appropriation (for example, Saposnek, 1983). More recently, Haynes's (1993) handbook on all-issues mediation, adapted by Fisher and Greenslade to the British legal, social and cultural context, is designed to be used in conjunction with training, professional regulation and insurance.

Family mediation has had to emerge from its innovative, empirical grass roots as an autonomous, professional practice independent of other professional interventions in the field of separation and divorce, such as therapy, counselling, social work and legal practice. This has necessitated the clarification and conceptualization of the nature of the mediation process and its distinctive features, as well as its essential professional and ethical operating principles in relation to family disputes. Good practice thus requires mediators to have not only a clear understanding of their primary goals and how to achieve them, but most important of all, a knowledge of the limitations of the process and of their role. Only then can there be practice of a kind that has proper regard for priorities and boundaries, and which is likely to be applied appropriately and therefore effectively. Kressel (1985, p.4) appraises the challenges involved in the settlement of divorce disputes as follows: 'The orchestration of a constructive process of divorce negotiation must be considered one of the most demanding tasks that rational beings are expected to perform.' The scale of the task therefore requires a modest approach with a full awareness of the obstacles. Nor, of course, is mediation a panacea or the only determinant of success in so far as the outcome of divorce is concerned. Many factors – personal, social, economic, as well as time itself – are influential.

As we come to mediation from different professional backgrounds and are trained in different settings, it is very important that there is common understanding of the process and its principles, however varied models of practice may be. No existing professional background can claim a monopoly of expertise in this field (Davis, 1983). The actual practice of mediation in family disputes is gruelling as well as creative – intellectually, emotionally and imaginatively. The dynamics of the process are fraught and many-layered.

Enthusiasm for mediation and expectations of its success are higher than ever. We therefore need to be clearer than ever about what mediation is and what it can achieve, as well as the limitations and obstacles that might render its use inappropriate.

Defining mediation

Mediation is a form of intervention in which a third party – the mediator – assists the parties to a dispute to negotiate over the issues which divide them. The mediator has no stake in the dispute, and is not identified with any of the competing interests involved. The mediator has no power to impose a settlement on the parties, who retain authority for making their own decisions.

The terms 'mediation' and 'conciliation' were often used interchangeably in the UK in the context of family disputes. They have different definitions in a labour relations context, where mediation is associated with the making of formal recommendations (ACAS, no date, para. 29). However, the term 'conciliation' has been used loosely to embrace a general approach to mitigating the harmful effects of family conflict. It was also used to cover a range of differing practices that were part of court procedure, as well as the voluntary and statutory services operating independently of the court. 'Conciliation' has been used to describe the conciliatory approaches of court personnel, such as in the preparation of welfare reports by court welfare officers, as well as the constructive bilateral negotiations conducted by some lawyers negotiating on behalf of their clients. In addition, the Family Law Bar Association set up what it called a Conciliation Board, which is in fact a document-based scheme of arbitration to settle disputes over property and finance. As in the USA a couple of decades ago, 'conciliation' in the UK became a 'buzzword' covering an array of different conflict-intervention processes and styles. For the public, the misunderstanding has been compounded by the frequent confusion of conciliation with *reconciliation*, which is concerned with the reuniting of estranged couples. Therefore, to ensure clarity, the term 'mediation' was adopted in the late 1980s because of its precise reference to a specific form of third-party intervention in the settling of disputes (in the family arena). The object of the process is consensual joint decision-making, authority for which is retained by the parties themselves.

What is mediation?

The most important point to remember when discussing mediation is that it is nothing more or less than a device for facilitating the negotiation process. Negotiations can and do occur without a mediator but mediation can never occur in the absence of negotiation. (Cormick, 1981)

These words, although written in connection with environmental mediation, are no less apposite in the context of family mediation. It is where the terms 'negotiation' and 'bargaining' are used interchangeably that misunderstanding is created. A failure to distinguish between the two processes could lead to the view that negotiation is too limited to accommodate the special circumstances of family breakdown, such as heightened feelings of distress and the needs of the children (for example, Shepherd et al., 1984, p.21). It is asserted, for example, that 'a straightforward bargaining model risks treating the children as inanimate possessions' (Robinson and Parkinson, 1985, p.375). Therefore, it is argued that you have to look to insights of the family systems approach and the techniques of family therapy in order to cater adequately for the special needs of those undergoing divorce or separation. It is also the reason why 'negotiation/bargaining' is relegated to a relatively minor and late phase in the conciliation process (Fisher, 1986).

'Bargaining' and 'negotiation' are not synonymous. 'Bargaining' and its associations with the cut and thrust of the marketplace, refers to the series of offers and counter-offers, demands and counter-demands, the 'trading' of concessions, which have limited applicability in this context, as the parents themselves would be the first to protest. 'Negotiation', on the other hand, is much broader in scope. Negotiation involves processes of communication, information exchange and learning. These are the means by which the dispute between the parties is placed, gradually, in a context of increasing

knowledge about all the circumstances, pressures, feelings, attitudes, perceptions and needs that surround it (Gulliver, 1979). Because this knowledge
leads to increasing understanding, there is a lessening of competition and
hostility, and therefore an adjustment and modification of expectations,
demands and preferences. A brief and final bargaining stage may be
included once all the groundwork of communication and learning has been
accomplished. As has been observed in another context, though also involving marital stress: 'persons mutually at odds are apt to cut each other off
intentionally or otherwise from the very information that might lead to a
healing of their differences' (Mayer and Timms, 1970, p.88).

If negotiation is successful, this learning process can lead to greater co-
ordination, even possibly co-operation, between the parties, resulting in a
mutually agreed settlement (see Gulliver, 1971, p.20). Negotiation is all about
learning. The parties begin to learn more about each other and their dispute.
This necessarily involves knowledge about feelings and the children who are
central to the dispute. In mediation, the parties also learn to negotiate, and so
to talk instead of fight.

In very simple terms, therefore, mediation is about getting the parties to
talk to one another again. Talking is, after all, one of the most important
means of avoiding trouble (Roberts, 1979, p.67). Talking provides an opportunity for the expression and release of feelings such as anger and bitterness.
However, the therapeutic effects of the expression of strong emotion must be
delicately balanced against the harmful effects of saying too much. Some
things are better left unsaid. Talking also provides the means of discussing an
end to the dispute and of reaching a settlement. Before the break-up, the
family made its own decisions on the important matters that affected it, and
settled its disputes in its own way (Maidment, 1984). Except in cases of risk to
the health and well-being of children, the autonomy of this 'self-contained
disputing arena' is not questioned (Dingwall and Eekelaar, 1986, p.55).
Conflict and distress interrupt the capacity to communicate, so that at a time
when it is difficult for people to talk to one another, but also when it is
imperative for vital decisions to be made, re-establishing communication
becomes of paramount importance.

This leads us briefly to outline the role of the mediator in the process of
negotiation. If, as we have seen, the essence of the process is the communication exchange between the parties, we also see that the mediator's task is to
facilitate this exchange. The mediator's role is therefore auxiliary to that of
the parties. Indirectly and unobtrusively, the mediator should clarify and
focus on the parties' own negotiations, and assist them in finding areas of
agreement and compromise. This requires a skilled exercise of creativity and
control, without being either passive or directive.

The main objectives of the mediator are:

- to re-establish contact between the parties;
- to provide a safe and neutral forum where the parties may meet face to face;
- to provide within that forum an impartial presence supportive of negotiation;
- to facilitate the exchange of information between the parties within a structured framework;
- to help the parties to examine their common interests and objectives, and the possibilities for reaching agreements that are practicable, acceptable and beneficial to themselves and their children.

The characteristics of mediation

The process of mediation has four fundamental and universal characteristics (McCrory, 1981, p.56):

- the impartiality of the mediator;
- the voluntariness of the process (because the mediator has no power to impose a settlement);
- the confidentiality of the relationship between the mediator and the parties;
- the procedural flexibility available to the mediator.

It is these characteristics that make mediation, as a method of dispute settlement, of value to the disputants. McCrory goes as far as to say that if these characteristics are altered or if one or more is absent, then the process cannot be characterized legitimately as mediation. These characteristics will be examined in more detail in the following chapters.

The premises of mediation

There are three requirements without which mediation cannot occur.

A willingness to co-operate

Without a modicum of willingness to co-operate, however reluctant, a mediated solution will not be possible. If people understand what mediation involves and enter the process voluntarily, they cannot do so without being prepared at least to *attempt* to negotiate. This does not mean that there need be an absence of conflict or hostility. In consumer research (Davis and

Roberts, 1988), it was found that although some people did not believe co-operation would be possible because of the degree of hostility, they were prepared to try mediation, and often managed to reach agreement on specific issues even against a background of continuing conflict. In many cases, this willingness to co-operate may be overlaid by other, perhaps competing, motives. One party, for example, may hope for a reconciliation, and may seek to use mediation, initially at any rate, to pursue that object. One party may want to use the occasion to resume fighting. If there is no desire to co-operate at all, then mediation becomes impossible.

Competence

The presumption of the competence of the parties to make their own decisions themselves is fundamental to mediation. However laid low people may be by circumstances and personal vulnerability, this does not mean that they are ill or incapable. In fact, mediation, by offering the parties the opportunity to take control of their own affairs, may provide them with the means of encouraging self-determination and autonomy and of enhancing adult and parental responsibility (Folberg, 1984). The implicit expectations of mediation – reasonableness, adult behaviour and mutual respect – are of most value precisely because circumstances may be bringing out the worst in people, who may be behaving childishly and selfishly, may be aware of this and its effect on their children, and yet have been unable to do anything about it until now.

This presumption of competence includes the premise that parents love their children, know their children better than anybody else, and are best able to decide what is in their interests, even though they may genuinely differ in their views about this. Their agreement over the arrangements for their children is regarded as the best safeguard for the children's welfare. It is continuing conflict between parents that has been shown to be detrimental to children (Wallerstein and Kelly, 1980; Cockett and Tripp, 1994).

There is no evidence to support the view that only the better educated can benefit from mediated negotiation. Whatever their social, economic or educational background, most people, given the opportunity, have the capacity to articulate their concerns and wishes, engage in discussion, and make their own decisions.

Equality of bargaining power

Even where there is a presumption of competence, mediation may be inappropriate where differences of power between the parties are substantial. The mediator has a fundamental ethical responsibility to end a mediation session when it appears that unfairness may result because of the exercise of duress by one party over another, or where cultural considerations deny women the capacity to negotiate in their own right at all (see pages 120–121 and 155–61; on the need of the mediator to avoid the coercive exercise of power, see Chapters 2 and 7).

Distinguishing mediation from other forms of intervention

What distinguishes mediation from other forms of dispute-settlement is, as we have seen, that in mediation, the authority for decision-making lies with the parties themselves.

Arbitration and adjudication both involve an appeal to a third party to impose a decision, because the parties themselves cannot agree. In arbitration, the parties invite the arbitrator to make this decision, and agree to honour the decision even though it is not legally binding. In adjudication, the judge imposes his/her decision, not by invitation of the parties, but by virtue of the office from which he/she derives authority (Roberts, 1979). Adjudication usually follows a hearing attended by formal rules and procedures, and the parties are represented by professional advocates. The order made by the judge is in favour of one of the parties, who is regarded as the winner. The loser is legally bound by the order, the implementation of which carries all the authority and sanction of the court. One professional mediator has summed up the differences as follows:

- *mediation* 'involves helping people to decide for themselves';
- *adjudication and arbitration* 'involves helping people by deciding for them'. (Meyer, 1960, p.164)

Negotiation by lawyers

Mediation must be distinguished from those negotiations, however conciliatory, conducted by lawyers. Many matrimonial disputes are formally settled by legal advisers representing the parties. These bilateral processes are conducted by professionals (whether solicitors or barristers), who act on their clients' behalf. The parties are not present, therefore they do not participate in the negotiations, the pace, substance and tone of which are controlled by the lawyers. In mediation, the parties conduct the negotiations themselves, and reach their own agreements with the help of the mediator.

Empirical research on lawyer negotiations is limited, most studies being based on (often self-serving) self-reports of lawyers following completed negotiations. Observational studies of actual negotiations are rare. North

American research on divorce negotiations has found these to be 'depressingly consistent' with negotiations in a variety of legal contexts (Menkel-Meadow, 1993a, p.369). The findings showed a desire not to bargain too hard, and to settle cases quickly for the 'going rate'. This was the case especially where lawyers were 'repeat players' with each other and sought to reach 'standardized solutions'. There was little evidence of problem-solving or focusing on the individual needs and interests of particular clients. The general evidence is that cases settle quickly, with little 'negotiation intensity' (often settling on the basis of first offers) or bargaining, of either a principled or unprincipled nature, as both sides try 'to cut a quick deal' that is often 'fairer' to the lawyers' payment incentives than to particular clients (Menkel-Meadow, 1993a, p.371).

In the UK, the vast majority of matrimonial legal disputes are settled by means of lawyer negotiations, which are private (see Chapter 11 for discussion of the impact of power imbalances on lawyer negotiation) and occur largely within the framework of litigation (Davis *et al*, 1994; Roberts, 1995a).

While some lawyers do undoubtedly exacerbate conflict, the combativeness of lawyers should not be exaggerated. The Code of Practice of the Solicitors Family Law Association, for example, reflects an awareness of the impact solicitors have on relations between their clients, and recognizes the need for solicitors to adopt conciliatory and settlement-making approaches in the interests of all the parties, including the children.

Mediation and social work

Differences between mediation and social work may appear less obvious than the differences between mediation and the processes of the adversary legal system, but they are no less significant.

Location of authority

The source of the social worker's authority has three possible locations:

- the employing agency;
- the law (for example, in the case of probation officers);
- the professional expertise derived from a specialist body of knowledge and skill.

The authority of the mediator derives from a tacit understanding between the parties and the mediator. The parties consent to participate with the mediator in the mediation process. The mediator is only there with the permission of the parties. To the extent that they are aware of their right not to participate if they so choose, the parties retain ultimate control.

The attributes and the skills of the mediator in promoting communication and assisting decision-making comprise a second source of authority. Furthermore, as Fuller (1971, p.315) has pointed out, one must not ignore the fact that 'the mediator's power may largely derive from the simple fact that he is there and that his help is badly needed'. Therefore, the mediator's authority may derive as much from the 'urgency' of the situation as from any special gifts of the mediator.

Self-determination

The ideal of self-determination as one of social work's fundamental values (McDermott, 1975) may appear to resemble superficially the 'party control' that is the central tenet of mediation, but 'self-determination' in social work practice refers primarily to the way the client may participate in the solution to problems and to the fact that the social worker will refrain from interfering, except 'in essentials' (McDermott, 1975, p.144, quoting Alan Keith-Lucas). In other words, the client is subject to the ultimate controlling authority vested in the social worker. The use of the term 'client' itself underlines the dependence inherent in the social work relationship, implying as it does an inability to identify one's own needs or discriminate between a range of possibilities (Mayer and Timms, 1970, p.15).

'Self-determination' is also used to refer to an increase in psychological insight gained by clients into their own needs and motives as a means towards, or condition of, furthering their own development (McDermott, 1975, p.134).

The precepts of mediation are, in contrast, the competence of the parties to define their disputes and assert their own meanings, their right and power to make their own decisions, and the opportunity to do so. The mediator is subject to their authority, not vice versa.

Expertise

The expertise of social workers is claimed to lie in the body of knowledge and skills from which their professional authority derives. In mediation in family disputes, the expertise of the mediator lies in a method of dispute-resolution that recognizes and protects the right of the parties to make their own decisions in matters over which they are expert – for example, their own children's lives. Where the parties themselves lack the expertise necessary for informed decision-making (for example, about legal, tax or welfare rights affairs), it is the responsibility of the mediator to ensure that this is included in the process. The expertise of the mediator, involving as it does no authority to impose an outcome or to give advice, determines the unique, even paradoxical nature of the professional relationship of the mediator with the parties. Only in the most exceptional circumstances should mediators find it necessary to contemplate asserting superior authority and using their specialist knowledge (for example, on child development) in order to influence the direction of negotiations.

Competence

The welfare ideology of social workers, and their proper preoccupation with pathological behaviour under the public law such as child abuse, occupies a different world from the decision-making processes of mediation, with its presumption of competence within the private law sphere of divorce where parental competence is not legally challenged. The parties to mediation and their children – to apply the Finer Report (1974, para.4.285) – should not be seen as 'clients' and still less as 'patients', but as 'subjects of rights', not as 'objects of assistance'. There is a view that the tensions and sorrows of divorce may result in a 'diminished capacity to the parent' (Wallerstein and Kelly, 1980, p.36). However, a preoccupation with one's own troubles is not a disqualification from competence to negotiate, nor a good reason to relinquish decision-making responsibility to others. Mediation should not be used by social workers as an excuse for extending surveillance over separating or divorcing couples and their families under the guise of 'child protection'.

Impartiality

Alliances between social workers and their clients are frequently established as one of the ways of building up trusting relationships, but a mediator must remain impartial between the two parties to the dispute, and must never form, or be perceived to form, an alliance with one or the other.

Assessments

Whatever the limitations of objective assessment in a child care context (Sutton, 1981), assessments are made by social workers as part of the process of determining strategies of treatment or action.

The concept of assessment is inappropriate in mediation, firstly because of its inseparability from the treatment which is carried out on its basis: 'assessment is impossible without treatment; treatment is an assessment' (Sutton, 1986, p.69); secondly, because it inevitably shifts the locus of knowledge, and therefore of power, from the parties to the person making the assessment (see, for example, Walker, 1986). Until recently, assessments in social work have been confidential, and remain so in a number of circumstances, for example where they are made by health professionals or where serious harm might result (Access to Personal Files Act 1987 and DoH Regulations and Circular LAC (89)2). In mediation everything is out in the open. If a record is kept it is of the bare facts and outcome and is not withheld from the parties. In fact some mediators encourage the parties to record such details themselves.

Short-term work

One of the features of family mediation is that it is time-limited. On average, children-only issues are mediated in one to three sessions, and four to six sessions cover all issues – financial, property as well as children issues. The short-term focus of the work is on the whole, in contrast with the longer-term nature of social work, involving, as it often does, building up the relationship between the social worker and their client. Some social work is, of course, short-term or 'task-centred', for example the provision of material assistance, though even a request for material help may be interpreted by some social workers as the 'presenting' problem (Mayer and Timms, 1970).

Focusing on the future

The mediation process looks to the future, for it recognizes that the past cannot be negotiated over. As Gulliver (1979) demonstrates, change is intrinsic to the dynamic process of exploration that negotiations involve. The mediation process itself involves a movement away from sterile interpersonal quarrelling and recrimination towards an examination of future options. While information about the past may well be relevant to an understanding of the dispute and should not be excluded, it should, in any event, come from the parties themselves. The mediator is not concerned to examine what went wrong, and so will often have to deliberately steer exchanges away from the minefield of the past, over which there will inevitably be differences of perspective; the facts of the past cannot be negotiated over, they can only be adjudicated over (see page 26). In social work practice, on the other hand, the case history, by definition retrospective in outlook, is an important tool for making judgements and determining strategies for the present and future.

Until 1989, when the principle of openness in relation to assessment, decision-making and intervention was implemented by giving social work clients the right of access to any personal information held on file, the case history was the property of the professionals, and was not available to those it discussed. While this change of attitude and approach to openness has been welcomed as a most significant development in social work, the low number of clients who have requested access raises questions. Several reasons for this have been suggested, including the number of grounds for excluding clients from access (for example, exemptions to protect sources of information and third parties), fears that files can be edited, lack of knowledge of the right of access to personal files, and difficulties of access for family members.

Mediation and family therapy

Mediation and family therapy are forms of intervention that are quite different, both in objective and in method. (For a full debate on this topic in *Mediation Quarterly*, see Roberts, 1992; Haynes, 1992; Amundson and Fong, 1993; also Robinson, 1991; Walker and Robinson, 1992.)

Family therapy has been described as a way of 'conceptualizing the cause and cure of psychiatric problems' (Haley and Hoffman, 1967, p.v). In the view of the family therapist, the 'site of pathology' is the family rather than the individual, and the set of relationships within which that individual is embedded (Minuchin, 1974). The scope of family therapy is wide. It involves not only 'a technical approach towards treatment . . . it is also a theoretical view of pathology giving rise to a whole range of treatment possibilities' (Walrond-Skinner, 1976, p.6).

The primary objective of family therapy is to modify 'dysfunctional' behaviour. It does this by challenging and changing the organization of the family in such a way that the perceptions and experiences of the family members change (Minuchin, 1974, p.13). Therefore, the basic assumption of family therapy is of psychiatric dysfunction in the family that requires treatment.

As far as mediation is concerned, marital breakdown and the disputes that arise from it are not regarded as symptoms of psychopathology, nor are the parties regarded as suffering from incapacities that render therapeutic intervention necessary; nor is it the object of mediation to challenge the perceptions of the parties. On the contrary, the parties are regarded as competent both to define the issues for themselves and to come to their own decisions. Their perceptions are seen as essential to an accurate understanding of their dispute and its context. The focus of mediation is modest, limited as it is to the negotiated settlement of specific substantive issues in dispute. If the process and outcomes of mediation lead to a reduction of bitterness and conflict in the relationship between the parties, then the process can be therapeutic in the widest sense, but that is a bonus, not the primary object.

The second fundamental difference between mediation and family therapy is that the therapist assumes a leadership role (overt or covert) (Minuchin, 1974, p.111; Walrond-Skinner, 1976, p.37); the mediator does not. Whatever method of family therapy is adopted (for example, Minuchin's structural approach, Haley's strategic approach, the Palo Alto Group of the Mental Research Institute's brief therapy, Epstein and Loos' dialogical constructivist approach or the Milan model of systemic family therapy), all adopt a mode of intervention that places the therapist as knowing expert in a position of exceptional power in relation to the family. This result is deliberate, for as one leading family therapist has stated, it is only from a position of leadership that the therapist has the freedom to manipulate the therapeutic system: 'The therapeutic contract must recognize the therapist's position as an expert in experimental social manipulation' (Minuchin, 1974, p.140). The systemic approach of the Milan method of family therapy exemplifies the leadership role of the therapist: 'When conducting the session the therapist must immediately demonstrate that he will lead it and dictate its form and pace' (Campbell et al., no date, p.16). Power also lies in the therapist's claim to have the monopoly on meaning. This monopoly involves explaining the problem in terms of the therapist's conceptual framework, which determines the diagnosis and method of treatment.

The mediator, on the other hand, affirms the supremacy of the parties' meanings and authority. The parties' control over the definition of the issues is fundamental to their control over the decision-making process and its outcome. One of the first tasks of the mediator is to gain an understanding of the issues as they are perceived by the parties themselves. This means giving paramount worth to the perceptions, feelings and meanings of the parties. The mediator has no privileged perspective on how to view and interpret experience. The skill of the mediator lies in facilitating the crucial exchanges of accurate and constructive information that lead, through adjustments of expectations and preferences, to greater understanding, co-ordination and order, and eventually to a settlement of the dispute (Gulliver, 1979), so the mediator's expertise lies in ensuring that the capacity of the parties to take responsibility for their own affairs is recognized and protected.

General systems theory, as applied to the analysis of the family, has been developed in the context of family therapy (for example, Walrond-Skinner, 1976; see also Minuchin, 1974, p.59). Systems thinking, in its application to family mediation, exemplifies this inextricable connection (Parkinson, 1986, p.126; James and Wilson, 1986, p.185).

In the 1980s, it was suggested that mediation practice could be expanded fruitfully by invoking the ideas and techniques of family systems thinking. It was claimed, in particular, that family systems theory contributed two valuable insights to the practice of family mediation:

- An integral aspect of family life was the interdependence of its members.
- Problems and tensions affecting one or more members of a family generally affected other members as well. (Parkinson, 1986, p.126)

No one would deny the soundness of the observation that an individual does not live in a personal, social or cultural vacuum. What could be challenged, however, was that these axioms of common sense were peculiar to systems thinking or family therapy. The stress and sorrow of individuals in conflict inevitably touches others – family members, and especially children, friends and colleagues. An understanding of the impact of the legal, economic, political, social, gender, cultural, ethnic, family and psychological environment of any dispute between individuals, particularly one involving children, is fundamental to the discussions that occur in mediation. The mediation process itself involves an examination of the implications for the parties and their families of various possible courses of action and their consequences. In other words, the recognition of the relevance of the interactive process is not a monopoly of the systems approach. Nor could it be assumed that the best means of helping people to appreciate the interpersonal and socio-cultural considerations of their predicament was by means of a family systems framework and/or the application of family therapy techniques.

Not only are the assumptions, objectives and methods of these two modes of intervention incompatible, there also seem to be a number of hazards associated with attempts to apply family therapy approaches to mediation:

Firstly, the boundaries between family mediation and family therapy could become dangerously blurred. The negotiation and decision-making processes of mediation could become tainted with the stigma of family dysfunction and treatment associated with family therapy. Furthermore, the values of mediation, such as the respect for the parties' capacity to behave as reasonable adults, could be undermined. One example of this danger is evidenced in the statement of a leading North American therapist/mediator: 'In many ways the mediator must act as a parent figure to the parents since their struggles are often not unlike those of siblings squabbling over joint possessions' (Saposnek, 1983, p.176).

Secondly, the terminology of family therapy may be imposed on mediation and its processes. The liberal application of the word 'system', for example, and the adoption of the typologies of family therapy (for example, the 'enmeshed', 'disengaged' and 'autistic' modes of classifying families) may be viewed as an attempt by one group of professionals to assume control and to appropriate mediation as an extension of their own activities as family therapists through the transforming processes of the specialist discourse.

Thirdly, some practitioners have drawn a distinction between the use of family therapy techniques in *therapy* and their deployment in *mediation*. It has been argued that at a time of crisis and stress such as attends family breakup, family therapy is a means of dealing with the underlying obstacles to rational communication. Family systems theory, in particular, is considered to be useful for dealing with intractable or irrational couples – those who are locked in destructive conflict. Haynes (1992), for example, outlines three conditions that should determine the use of such strategic interventions:

● an awareness of the specific strategy;

- an understanding of the anticipated outcome of the strategy;
- an immediate return to mediation when that strategy has been implemented.

The determinist behavioural assumptions that inform family systems thinking affect the techniques that are used to bring about change – for example, circular questioning, hypothesizing and paradoxical interventions. The systems view is that challenging and changing behaviour will lead to changes in perceptions and experience. This is the reverse of the process by means of which change is perceived to be brought about through learning and an improvement of understanding (see, for example, Deutsch, 1973; Eckhoff, 1969; Gulliver, 1979; Stevens, 1963; Stulberg, 1981).

In a systems approach, the therapist seeks to effect a change in 'belief system' by means of changing the system's behavioural interaction. This requires the use of techniques designed to manipulate behaviour patterns in order to modify perceptions. These techniques are therefore designed to place the therapist in a position of power, and are acknowledged to be intentionally manipulative – that is, covert (Campbell et al., no date., pp.21 and 36; Minuchin, 1974, p.140; Walrond-Skinner, 1976, p.149). The application of such techniques (for example, family assessment, the questioning techniques of the Milan method and the use of one-way mirrors and concealed video recorders) in mediation is not what the parties expect, and with or without their express knowledge and prior consent, they serve only to increase the controlling power and manipulative apparatus of the therapist/mediator.

Systems therapists do not aim to engage the informed participation of their patients. As a result, the family remains essentially passive, unable to recognize the exact nature of the demands made upon it. In some cases, this may involve the therapist engaging in a covert, adversarial power struggle with the family if they prove 'resistant' (Howard and Shepherd, 1987). Obviously, there is a tension between this approach and the view that one of the crucial characteristics that distinguishes human beings is their capacity to form intentions, become aware of alternatives, make choices and acquire control over their own behaviour (Lukes, 1973). The presuppositions underlying a systems approach negate the significance of human intention in the interactive process (Watson, 1987). It is precisely this component of intention that is central to mediation. As such, the systems approach is incompatible with the assumptions and goals of mediation. As Lukes (1973, p.133) notes: 'We cease to respect someone when we fail to treat him as an agent and a chooser, as a self from which actions and choices emanate'.

In the 1990s, the 'postmodern' discussions of family therapy reflect a general move towards an awareness of the ethical implications of power and control and a move away from open attempts to assert an expert role in the treatment process (for example, see Epstein and Loos, 1989; Goolishian and

Anderson, 1992; Larner, 1995). Notwithstanding these theoretical shifts, in practice the degree to which opportunities for professional domination are reduced, must remain in doubt.

Finally, the therapist is concerned with the underlying dynamics of behaviour. Therefore, there can be a tendency to regard the specific disputes focused on in mediation as 'presenting' problems, symptoms of the more profound, 'real' conflicts (Kressel, 1985, p.76). This view has three important implications for mediation:

- The insights of the therapist/mediator in deciding what is 'real' may be regarded as more valid than those of the parties.
- In making such interpretations, there is a risk of escalating conflict and antagonizing the parties. Kressel (1985, p.33) cites the example of a well-meaning divorce mediator who tried to break an impasse in negotiations over a custody dispute by suggesting to the husband that his inflexible bargaining position might be the product of his understandable hurt and anger at being rejected by his wife, rather than because of any doubt about his wife's ability as a parent. The husband refuted this interpretation vehemently, and accused the mediator of partiality and lack of understanding. Consumer research in the UK confirms that the parties resent such attempts at psychological interpretation as presumptuous and often erroneous (Davis and Roberts, 1988).
- The therapist's traditional 'assumption of repressed feelings' may be inappropriate in mediation (Saposnek, 1983, p.45). Those who adopt this assumption do so in the belief that some emotional catharsis is necessary if ambivalence or other unresolved feelings about the divorce are to be sorted out; only then, it is argued, will constructive negotiation on the issues in dispute be possible. Although tension may be lowered by the expression of strong feelings, excessive emotional 'venting' without leading on to any resolution of the problem can be destructive. Mediators usually discourage the expression of negative emotion for this reason. In any event, at least one of the parties will often refuse to discuss the emotional aspects of the breakup.

Even as an advocate of the therapeutic orientation in mediation, Kressel (1985, pp.275–8) cautions against its application in practice:

- because of the demands it places on the diagnostic competence of the mediator;
- because of the complications it adds to the already difficult role of the mediator;
- because of the risks it runs of alienating the parties;
- because it is likely to be ineffective; long-standing patterns of relating cannot be changed by short-term 'task-focused' intervention.

In this context, Kressel (1985, p.277) cites the advantages of the clarity, simplicity and 'time honoured interpretation of the mediator's role' – the modest profile of the mediator, the encouragement of the parties' autonomy, and the avoidance of the adoption of standards of settlement foreign to the parties.

2 The emergence of mediation in family disputes

One word more, one word.
This tiger-footed rage, when it shall find
The harm of unscanned swiftness, will, too late,
Tie leaden pounds to heels.
Proceed by Process.
Lest parties – as he is beloved – break out,
And sack great Rome with Romans.
(William Shakespeare, Menenius, *Coriolanus*, Act III(i), lines 319–21)

Since the Second World War there has been a general increase in the number of divorces in the UK. While over the past two decades the number of divorces in England and Wales has doubled, the most recent figures show that the number of divorces fell between 1993 and 1994, from 165,000 to 158,000 – the first fall since 1989 (Family Policy Studies Centre, 1996). Over the same period, the marriage rate also dropped dramatically by 50 per cent. Estimates indicate that 41 per cent of marriages in England and Wales will end in divorce, and about one in four newborn children will see their parents divorce (*Hansard*, parliamentary written answer 9601, 17 January, 1996). In 1993, the numbers of children under 16 affected by divorce rose to a new high of 175,961 (Office of Population Censuses and Surveys, 1995). The UK currently has the highest divorce rate in the European Community.

Although divorce may have become an everyday event, for all those affected by it, it is a crisis, painful and uniquely personal, and considered to be, after bereavement, the second most stressful life event. The ending of intimate ties unleashes powerful emotions, such as feelings of betrayal, rejection, failure, grief, anger and guilt, as well as relief and a sense of victory. At the same time, harsh and exhausting changes in the circumstances of daily life are often precipitated, resulting not infrequently in lowered standards of living, financial hardship and ill-health. These changes, such as moving house, having less money and increased child care responsibilities, would be demanding at the best of times, but there is a risk of exaggerating the emotional instability or irrationality of divorcing or separating individuals in these circumstances (Kressel, 1985). Selfish, even destructive behaviour should not be given greater emphasis than those qualities of courage, resilience, strength and forbearance that are also shown, both by adults and by children, in these testing times (Burgoyne, 1984).

Many writers (Bohannan, 1971; Haynes, 1981b; Kressel, 1985; Wallerstein and Kelly, 1980; Clulow, 1995) acknowledge that divorce is not simply the legal 'rite of passage' that obtaining a decree absolute involves, but 'a complex social phenomenon as well as a complex personal experience' (Simpson, 1994; Bohannan, 1971, p.33). In what he terms 'the six stations of divorce', Bohannan describes the overlapping experiences that constitute, in varying order and degrees of intensity, the processes involved in divorce. He describes these as follows:

1 *the emotional divorce*, characterized by feelings of hurt, anger, loss of attraction and trust;
2 *the legal divorce*, which creates remarriageability;
3 *the economic divorce*, which marks the reorganization of the financial and property arrangements;
4 *the 'co-parental' divorce*, which involves matters of residence of and contact with children, and which produces, in his view, the most enduring pain of divorce – for example, because parents have to come to terms with the realization both that there can be no 'clean break' where there are children, and that, bar situations of moral and physical danger, the relationship between one parent and their child ceases to be any business of the other parent;
5 *the community divorce*, which covers the impact of divorce on the social life of divorcees – for example, the way married friends treat divorcees and the organizations available to meet the needs of information and friendship of divorced people;
6 *the 'psychic' divorce*, which describes the means by which individual autonomy is recovered – this is thought to be the most difficult yet the most constructive achievement of all.

A high incidence of divorce is now accepted as an inevitable fact of life. The focus of attention has been not on divorce itself, but on the post-divorce period, especially on the need to mitigate some of the harmful consequences of divorce, particularly for children. Two government committee reports exemplified this concern by espousing a new spirit in which family breakdown should be viewed. The Finer Report (1974, para.4.313) affirmed the need to 'civilize' the consequences of breakdown by recommending that the 'winding up' of marriage failure should be accomplished by the couple making the most rational and efficient arrangements for their own and their children's future. The report first gave public recognition to the idea of conciliation in family disputes, which it defined as:

> the process of engendering common sense, reasonableness and agreement in dealing with the consequences of estrangement ...
>
> ... assisting the parties to deal with the consequences of the established breakdown of their marriage, whether resulting in a divorce or a separation, by reaching agreements or giving consents or reducing the area of conflict upon custody, support, access to and education of the children, financial provision, the disposition of the matrimonial home, lawyers' fees and every other matter arising from the breakdown which calls for a decision on future arrangements. (Finer Report, 1974, paras 4.305 and 4.288).

The idea of conciliation contained in the Finer Report thus expressed this fresh approach to family breakdown in terms of two objectives. Firstly that it should be approached in a quiet restrained way with the least possible bitterness and fighting; and secondly, that the parties themselves should take primary responsibility for resolving their own disputes (Roberts, 1983a). The Booth Committee (1985, para.3.10) reinforced these recommendations:

> It is of the essence of conciliation that responsibility remains at all times with the parties themselves to identify and seek agreement on all the issues arising from the breakdown of their relationship.

From the 1930s until 1971, the terms 'conciliation' and 'reconciliation' had been used interchangeably in English family law to refer to the repair of failing relationships (Dingwall and Eekelaar, 1988). Then, in *Practice Direction* [1971] 1 All ER 894 on matrimonial conciliation, issued by the President of the Family Division, conciliation was distinguished for the first time, both from reconciliation and from the preparation of welfare reports for the court (Parkinson, 1983). It is in the context of industrial relations, however, that conciliation as a form of alternative intervention has had the longest history, dating from the Conciliation Act 1896.

Following the Booth Committee (1985), continuing concern, both about the current prevalence of divorce and that the divorce process was making things worse for couples and their children, resulted in the publication in 1988 by the Law Commission of *Facing the Future – A Discussion Paper on the Ground for Divorce* (Law Com. No.170). The Law Commission's findings were that the present law was confusing and unjust and fulfilled none of its original objectives, namely the support of marriages with a chance of survival, and the decent burial of those marriages that were dead, with the minimum of bitterness, embarrassment and humiliation. Extensive consultation with professional groups and representative sectors of the public, plus additional research, endorsed the findings of Law Com. No.170, which went on to publish its divorce reform proposals, *Family Law: the Ground for Divorce* (Law Com. No.192) in 1990. These included two further objectives of a 'good' divorce law:

- to encourage, as far as possible, the amicable resolution of practical issues relating to the couple's home, finances and children, and the proper discharge of their responsibilities to one another and their children;
- to minimize the harm that the children may suffer, both at the time and in the future, and to promote, so far as possible, the continued sharing of parental responsibility for them (Law Commission, 1990, p.2); this objective was also fundamental to the Children Act 1989.

Law Com. No.192 recommended that irretrievable breakdown of marriage should remain the sole ground for divorce. In a radical departure from the existing law, the report and its accompanying draft bill introduced, with the overwhelming support of the vast majority of consultees, the period for reflection and consideration – the 'cooling off' period or breathing space – as a new way of demonstrating irretrievable breakdown of marriage. Within this period for reflection and consideration, the parties' own responsibility for decision-making was given central emphasis. The other radical innovation of the proposals was the incorporation of mediation as 'an important element in developing a new and more constructive approach to the problems of marital breakdown and divorce' (Law Commission, 1990, para.7.24). These proposals were subsequently incorporated into the Green Paper (1993), the White Paper (1995) on divorce reform (both of which were entitled *Looking to the Future: Mediation and the Ground for Divorce*) and then the Family Law Act 1996 (which is unlikely to be implemented before 1998 at the earliest). (For more detailed consideration of these and other legal developments, see Chapter 3.)

Two themes, often intertwined, provide the impetus behind the present official enthusiasm for mediation in family disputes and in the civil justice system (Woolf Report, 1995). The 'warm theme' celebrates mediation as a superior method of dispute-resolution, and refers to the 'impulse to replace adversary conflict by a process of conciliation to bring the parties into mutual accord' (Galanter, 1984, p.2). The 'cool theme' emphasizes administrative efficiency and cost savings (for example, in the reduction of court hearings or welfare reports) at a time when matrimonial disputes account for two-thirds of the civil Legal Aid outlay and the civil justice system is indicted by its own most senior judge as being too expensive, too slow, too complex and too unequal (Woolf Report, 1995).

The advantages of mediation in family disputes

The decisions in mediation are made by those who have to live with them, rather than by some third party, however wise and well-meaning. Retaining control over their own affairs also assists the parties to recover self-respect and dignity. Although there may appear to be temporary relief in legal representatives taking over problems, the limitations of this soon become apparent. While the law provides necessary protection from state intrusion and individual violence, as Auerbach (1983, pp.viii and 13) reminds us: 'although a lawyer can provide reassuring guidance, "in loco parentis", the price of protection is still dependence ... [the law itself] also encourages the isolation that makes protection necessary.' The parties, locked into a relationship of dependence, can find themselves more lacking in control than ever. A mediated agreement, because it is consented to voluntarily, is more likely to be satisfactory to the parties and therefore to be adhered to by them (Emery, 1994). Even where no agreement is reached, mediation as a process is likely to be of value to the parties in providing improved opportunities for communication.

Mediation straddles traditional professional boundaries, allowing recognition of the legal, ethical, emotional and practical aspects of disputes. The legal system is limited by the fact that it recognizes only legal norms, and cannot fulfil the psychological requirements as well as the requirements of legal justice for the parties and their children (Saposnek, 1983). The parties can draw up their own agendas and define issues in their own terms, incorporating what might be important to them, ethically or emotionally, however irrelevant these may be in law.

The opportunity provided in mediation for the expression of feelings can be an important advantage over the legal system, though if this is excessive or prolonged, it may seriously impede rational exchange and lead to a deterioration of relations, rather than any improvement. It does not follow that mediation deals with the emotional side of divorce and lawyers with its rational side. Rational decision-making is the objective of mediation, achieving this by its 'person-oriented' perspective, rather than by the 'act-orientation' of litigation (Fuller, 1971).

One of the special features of family disputes involving children is that there are usually two disputants involved – the parents in most cases. Fuller's analysis of mediation appraises 'the dyad' as the 'home ground' of the mediation process (p.310). Another special feature is that they are bound together through their children in a continuing and interdependent relationship, whether they like it or not (unlike a relationship that involves only a brief interaction occasioned by a one-off encounter, such as a car accident or business transaction).

The two parties are locked in a relationship that is virtually one of 'bilateral monopoly'; each is dependent for its very existence on some collaboration with the other (Fuller, 1971, p.310).

This relationship creates the 'internal pull towards cohesion' which mediation by its nature presupposes (Fuller, 1971, p.314). In family disputes the 'heavy interdependence' occasioned by this intermeshing of interests is likely to be of an intensity sufficient to induce in the parents a willingness, however minimal or reluctant, to collaborate in the mediation effort and reach some sort of accommodation (Fuller, 1971, p.310). This is because the parties' common interests (namely their children) may be seen, or may come to be seen, as more important than who is right or who is wrong. This creates a strong pressure to follow the Confucian 'middle road', a tradition that embodied the duty of everyone, as his or her first obligation, to achieve harmony with others and with nature (Shapiro, 1981).

The mediation process is, in essence, forward-looking (but see also Chapter 11). Whereas the judge looks backwards to events of the past and makes a judgment on those facts in terms of the legal norms connected with them, the mediator looks forwards to a consideration of future options and the consequences of alternative courses of action (Eckhoff, 1969). That is what makes the mediation process singularly appropriate to negotiation over family disputes concerning children, where future child care arrangements have to be determined over several years, and where co-ordination between the parents is necessary to achieve this (Sander, 1984). This is in contrast to the powerful but once-and-for-all nature of court decision-making. While it should be noted that family jurisdiction is different from other jurisdictions in that it is almost entirely discretionary, it is still the judge who makes the decision.

There are dangers in failing to acknowledge that family proceedings are to a large extent conducted on an inquisitorial basis, as well as in exaggerating the destructive influence of lawyers. Nevertheless, the adversary mould of our legal system does inevitably encourage competitive rather than co-operative attitudes and exchanges. Lawyers are meant to act as partisans, championing their own client's interests (Davis, 1988). Limited disclosure, communication through third parties, the translation of everyday language into legal discourse, the transformation of the client's objectives into legal categories plus the win/lose nature of the judge's order – all these processes impede not only a search for truth, but any expression of concern for the person on the other side (Gilligan, 1982). The process of mediation, in comparison, facilitates direct communication and confidentiality, which are more likely to reduce misunderstanding and conflict, and can nurture a potential for co-operation that might not otherwise be realized. More practically, evidence indicates that disputes are resolved more quickly in mediation than by adversarial means, and legal costs are more predictable and lower than either lawyer negotiation or adjudication (Emery et al., 1991; Walker et al., 1994; Glasser, 1994; McCarthy and Walker, 1996a).

Any agreement reflects arrangements at a particular moment. But circumstances and minds do change. Not only does mediation enable specific practical disputes to be settled, it can also be an important 'learning experience' (Sander, 1984, p.xiii). The parties learn how to negotiate, and this improved capacity means that in the longer-term, future differences and changing circumstances can be accommodated in modified or new arrangements (Davis and Roberts, 1988). Recent research concludes that reaching agreements in mediation is a vital component in making and maintaining co-operation relationships between divorcing parents (McCarthy and Walker, 1996b).

The intact family – whatever its form at a given historical point – has usually made decisions without interference (except in the rare, extreme case of risk to a child). Where conversations have been disrupted by family breakdown, mediation enables these to be resumed and this 'private ordering' process to be sustained, not only between couples, but across generations – for example, in disputes between grandparents and fathers or mothers in relation to contact over grandchildren. Family break-up should not be an excuse for external agencies to interfere and take control. (See Chapter 10 for further discussion of children's rights and representation.)

Competing tensions within family mediation

Mediation is practised in a political, legal, ethical and economic environment. This inevitably gives rise to a number of tensions which the mediator must constantly bear in mind.

Political pressures

With the exception of the reservations of a few academics and feminists (Freeman, 1984; Davis and Bader, 1985; Roberts, 1983a, 1986; Bottomley, 1984, 1985; Matthews, 1988), enthusiasm for mediation in the UK has not been lessened by the more widespread criticisms that have emerged in the USA (for example, Abel, 1982; Auerbach, 1983). Findings there examined the political implications of 'informal justice', and suggested that in some cases, alternative dispute agencies, such as Small Claims Courts and Landlord and Tenant Courts, served to divert the legitimate claims of the more vulnerable groups in society (the poor, blacks and women) away from legal channels into forms of second-class justice that lacked the safeguards of due process, and increased covert state regulation. It was claimed that while 'informal justice' processed the small claims and minor disputes of the poor, justice according to law was reserved for the rich. This concern has been focused on the public mediation programmes, though not specifically on family mediation. Ironically, concern is also directed at private fee-for-service family mediation, which, it is claimed, has been available only to the rich (Folberg and Taylor, 1984).

Family mediation in the UK, particularly in the light of recent developments in family law, cannot escape these concerns. Davis and Bader (1985) highlighted the pressures and powerlessness experienced by the parties in the context of 'conciliation' on court premises. Out-of-court services increasingly risk incorporation within the judicial system. *Practice Direction* [1986] 16 Fam. Law 286 of the Principal Divorce Registry directed judges and registrars to consider referring contested cases to local conciliation services, where these exist. With mediation as the main plank of divorce reform (Family Law Act 1996), accompanied by government proposals for legal aid reform (Green Paper, 1995, *Legal Aid: Targeting Need*; White Paper, 1996, *Striking the Balance: The Future of Legal Aid in England and Wales*), public funding for independent family mediation services has become a reality for the first time. There are consequent risks to be guarded against. External funding, while bringing much-needed financial security to struggling service providers, will inevitably bring demands of accountability and quantifiable measures of effectiveness (for example, see Power, 1994), as well as pressure on legal aid recipients to mediate as the officially preferred approach to settling disputes. Backdoor coercion into mediation must be resisted, along with any undermining of professional autonomy over policy, principles and quality assurance.

Rights versus responsibility

Mediators must be the first to acknowledge that the better informed both parties are, the better able they are to negotiate. Knowledge of their legal rights is an essential prerequisite for mediation. However, individual rights associated as they are with the pursuit of legal interests, exist in tension with the ethics of collaboration and mutual responsibility associated with mediation (Gilligan, 1982). Under the banner of children's rights, and in particular article 12 of the UN Convention on the Rights of the Child (the right of the child to express an opinion and to have that opinion taken into account), recent attempts to expand the role of guardians ad litem to the private law proceedings of divorce have complicated the picture still further (see Chapter 10 for further discussion).

A mediated agreement, if it is to be fair and satisfactory to both parties, and in the children's interests, somehow has to balance the demands of these apparently competing approaches.

Objectives and reality

Kressel (1985, p.204) has drawn attention to the lofty nature of the mediator's goals, the fulfilment of all of which would constitute no mean achievement. They apply as much to the mediation of international disputes between nations as to family disputes. In the context of family mediation, these goals – difficult enough to meet at the best of times – must be striven for in circumstances of enormous personal stress and practical, social and economic difficulty:

> With regard to the parties, the mediator is expected to establish and maintain trust and confidence; to demonstrate empathy and understanding for the positions of each side; to be highly expert on substantive and procedural issues, but to use that expertise to guide and counsel, not to impose personal views or take sides. With regard to the process, the mediator is expected to foster a procedure of dispute resolution: in which neither party gets all that it is asking, although neither ends up feeling humiliated or defeated; that engages all parties in an active process of give and take, albeit one that is sufficiently controlled so that the risks of conflict escalation are kept to the minimum; and that is based on an objective and realistic assessment of the forces and interests at play. With regard to the settlement, the mediator is expected to promote agreements that both sides can defend publicly; that each can view as reasonably fair; and that lay the groundwork for improved interaction.

Parental autonomy and state intervention

Officially, parental autonomy and private ordering are encouraged (see Chapter 3). But at the same time, the court has a duty to protect the interests of children in matrimonial proceedings in both contested and uncontested cases (Matrimonial Causes Act 1973, s.41; Family Law Act 1996, s.11). The Children Act 1989 removed the duty of district judges to make any judgment as to the satisfactoriness or otherwise of the arrangements for children at the Children's Appointment. Whether the court would use its power to refuse to accept an agreement made by the parties themselves remains uncertain. There is also uncertainty about the grounds on which the court's supervisory jurisdiction ought to be exercised (Maidment, 1984).

The principle of the welfare of the child as the paramount consideration guides the court in making decisions over children (Children Act 1989, s.1). This principle, while not one of the basic premises of mediation, informs the legal and ethical framework within which decision-making in mediation takes place (Finer Report, 1974). However, the principle of party authority is fundamental to mediation. Research findings (Lund, 1984; Wallerstein and Kelly, 1980), showing that the basis of what is best for the child lies in an agreement between the parents, resolve (in practice) these tensions of principle.

The organizational framework within which mediation is practised

Many different organizational arrangements characterize the practice of mediation in the UK. Broadly speaking, a distinction can be drawn between services that are directly linked to the court and those that are independent of the court, based in the community. In fact, the picture is more complex and the influence of the court more pervasive, intruding even into the practice of out-of-court services (for example, in their accepting court referrals and in the presence of members of the judiciary on their management committees). Nevertheless, the degree of involvement in the judicial process is still a useful index for determining the fundamental differences between the services.

Court-based settlement practices

A variety of practices, termed variously 'conciliation', 'mediation', 'settlement-seeking' and 'dispute resolution', are conducted either at the direction of the court or on the court premises. At least five of these were identified in the County Court (Ogus et al., 1987, p.66). Examples of such court practices are set out below.

The conciliation appointment before the registrar and the court welfare officer

Here, conciliation is an integral part of the legal process and takes place under the authority of the registrar.

The first experimental scheme of this kind was set up by Mr Registrar Parmeter at the Bristol County Court in 1977, in order to reduce the number of defended divorces. It was extended in 1978 to some custody and access disputes in undefended divorces. The appointment was to take place before affidavits were filed and before the case was set down for a full hearing. The parties and their solicitors would attend a meeting with the registrar and a welfare officer in order to clarify the exact nature of the dispute. If there seemed to be a prospect of agreement, the parties and the welfare officer would have a private discussion in another room for about forty minutes. These discussions would be legally privileged, and so could not be subsequently disclosed (*Practice Direction* [1982] 3 All ER 988). Should an agreement be reached, the registrar would make an order giving effect to it. Otherwise, he/she would give directions for the trial of the dispute.

Since then, several courts have introduced similar schemes, including the one introduced in 1983 at the Principal Registry of the Family Division. This scheme was extended to include referrals from a judge at the Children's Appointment.

Research by Davis and Bader (1985) into conciliation appointments at Bristol County Court revealed that what actually took place was a stressful encounter involving the spouses, mostly in the overcrowded public waiting area of the court, under the threat that failure to agree would result in the imposition of further costs and delay. Solicitors spoke on behalf of their clients, and there was little direct negotiation between the parties themselves. The parties' experience of in-court conciliation was therefore of a coercive and excluding process, with little attention being paid to their own under- standings and interpretations of their circumstances. From the standpoint of the courts, these appointments provided an efficient means of rationalizing cases, diverting them away from judicial hearings. Settlement-seeking pressures (including those from the parties' own solicitors) dominated at the expense of the quality of those settlements.

Conciliation before a judge

Some judges sometimes attempt to mediate if both parties are present at the Children's Appointment (Matrimonial Causes Act 1973, s.41), but they do not divest themselves of their judicial authority by assuming a mediatory role.

Settlement-seeking by a court welfare officer during the preparation of a welfare report

The main traditional duties of court welfare officers have been their statutory duties to investigate and report, providing information to the court on matters relating to the welfare of children. Additional duties have included the supervision of arrangements for children (James, 1988). The court welfare officer occupies a position of formal authority as an officer of the court whose primary responsibility is to assist the judge (or magistrate) in judicial decision-making. The officer does this by acting as the 'eyes and ears' of the court, investigating all the circumstances and reporting back to the court so that an informed judgment can be made by the judge. This will inevitably involve providing the judge with an account of the circumstances of the family concerned.

Some court welfare officers, pursuing practices influenced by notions of systemic family therapy, see their primary objective as effecting a change in the dysfunctional family, rather than meeting the requirements either of the judicial process (for determining parental disputes) or of the families and their perceptions of their needs (James and Hay, 1993). These court welfare officers (for example, Howard and Shepherd, 1982) deny that their reports to the court need include recommendations involving value judgements. While it must indeed be desirable for the court welfare officer to avoid a moral judgement on the conduct of the parents, a recommendation as to the course of action which is in the best interests of the child is unavoidable if the report is not to be useless as an aid to adjudication. Moreover, these practitioners, in claiming the right both to exercise their professional judgement independent of legal or judicial constraint as 'free floating professionals' (James and Hay, 1993, p.119) and to use their power as court welfare officers to impose their methods on disputants, simultaneously *deny* and *exploit* their statutory authority.

A conciliatory approach adopted by a welfare officer in the course of investigatory duties may indeed bring about some, or even total agreement between the parties to a dispute. However, there are fundamental differences of objective and practice in the tasks of welfare investigation and mediation. It is important to remember that the parties' participation in the court investigation is mandatory – depending not on their consent, but on the need of the court to inform itself when called upon to make orders affecting children – and that discussions are not privileged. Nor is it possible for the court welfare officer to be impartial *vis-à-vis* the parties, for, as we have seen, in the absence of an informal agreement, the officer must subsequently prepare an influential report in which his/her own opinions predominate. The principle of party competence of mediation is also subservient to the court welfare officer's statutory child protection role.

For all these reasons, attempts by a court welfare officer to mediate from this powerful position of formal authority tend to place the parties, especially if reluctant to agree, under considerable pressure at a time when they may already be feeling vulnerable and overawed by the formality and unfamiliarity of proceedings and the authority of the court. These dangers of coercion are compounded by risks of manipulation in the covert use by some court welfare officers of family therapy techniques (including the frequently secret use of one-way mirrors and video recorders) often employed with neither the prior knowledge nor the consent of the parties, as a means of assessing families and their relationships (for example, Howard and Shepherd, 1982).

The Booth Committee (1985, para.41.2) strongly recommended the separation of report-writing and mediation, going as far as to describe these two activities as 'so different as to be incompatible'. Mr Justice Ewbank (*Re H: (Conciliation: Welfare Reports)* [1986] 1 FLR 476) first gave this viewpoint judicial backing by stating:

> conciliation and reporting as a court welfare officer are different functions. Conciliation is the helping of parties to resolve their disputes. The duty of the welfare officer is to help the court to resolve disputes that the parties are unable to resolve. Both functions are of great value but they are not functions which are to be mixed up. Probation officers who are involved in conciliation are not subsequently

to investigate and write welfare officers' reports. This is a fundamental point which has been made on many occasions . . .

Practice Direction [1986] 16 Fam. Law 286 of the Principal Registry of the Family Division officially endorsed the need for the separation of these two functions by directing that the same officer should not act both as report writer and as conciliator in the same case. Home Office policy now confirms this prohibition (see *National Standards for Probation Service Family Court Welfare Work*, Home Office, 1994). This policy document attempts to clarify the respective functions of the court welfare officer. Section 4.3 on the purpose of the welfare report states:

> Where in the course of preparing the report the court welfare officer identifies opportunities for helping the parties to reach agreement, these should be pursued in line with the general principle of promoting parental responsibility *but it is not the role of the court welfare officer to set out to resolve disputes when preparing a welfare report.*

Mediation, on the other hand, is described as a process of dispute-resolution. It is privileged, to be undertaken only at the request of the court and when the parties have given their informed consent: 'It may take place on court premises or elsewhere. Research suggests that mediation is more effective away from court premises.' (Home Office, 1994, s.5.34).

The court welfare officer may also have a settlement-seeking role in relation to Directions Appointments. These discussions are distinguished from mediation in that they are not privileged and are normally brief (Home Office, 1994, s.5.23). Outcomes must be reported to the court (Home Office, 1994, ss.2.6 and 2.7).

However carefully these different functions are clarified and respected, attempts at promoting legal settlement as part of court proceedings must be distinguished from the offer of mediation. That offer must be kept independent of the court process and therefore of its coercive powers. Where court officials act as mediators, the parties are inevitably exposed to such unsatisfactory pressures. The dangers of coercion in the mediation process and of impairment of judicial authority where these functions are combined have been highlighted by Roberts (1986).

Recent research (James and Hay, 1993) confirms that court welfare work is characterized by a wide variety of practices – nationally and locally, between areas, teams and individual officers. Their findings suggest that this variety reflects divergent philosophical and theoretical views as to the objectives, values, functions and skills that should underpin this area of work. The lack of clarity as to overall aims and objectives and the absence of 'any coherent and evidentiary framework' within which court welfare is located (James and Hay, 1993, p.178), has been addressed by the introduction in 1994 of a policy of uniformity, embodied in the Home Office's *National Standards for Probation Service Family Court Welfare Officers* (Home Office, 1994). While on the one hand James and Hay (1993, p.119) state 'there are as many approaches to court welfare work as there are court welfare officers', they also identify emerging common features of practice: for example, the pervasive influence in court welfare work of family therapy; the almost universal hostility to the court process and its perceived destructiveness; the concommitant view as to the importance of diverting disputants away from the court; a growing interest in issues of race, gender and power, and an increased focus on dispute-resolution co-existing with the traditional investigative role.

As James (1988) has pointed out, the development of in-court conciliation, *ad hoc*, local and piecemeal as it has been, is undeniably a major practice innovation new to probation work, which has traditionally been individual work, rather than co-working in joint sessions. James (1988, pp.58–62) refers to the substantial confusion resulting from this development, surrounding not only the use of terminology, but also concepts, structures and management. Conciliation has had to be 'smuggled' into court welfare work for two reasons: because of the absence of any authority to provide for or resource its development, and because of the powerful and unanimous legal and judicial consensus, supported by researchers such as Davis (1985), on the basic incompatibility between the use of conciliation/mediation and the task of welfare investigation.

Out-of-court mediation provision

Following the publication of the Finer Report in 1974, the initiative was taken to offer mediation in the out-of-court, independent, voluntary (or charitable) sector of provision. The first of these out-of-court services was the Bristol Courts Family Conciliation Service (BCFCS) established in 1978, funded by the Nuffield Foundation and other trusts. Initially a pre-court service, it was intended to complement the in-court conciliation at Bristol County Court. The use of 'courts' in its title was confusing, for the BCFCS had no formal connection with the local courts (Parkinson, 1986). No doubt it was thought that this judicial association would lend greater authority and status to its activities, and win the support (in the form of referrals) of the legal profession. This was ironic in view of the fact that the chief advantage of the service lay in its independence of the court. The second full-time out-of-court service, the South-East London Family Conciliation Bureau, was set up in 1979 in Bromley. Funding was dependent on a variety of charitable and local authority sources, as well as strong Probation Service support. Administratively and financially linked to the Civil Work Unit of the

Probation Service, it took great pains to demarcate and maintain clear information and professional boundaries in order to preserve its independence of the court. This was because its co-ordinator and some of the mediators were then also court welfare officers. The mediators were mainly drawn from a variety of professional backgrounds (legal, personnel, social work, psychology and counselling).

This interdisciplinary mix was unusual then, as the mediators who first staffed the early out-of-court mediation services came from professional backgrounds in social work, counselling and therapy, which focused on child welfare protection. This professional ideology, and the Law Society's determination to confine dispute-resolution to the sphere of legal activity and therefore the control of lawyers, influenced the terms in which mediation in these early days was then perceived – as a form of welfare activity primarily concerned with issues concerning children.

Since then, the situation has been transformed, and developments have been dramatic, organizationally, professionally, legally and politically. There are now 68 Family Mediation Services (FMS) in England, Wales and Northern Ireland, forming an association under the umbrella of National Family Mediation (NFM), the largest provider of out-of-court family mediation in the country. NFM, having secured the identity of the core process in its professional requirements, has moved on to consolidating the distinctive environment of family mediation practice in its developments in quality assurance, supervision training, the consultation of children in mediation and screening for domestic violence. The most recent statistics (NFM, 1994b) show that in 1994, NFM services dealt with 16,500 referrals and mediated in relation to 6,500 couples (in some areas between 10 per cent and 20 per cent of the divorcing population); 17,000 children were the subjects of such mediations, of whom 4 per cent were consulted directly; 23 per cent of couples had never been married, compared to 41 per cent who had been married, the former proportion increasing year by year. With only 11 per cent still together, the proportion of those who were already separated (over half with one partner already cohabiting) – 82 per cent of couples – is striking. All or some issues were resolved in 70 per cent of cases. Reconciliation occurred in 10 per cent of cases where the couple were still living together and 6 per cent of those who brought to mediation reconciliation as an issue for decision. Only 1 per cent of couples already separated reconciled.

All NFM services provide mediation regarding issues relating to children, and the organization prides itself on its focus on the importance of the perspective of children in parental discussions during the process of mediation. Increasing numbers of services offer all-issues mediation (AIM) – the mediation of the detailed arrangements concerning financial, property as well as children issues. Agreement rates are consistent with those in other countries: 70 per cent of couples agreed arrangements in respect of their children, and

80 per cent reached agreement on all issues (Joseph Rowntree Foundation, 1994).

Each Family Mediation Service is an autonomous charity, funds for which are drawn from various sources – client fees, the local authority, the Probation Service, some children's charities (NCH Action for Children and Barnardos), other trusts and charities and from small Legal Aid disbursements to solicitors for reports which clarify the issues for their legally-aided clients. Charitable status ensures that nobody is denied mediation because of lack of money.

Over 700 mediators work in NFM services, mainly on a sessional basis. Each mediator has to satisfy the professional requirements of NFM's national regulatory framework, which consists of affiliation criteria for services, and national procedures for the selection, training, supervised practice and accreditation of mediators. This regulatory framework provides the means by which uniform standards are set and monitored. The achievement of these standards depends in practice upon the local service base, which recruits mediators, provides the necessary infrastructure for securing referrals of cases, and oversees the quality and accountability of work by local supervision procedures. Moreover, the service base for the provision of family mediation ensures that a balance is maintained between the demand for mediation and the supply of mediators.

What has characterized these developments is mediation's struggle to emerge and become recognized as an independent activity distinct both from the practice of therapy and welfare professionalism and from legal practice and process. It was not until 1989 that mediation broke free from this confusing inheritance which reflected:

> a mental universe dominated by the now aging dyad of 'justice' and 'welfare' and while there is obviously nothing wrong with either 'justice' or 'welfare', mediation is about something else. It is primarily directed towards the support of private ordering in seeking to facilitate joint decision-making through party negotiations. (Roberts, 1993a, p.6).

In 1989, the distinctive nature of mediation, embodied in its own ancient tradition, was affirmed officially, both in its incorporation as the basis of the first national mediation training programme and in the definition in the report from the Lord Chancellor on the costs and effectiveness of conciliation:

> The distinguishing feature [of mediation] should be *to enable couples to retain control of the decision-making process* consequent on separation or divorce, encouraging them to make their own agreements. (Conciliation Project Unit, 1989, para.20.19; emphasis added).

This clarification of the significant characteristics of mediation as a decision-making process was confirmed by the adoption in 1991 of new selection criteria for eligibility for training with NFM. Aptitude for mediation, analysed and demonstrated via a range of specific performance-based selection exercises and procedures, became the primary determinant of suitability for training for mediation, rather than any particular educational or professional qualification and experience. This was in line with the recommendations of the North American Society of Professionals in Dispute Resolution (SPIDR Commission, 1989). The SPIDR Commission on Qualifications found that no particular type or degree of prior education or job experience was shown to be an effective predictor of success as a mediator, arbitrator or other professional 'neutral'. Terminological clarification ensued too, when, by 1989, the term 'mediation' began to replace 'conciliation', preferred because of its greater precision.

At about this time, the Family Mediators Association (FMA) was set up, offering mediation on all issues in the private sector. This body grew out of the earlier initiative of a small group of solicitors and a social worker, operating under the title Solicitors in Mediation. The FMA, an association of individual practitioners (rather than services), adopted a model of practice based on a lawyer and mental health professional co-working together. Unfortunately, this approach perpetuated the old 'mental universe' that had hitherto confused mediation.

The FMA's monopoly in the private sector is being challenged by the rapid proliferation of lawyer-dominated training programmes, including those offered by the Solicitors Family Law Association (SFLA) with the support of the Law Society, itself anxious to extend its remit over mediation. The risk to the public of unregulated practice is one of the reasons for the creation of the UK College of Family Mediators by the three main family mediation providers, National Family Mediation, Family Mediation Scotland and the Family Mediators Association (see Chapter 11).

Distinguishing features of independent mediation services compared to those annexed to the court

- Referrals come from many sources, which include self-referrals, Citizens' Advice Bureaux, solicitors, health workers, as well as the court or Court Welfare Service.
- These schemes are not restricted to those involved in matrimonial proceedings. Unmarried couples also have access to them.
- Mediation is available at an early stage while couples may still be living under the same roof, before divorce petitions are filed, or even before legal advice has been sought. Independent mediation services are also

available later on, long after legal proceedings over divorce are completed.

- Even the busiest independent services can offer appointments at short notice, which is of special value in moments of crisis – for example, if a teenager refuses to return home following a contact visit.
- The length and number of sessions can be determined by the agency itself, according to its own objectives and the particular needs of the consumers.
- Confidentiality can be more readily assured in an out-of-court service, where there is less danger of the parties confusing the role of the mediator with that of the court welfare service in cases where a report has also been ordered by the court.
- Mediation, as practised in independent agencies, can better ensure that the authority of the parties to determine their own arrangements over their own affairs in their own way is protected. This fundamental requirement of mediation cannot easily be reconciled with court-directed or court-annexed mediation, where the ethos of the court, characterized as it is by the surrendering of decision-making authority to a judge, prevails.

3 The legal context

Marriages do break down and ... the civil legislator must take account of this fact and provide the best framework of law to cater for this. (Lord Chancellor, House of Lords, *Hansard*, Vol.567, No.10, 30 November 1995, p.704)

An all-pervasive legal and 'adjudicative bias' has conditioned thinking about dispute-resolution in our society (Effron, 1989, p.480). Not only has this been detrimental to the effective resolution of family disputes, but it has also, until recently, disabled many from contemplating dispute-resolution processes such as mediation, which do not enjoy the privileged position of adjudication in the legal process and which lie outside the monopoly of control over those processes by legal professionals.

Many decisions following family breakdown are negotiated between the parties themselves, with or without the assistance of lawyers. The prevalence of this private negotiation has been officially recognized and encouraged in the value of personal autonomy that was first proclaimed in relation to family conflict in the Finer Report (1974), followed by the Booth Committee (1985). This comparatively new approach to the management of disputes in the field of family breakdown is now an acknowledged part of legal policy and of the substantive law, culminating most recently in the divorce reform proposals included in the Family Law Act 1996. These proposals accord primary responsibility for decision-making to the parties, and are therefore in line with the Children Act 1989. The Children Act, in introducing its two innovatory principles of parental responsibility and non-intervention of the court, embodied for the first time a view of the public interest that was defined, certainly in the private law, in terms of settlement through agreement (Bainham, 1990). In presupposing that the public interest is best served by the facilitation of parental agreement, coupled with the discouragement of the intervention of the court, a premium is placed on mediation as part of this movement away from legal process and towards alternative dispute-resolution processes.

This trend became apparent when the introduction of 'irretrievable break-down' as the sole ground for divorce (subject to proof of one of the five 'facts') officially removed the former fault basis of divorce (Matrimonial Causes Act 1973, s.1). Furthermore, with the introduction in 1977 of the Special Procedure and the way undefended divorces are processed, the usual judicial decision-making function of the court was replaced. Although a decree nisi was awarded in open court and a decree absolute granted only if the court declared itself satisfied about the arrangements for the children, the privately-negotiated settlements made by divorcing couples were merely rubber-stamped by the court (Davis et al., 1983). The court does, of course, still offer adjudication in disputes involving the decree, money and children to those who require it, but the large majority of cases are settled prior to trial, and only a tiny percentage are concluded in adjudication.

Mediation is part of this movement towards 'private ordering'. But all private negotiations in family matters – bilateral party negotiations, medi-ated negotiations or lawyer negotiations – take place within the 'shadow of the law' (Mnookin and Kornhauser, 1979). In theory, this provides the 'defin-ing context' within which mutual actions, expectations and decisions occur (Hamnett, 1977, p.5). Research reveals that in practice, so far as lawyer negotiations are concerned, many cases settle for reasons that have nothing to do with moral or legal standards (Menkel-Meadow, 1993a).

The mediator needs to have an understanding of the substantive law and of the procedural stages of divorce, and how these affect negotiations. Marriage is, on one level, a legal contract between a man and a woman; divorce defines the process by which the legal obligations and privileges of a man and woman towards one another are changed (Bernard, 1971).

Current divorce law

Although, as already noted, irretrievable breakdown is the only ground for divorce, three of the five 'facts' by which it is proved are fault-based and derive from the old matrimonial offences of adultery, cruelty and desertion (Cretney and Masson, 1997). The large majority (about 75 per cent) of divorce petitions are based on adultery or unreasonable behaviour, less than 20 per cent on two years' separation, and fewer than 6 per cent on five years' separa-tion (White Paper, 1995). Women are the petitioners in most cases. As the White Paper (1995, para.2.10) states: 'not surprisingly, the subtlety that the facts are not grounds for divorce, but merely evidence of breakdown, is seldom grasped by those who are sued for divorce'. 'Unreasonable behav-iour'[1] is most frequently cited as a 'fact' because that is the quickest way of getting a divorce. It also causes the most trouble. Research shows that disputes about children seem to be more common in divorces based on unreasonable behaviour than in others (Green Paper, 1993, para.5.12). Unless that tactical purpose behind its frequent use is clear, especially to the respondent, the repercussions are often serious. Many disputes are exacerbated by a spouse's outrage at receiving a petition cataloguing a history of 'unreasonable behaviour'. The concern is that animosity is likely to be increased and litigation protracted if the respondent seeks to defend the petition as a means of refuting these allegations.

What the parties need to know in these circumstances is that most allegations about conduct as a spouse do not prejudice the respondent's position, either *vis-à-vis* the children or *vis-à-vis* property and financial rights and obligations. Conduct is disregarded by the court unless it would be inequitable to do so, and this occurs only exceptionally. In deciding how to respond to a petition based on unreasonable behaviour, the respondent also needs to know that there is no public hearing if the petition is undefended, and that the decree absolute makes no reference to any of the facts required to prove irretrievable breakdown (Grant, 1981). Clarification of these issues by the mediator can help to prevent misunderstanding and the escalation of conflict.

The Children Act 1989

The main aims of the Children Act were twofold: to establish a single body of law relating to the care and upbringing of children, and to provide a consistent set of legal remedies for all courts and in all proceedings.

Principles of the Children Act 1989

The Act sets out the basic principles upon which the *courts* shall decide issues relating to children.

The welfare principle (section 1)

The 'welfare principle' has been described as 'the golden thread which runs through the whole of this court's jurisdiction' (*Re D*. 1977). In deciding any question relating to the upbringing of children or the administration of a child's property, the court has to make the welfare of the child its paramount consideration. The child's welfare is considered 'first, last and all the time' (*Re D*. 1977). It applies in both the private and the public law, and has been the cardinal principle guiding the court in relation to decisions over children since the Guardianship of Minors Act 1971 (re-enacting the Guardianship of Infants Acts of 1886 and 1925).

Parental responsibility (section 3)

'In this Act "Parental Responsibility" means all the rights, duties, powers, responsibilities and authority which by law a parent of a child has in relation to the child and his property' (Children Act, s.3(i)). This was a fundamentally new principle of the Act. 'Parental responsibility' and the primary status it accords to parenthood replaced the old concept on which the law was based – 'parental rights'. In contrast, parental responsibility gives significance to the everyday practical responsibilities of caring for children – bringing up the child, caring and making decisions. Parental responsibility rests automatically on both parents if they are married when their child is born, or if they have been married to one another at any time since the child's conception. It is an enduring status that is not lost on separation or divorce (or when a child is in the care of the local authority). On divorce, therefore, both parents continue to have parental responsibility, which resides independently in each. This has the following implications:

- It replaces a 'rights' approach to parenthood, which tends to foster a competitive, adversarial approach.
- A person with parental responsibility does not cease to have it solely because another person has it.
- It preserves the equal status of each parent.
- It gives each parent the authority to act independently of the other in relation to the children (unless the court orders otherwise). Therefore, parental responsibility can be met alone.
- It is intended to encourage *both* parents to feel responsible for the welfare of their children and to have a continuing role to play in relation to the children.
- It removes one important area of dispute during divorce – the issue of legal custody.
- It is intended to reduce conflict, and therefore enhance the continuing involvement of both parents in the care and upbringing of their children.
- In promoting agreement, it is intended to advance the welfare of children.
- Parental responsibility may not be surrendered or transferred. Some or all of it may be delegated, but it always remains intact (unless removed by adoption). This means that a parent with parental responsibility will always be responsible for ensuring adequate arrangements for the care of the child. If a Care Order is made, the local authority shares parental responsibility with those who already have it.
- Local authorities have a duty to consult parents, the child and non-parents with parental responsibility. There is no equivalent legal duty

in the private law for those with parental responsibility to consult *each other*. The Law Commission (1990) considered this to be both 'unworkable' and 'undesirable', likely to lead to an escalation of disputing.

Non-interventionism of the court (section 1(5))

Where a court[2] is considering whether or not to make one or more orders under the Act with respect to a child, it shall not make the order or any of the orders unless it considers *that doing so would be better for the child than making no order at all.* (Children Act, s.1(5); emphasis added)

This is the second radical new principle of the Act. It reinforces the principle of parental responsibility in its presumption that there is no need for a court order at all, except where an order is the most effective way of safeguarding or promoting the welfare of the child. In other words, the order must positively contribute to the child's welfare. This presumption against the making of court orders is based both on the expectation that the meeting of parental responsibility will lead to a reduced need for court intervention, and on the view that the court does not necessarily know what is best. The court does not have the right to impose its own values.

In both the private and the public law, the assumption that the court should make an order is removed. The converse is presumed – that parents are the best carers of their children (unless there is a risk of harm), and that just because they are separating or divorcing, there is no need to assume that the court should make an order. The court will make an order if there are circumstances when making an order would be better for the child than making no order.

Delay is bad for children (section 1(2))

The court must have regard to the general principle that any delay in determining the question is likely to prejudice the welfare of the child. (Children Act, s.1(2))

Delay is considered to be bad because it creates uncertainty and harms the relationship between parents and their capacity to co-operate in the future. This principle embodies the only explicit value judgement in the Act. What this means in practice is that the court will be much more involved in the conduct of each case. It is the court that controls timetabling (not the parties), so that drifting as a result of unnecessary adjournments and/or delay is prevented.

Notwithstanding concerns about the detrimental effects of delay, good reasons for delay have been endorsed by the courts, such as the advantages of allowing 'things to settle down' (*S. v. S.* 1992) and of monitoring a programme for interim contact (*Re B.* 1994).

Provisions of the Children Act 1989

The private law orders available under the Act are available in all 'family proceedings'. Family proceedings include proceedings under the inherent jurisdiction of the High Court and a number of different Acts (Children Act, s.8(3) and 8(4)).

Section 8 orders – residence orders, contact orders, specific issue orders and prohibited steps orders – are designed to resolve concrete, practical issues relating to the care and upbringing of children. They are not designed to confer rights. Section 8 orders are not made once a child has reached the age of 16, except in exceptional circumstances.

These orders incorporate in one enactment, with one common procedure, a wide variety of different remedies formerly requiring access orders, injunctions, custody and custodianship orders and others. The aim is to simplify cases, particularly where more than one remedy is sought.

The court is not bound by or confined to what has been asked for. It has the duty to consider all the powers open to it, and has the utmost flexibility in exercising its powers. It must choose the most appropriate order in the particular case, not necessarily the order sought (Children Act, s.1(3)(g)). The court may add conditions, give directions and make any other provision it thinks fit. Even if there is no dispute, if a child needs an order for purposes of security or stability, then the court will make an order. In family proceedings, therefore, section 8 orders can be made by the court of its own motion, even if no other family proceedings are being undertaken.

The object of section 8 orders is to preserve as much as possible of each person's independence in meeting his/her parental responsibility. They are designed to encourage the continuing involvement of both parents in their children's lives. They are not therefore the equivalent of a joint custody order, with its right of veto by one parent over important decisions by the parent with care and control. Residence and contact orders are not the same as the old custody and access orders. Their purpose is to promote parental responsibility by encouraging parents to try to resolve disputes themselves, and not to regard custody as a first prize and access as a consolation prize – their aim is to lower the stakes where there is disagreement. In addition, a residence order is different from a custody order, in that it is more flexible (different arrangements are possible) and is separate from parental responsibility. A residence order regulates the practical arrangements relating to where a child lives. It does not transfer or re-allocate parental responsibility, which continues in both parents. If there is agreement, there is no need for a court order.

Residence orders confer parental responsibility, and therefore legal security, on those who do not already have it, for example, unmarried fathers, non-parents or relatives. Residence orders provide a link between the private and public law. They are a means by which, for example, foster-parents may acquire parental responsibility and hence legal status in relation to fosterchildren. They are also a means whereby, for example, grandparents can care for a child at risk who might otherwise go into care. A residence order discharges a care order, and vice versa.

Once a residence order is in force, the child may not be removed from the UK or have his/her surname changed without the written consent of every person with parental responsibility, or without the leave of the court (Children Act, s.13(1)). While a residence order imposes an automatic restriction on the removal of a child from the UK, this does not prevent the removal of a child for a period of less than a month by the person with a residence order. There is no limit on the number of short trips that may be taken, but if there is a fear of abduction, a prohibited steps order may be necessary.

Residence orders may be made in favour of two or more persons who do not live together. The order may specify the periods for the different households concerned (Children Act, s.11(4)). The view of the court is that shared residence orders are 'non-conventional' orders, and should be made only where it can be clearly demonstrated that there is a positive benefit to the child (*A. v. A.* 1994).

Contact orders are intended to be wider than the old access orders, also covering arrangements other than physical contact, such as letters. The contact order is also more child-centred, in that it allows the *child* to visit or stay or have other contact with the person named in the order, rather than the other way round (Children Act, s.8(1)). Contact with a parent is a fundamental right of a child, save in exceptional circumstances (*Re W.* 1994). There may be more than one contact order, made out to anyone – that is, anyone with a serious interest in the child.

Recent case decisions confirm the courts' endorsement of the principle that it is important to preserve the child's contact with both parents. This principle of continuing contact is enshrined in article 9 of the United Nations Convention on the Rights of the Child (*Re R.* 1993).

Specific issue orders and prohibited steps orders cover decisions the court would make, for example, over which school a child is to attend, whether or not a child is to undergo an operation, whether a child may be taken abroad, etc.[3] A prohibited steps order can be made against anyone. That person does not have to be a party to the proceedings (*Re H.* 1995).

The checklist (section 1(3))

The checklist is a checklist of *factors* (*not* a set of guidelines) relating to the child's needs that the court must have particular regard to in making an order that places the welfare of the child as paramount. The checklist applies only in contested private proceedings (part II) and any proceedings under part IV of the Act.

The factors to be considered are:

- the ascertainable wishes and feelings of the child concerned (considered in the light of his/her age and understanding);
- his/her physical, emotional and educational needs;
- the likely effect on him/her of any change in his/her circumstances;
- his/her age, sex, background and any characteristics of his/hers which the court considers relevant;
- any harm which he/she has suffered or is at risk of suffering;
- how capable each of his/her parents and any other person in relation to whom the court considers the question to be relevant, is of meeting his/her needs;
- the range of powers available to the court under this Act in the proceedings in question.

In enshrining in law for the first time (other than in adoption proceedings) the principle that in family proceedings the child's wishes and feelings must be ascertained, the perspective of the child assumed a new significance and became the central focus of the Act. Case law has clarified the question of the weight to be attached to this factor, and whether the fact that it features first on the checklist gives it a predominance over the other factors.

> The courts, over the last few years, have become increasingly aware of the importance of listening to the views of older children and taking into account what children say, not necessarily agreeing with what they want nor, indeed, doing what they want, but paying proper respect to older children who are of an age and the maturity to make their minds up as to what they think is best for them. (*Re P. (A Minor) (Education)* [1992] 1 FLR 316, 321 BUTLER-SLOSS LJ).

Therefore, important though the child's wishes are when determining what, if any, order ought to be made, they are ultimately but *one* of the factors that have to be taken into account under the statutory checklist (see also *Re R.* (1995)). In this case, notwithstanding the expressed wish of the children to stay with their mother in the UK, the court ordered their return to the USA, where custody proceedings were taking place.

The checklist is intended to achieve consistency among courts in their orders relating to children and their welfare. Although limited in its application to contested proceedings, the checklist is useful where out-of-court settlements are being negotiated (by solicitors or the parties themselves), bearing in mind what factors the *courts* will look at in making decisions. The checklist is not an invitation to solicitors, mediators or social workers to apply it themselves in interviewing children or making assessments, etc.

The Lord Chancellor warned of the need for care in the application of the checklist:

> The Act sets out important principles many of which require those applying them to think as carefully about their attitudes and values as about legal concepts. The checklist in section 1 is a prime example: to evaluate a child's physical, emotional and educational needs, the effect on him of change, or any harm he may have suffered or is at risk of suffering – *these are complex questions, as complex as life itself*. No one profession can provide the answers to all of them but by working in partnership, a better answer for the child may emerge upon which the court may then act. (emphasis added)

Matrimonial Causes Act 1973 (s.41) (Children Act 1989, schedule 12, 31)

The policy of protecting the child in matrimonial proceedings is embodied in section 41 of the Matrimonial Causes Act 1973, which requires the court to consider the interests of the children before making absolute a decree of divorce or nullity, or before granting a decree of judicial separation. The court has to declare itself satisfied that where there are children of the family, arrangements for the welfare of each child have been made. To enable the court to discharge these duties, the petitioner is required to file with the petition, a 'statement as to the arrangements for children'.

Until amended by the Children Act 1989 (schedule 12, 31), section 41 required the court to make a declaration as to whether the arrangements were satisfactory or 'the best that can be devised in the circumstances' (Matrimonial Causes Act, s.41(1)(i)). The Children Act 1989 removed this requirement to make a declaration of satisfaction, replacing it with an increased duty on the petitioner to provide more detailed information about arrangements for children.

The Children Act 1989 makes no attempt to influence the nature or content of parental agreements, and the court is unlikely to interfere with agreements made by the parties except in exceptional circumstances. However, the increased disclosure requirements of section 41 mean that divorcing parents must provide the court with details of the proposed arrangements for their children. This means that although the Children Act removed the requirement for the court to make a judgment as to the adequacy of those arrangements, more is expected of parents in considering carefully and comprehensively the vital arrangements affecting their children. The Family Law Act carries this expectation further – under the new divorce reform proposals, such arrangements will have to be sorted out *prior* to obtaining a divorce decree (Family Law Act, s.7(1)(b)).

The Children Act 1989 attempts to redress a historical imbalance that has, in the past, favoured the protection and welfare of children over their autonomy and rights. This is a qualified autonomy, however. Children are entitled to participate in the decision-making process, but they are not to have the final say. The difficult balance must always be struck, whatever process of decision-making is adopted, between the need to recognize the child as an independent person and the risk of imposing on the child the burden of responsibility for making choices. The important point is that the law upholds the principle that children are persons to whom duties are owed, rather than objects of welfare, or possessions over whom power is wielded.

The Child Support Act 1991

The Child Support Act 1991 introduced, for the first time, an administrative formula approach to the calculation of child maintenance, instead of relying on the jurisdiction of the courts to determine, vary and enforce individual settlements. A new government agency, the Child Support Agency (CSA), was set up under the Act to apply and collect Child Support. The aim of the legislation was to increase the level and reliability of Child Support payments, and thereby reduce the amount of Income Support and other benefits paid to single parents. In theory, the Act upheld the uncontroversial political principle that parenting is 'for life', and that parents should, as far as possible, take financial responsibility for their dependent children, even when they do not live with them. The economic goal, born of the view that lone parents who received regular maintenance payments were more likely to take paid work, was also a powerful impetus behind the Act.

In practice, the application of the Act has been fraught with problems – largely foreseen – and the result both of flawed original proposals and incompetent implementation. A number of criticisms have been identified, including the following (Utting, 1995):

- The child support formula is over-complicated and draconian in its effects.
- Disincentives to work have been created.
- 'Clean break' capital settlements made prior to the Act (for example, giving sole ownership of the family home to the parent with care of the children) are not taken into account when calculating payments.
- The financial commitments of non-resident parents and their new families are inadequately recognized by the formula, creating difficulties and pressures for stepfamilies.
- Because maintenance obtained from the non-resident parent is

deducted pound for pound from benefit, lone parents on Income Support have little incentive to co-operate with the CSA.

- Long delays in issuing maintenance assessments have resulted in demands for the payment of large sums in arrears.
- Errors in calculation of the formula (reckoned to occur in two-thirds of cases) and delays in securing payments have created hardship for resident parents.
- Government targets for the number of claims to be processed and the amount of benefit to be saved in the first two years of the CSA were unrealistic.

Mediation and the Child Support Agency

When couples use mediation to sort out finance and property as well as children issues, they must take full note of the impact of the Child Support Act on their negotiations. Mediators therefore have a responsibility to ensure that couples are informed about the possible impact of the Child Support Act formula upon all their arrangements. If either party is already on Income Support, or is likely to become dependent on state benefit as a result of separation or divorce, they are informed of the way the CSA operates, and in particular that no calculations will be made without an accurate maintenance figure being obtained from the CSA. It is the *parties'* responsibility to obtain this calculation. In all cases, whether or not one or both parties is or is likely to apply for Income Support, the possibility of the operation of the Child Support Act should always be examined. As a benchmark for negotiations, a 'ballpark' figure for what the maintenance calculation might be, based on the couple's existing circumstances, will be used. This ballpark figure may be obtained from a variety of sources, such as the Citizens' Advice Bureaux, solicitors, legal consultants or the mediators, usually calculated outside the session.

The effect of the Child Support Act on mediation practice has been problematic. It can increase anxiety, mistrust and tension, and can inflame disputes over children. While one advantage of the formula is that it establishes the expectation of realistic financial support for children as a fixed item in an otherwise negotiable array of items, it can inhibit the development of options. Its overall impact on mediation is undoubtedly to complicate and possibly prolong negotiations. On the other hand, greater understanding about the Child Support Act and its impact may be achieved in the joint discussions of mediation, leading to a reduction of suspicion and fear.

Divorce reform

The government's proposals for divorce law reform were published in April 1995 in the White Paper entitled *Looking to the Future: Mediation and the Ground for Divorce*. This publication of policy followed an extensive two-year consultation process initiated by suggestions for reform published in the Green Paper of December 1993. The Family Law Bill, announced in the Queen's Speech on 15 November 1995, was enacted in July 1996, to be implemented in 1999. Parts I and II of the bill introduce the government's proposals for reform of the law of divorce as set out in the White Paper (1995). Part III deals with Legal Aid for mediation in family matters, and part IV incorporates an amended version of the Family Homes and Domestic Violence Bill 1995, covering the occupation of the family home in cases of domestic violence, the prevention of molestation, and other related matters.

Criticisms of the existing divorce law

The White Paper (1995) sets out the objectives that should be fulfilled in a good law of divorce, and which the present law, it argues, fails to meet in a number of respects.

The White Paper identifies five such objectives. In doing so, emphasis is placed on the importance of the consequences of divorce for the parties, and especially for their children. The objectives are:

- to support the institution of marriage;
- to include practicable steps to prevent the irretrievable breakdown of marriage;
- to ensure that the parties understand the practical consequences of divorce before taking any irreversible decision;
- where divorce is unavoidable, to minimize the bitterness and hostility between the parties and reduce the trauma for the children;
- to keep to the minimum the cost to the parties and the taxpayer. (White Paper, 1995, para.3.5)

The White Paper argues that not only is the present law not working well, but that it fails to meet the above objectives. The main criticisms of the current law are set out below (White Paper, 1995, paras 2.12–2.30):

- The system does nothing to help save savable marriages. In 75 per cent of cases, the fault facts of unreasonable behaviour and adultery are used to establish irretrievable breakdown in order to obtain a quick and easy divorce. The citing of allegations of bad behaviour militates against reconciliation, and exacerbates hostility. In many cases, the consequences of the dissolution of the marriage – for example, the financial reality and the loss of day-to-day contact with children – are not faced until it is too late. Arrangements relating to children, finance and property can take up to two years to sort out after divorce. The present system requires the couple to take up opposing positions, which again creates hostility and increases conflict. Even where solicitors representing the parties adopt conciliatory approaches to negotiation, the divorce process itself requires the parties to sue each other and to make allegations. Furthermore, arms'-length negotiations and litigation reduce communication between the couple, and can increase or create misunderstandings – another source of conflict.

- Divorce can be obtained without proper consideration of the consequences and implications. The present system makes no requirement for couples to sort out the arrangements for their separate lives before the divorce is granted.

- The system makes things worse for children. The conflict inherent in the casting of blame necessary in seeking a quick divorce or the prolonged uncertainty involved in waiting two years for a consensual divorce, or worse, five years on the basis of separation, are damaging to children. Research has shown that children suffer and are damaged as a result of conflict between parents, whether they are living together or apart.

- The system is unjust. The petitioner for divorce is construed by the law as the 'wronged party' and the respondent as the 'wrong-doer', which can create a powerful sense of injustice. This can be increased by the difficulty and expense involved in defending a divorce. The fault 'grounds' alleged are frequently exaggerated, and may be due to mental illness, disability or incompatible lifestyles – they are not necessarily 'faults' at all.

- The system is confusing, misleading and open to abuse. The central confusion lies in requiring the single no-fault ground for divorce (irretrievable breakdown) to be established by fault facts in most cases. Such allegations of fault, as already mentioned, are likely to be exaggerated, uncorroborated or irrelevant to the breakdown of the marriage.

- The system is discriminatory. The option of a consensual divorce relying on two years' separation is available only to those who have the means to separate and arrange separate accommodation before divorce. Those of limited means therefore have no option but to rely on allegations of fault.

- The system distorts the parties' bargaining positions. The party who does not want to divorce is in a stronger bargaining position because he/she can exact concessions over finance and the children, especially in separation cases, in return for their consent to the divorce.

While the White Paper (1995) focuses on the use of family mediation in the context of divorce proceedings, it recognizes that the advantages of mediation are not confined to divorce. Mediation may be appropriate for resolving issues relating to children as well as property and finance, in situations other than divorce (para.8.1).

The Family Law Act 1996: Divorce reform

The general principles underlying the Act (part I, section 1)

The Act sets out four main principles to which the court or any person exercising functions under Part II (divorce and separation) and Part III (Legal Aid for mediation in family matters) shall have regard. These are:

(a) that the institution of marriage is to be supported;
(b) that the parties to a marriage which may have broken down are to be encouraged to take all practicable steps, whether by marriage counselling or otherwise, to save the marriage;
(c) that a marriage which has irretrievably broken down and is being brought to an end should be brought to an end –

    (i) with minimum distress to the parties and their children;
    (ii) with questions dealt with in a manner designed to promote as good a continuing relationship between the parties and any children affected as is possible in the circumstances; and
    (iii) without costs being unreasonably incurred in connection with the procedures to be followed in bringing the marriage to an end; and

(d) that any risk to one of the parties to a marriage, and to any children, of violence from the other party should, so far as reasonably practicable, be removed or diminished. (Family Law Act, part I, s.1)

Marital breakdown (section 5)

Irretrievable breakdown remains the sole ground for divorce (Family Law Act, s.5). What is new is that no facts requiring allegations of fault are necessary to establish irretrievable breakdown. There is therefore no legal requirement to prove fault. Irretrievable breakdown is to be established by an objective test of breakdown – the sole fact of the passage of a period of time, a period to be used for the purposes of reflection (on whether the marriage has broken down irretrievably) and consideration (of the consequences of breakdown). The primary purpose of the period is to demonstrate adequately and with certainty that the marriage has broken down irretrievably, as well as to make arrangements for the future.

The period for reflection and consideration (section 7)

This demarcated period is 'a period with a purpose' (Consultation Paper, 1993, Foreword). During this period, initiated by a Statement of Marital Breakdown (Family Law Act, s.6), the opportunity is created for reflection and consultation, with the aim of rescuing savable marriages where possible, and ensuring that the parties, where they do decide to proceed to divorce, understand the practical consequences for themselves and their children *before* taking irreversible decisions. It is in considering what arrangements should be made for the future (Family Law Act, s.7(1)(b)) that the main opportunity for mediation is provided, and for which, in Part III, Legal Aid is made available.

A further opportunity for mediation is provided under section 13, where the court, on its own initiative or on the application of either of the parties, may give directions with respect to mediation to enable each party to attend a meeting to receive an explanation about facilities for mediation and to have the opportunity to agree to participate in it (Family Law Act, s.13(1)(a) and 13(1)(b)). There is no *requirement* to participate in mediation.

The original recommendation was that the period for reflection and consideration should be one year. This had the beauty of simplicity, and made sense practically and psychologically, especially for children. The complexity that now characterizes the Act in this respect creates new scope for legalistic manoeuvre. The period for reflection and consideration is nine months (Family Law Act, s.7(3)). This follows the three months between the Information Meeting and the making of the Statement of Marital Breakdown. However, where there is a child of the family under the age of 16, the period is extended by six months, as it is where one of the parties requests such an extension (Family Law Act, ss.7(11) and 7(13)). This extension is subject to exceptions – where it would be significantly detrimental to the welfare of any child of the family, or where an Occupation Order or Non-molestation Order is in force in favour of the applicant or of the child, made against the other party (Family Law Act, s.7(12)). So the period for reflection and consideration now amounts to 18 months where there are children of the family.

The extension of the period occurred despite the strong support for the one-year period that emerged during the consultation process. While it was argued on the one hand that a longer period could protect the interests of children by making divorce harder, this view was outweighed by those who argued that making divorce more difficult for those with children would not alleviate the problems of marital breakdown, and furthermore, that such delay was likely to harm children, especially if the parents blamed the children for the delay. A longer period would discriminate against those with children 'locked in unhappy marriages' (White Paper, 1995, para.4.18).

The Information Meeting (section 8)

Those who wish to make a Statement of Marital Breakdown must, except in prescribed circumstances, *first* attend an Information Meeting. Attendance at such a meeting is compulsory for the party making the Statement of Marital Breakdown, and must have taken place not less than three months *before* the making of the statement (Family Law Act, s.8). It is envisaged that meetings will be on a one-to-one basis, and not conducted in groups (although a husband and wife may attend together if they choose). Where one party has made a statement, the other party (also except in prescribed circumstances, such as situations of domestic violence) must also attend an Information Meeting before making any application to the court in relation to the child(ren) of the family or in relation to property or financial matters, or contesting any such application (Family Law Act, s.8(5)).

The Information Meeting must be conducted by an approved and qualified person who has no financial or other interest in any marital proceedings between the parties (Family Law Act, s.8(7)).

The purpose of the Information Meeting is to ensure not only that information is made available to people (both those whose marriage has not yet reached a crisis point and those who are already contemplating divorce), but also that 'they have assimilated the information as it affects them' (Lord Chancellor, 1995).

The Act sets out the information which is to be made available:

- marriage counselling and other marriage support services;
- the importance to be attached to the welfare, wishes and feelings of children;
- how the parties may acquire a better understanding of the ways in which children can be helped to cope with the breakdown of a marriage;
- the nature of the financial questions that may arise on divorce or separation, and services which are available to help the parties;
- protection available against violence, and how to obtain support and assistance;
- mediation;
- the availability to each of the parties of independent legal advice and representation;
- the principles of Legal Aid, and where the parties can get advice about obtaining Legal Aid;

- the divorce and separation process. (Family Law Act, s.8(9)).

The three months that must elapse between attendance at the Information Meeting and the making of the Statement of Marital Breakdown is intended to allow the parties time to reflect on their marriage in the light of the information received, and to encourage them to take every opportunity of saving their marriage by seeking appropriate help, as well as to take early advantage of the provision of mediation, where appropriate.

Mediation

Family mediation is introduced in both the Green Paper (1993) and White Paper (1995) (as their titles highlight: *Looking to the Future: Mediation and the Ground for Divorce*) as the major element in the development of a more constructive approach to the problems of marital breakdown. In line with the Children Act 1989, the proposals extend to divorce the principle that primary responsibility for decision-making should lie with the parties themselves. Mediation, premised on presuppositions of party competence and party authority for decision-making, and envisaged as a new part of an integrated divorce process, is to be available as a resource, supportive of the parties' own decision-making. Issues to be decided include the primary question of whether or not the marriage is over (with the possibility of reconciliation that this entails), and the arrangements relating to finance, property and children that must be settled as a precondition of the granting of the Divorce Order.

Mediation, it is acknowledged, should not be compulsory – 'compulsory mediation quite simply does not work, and is a contradiction in terms' (Lord Chancellor, 1995, p.704). However, it is to be given 'definite encouragement' as the means of providing a 'decent and civil' way of ending the marriage (White Paper, 1995, paras 5.21 and 5.22). In this way, it is envisaged that the parties will retain control and responsibility, will deal with fault and other relevant matters themselves in face-to-face discussions which will encourage direct communication, and as a result reduce misunderstanding and conflict. In supporting more direct negotiation between the parties, assisted where necessary by mediation, the White Paper expects that there will be less need for arms'-length negotiations *on behalf of clients* by lawyers, with the associated litigation, increased costs and increased conflict.

The Family Law Act creates four primary opportunities for mediation to take place:

- following the compulsory Information Meeting (s.8);
- following the Statement of Marital Breakdown; the central purpose of the period for reflection and consideration, once it is decided that there

is no hope for the survival of the marriage, is for the parties to make joint decisions about arrangements for the future; this is likely to be the main occasion for resort to mediation (s.7(1)(b));

- following the direction of the court once a statement has been made (s.13);
- when civil Legal Aid in respect of legal representation is being determined for financially eligible clients (s.29).

It is important to reiterate that participation in mediation remains a matter of choice for the parties. In upholding the principle of voluntariness of participation in mediation, the Act recognizes the fact that mediation will not be appropriate in all cases, including domestic violence. However, the court may direct that a party must attend a meeting for the purpose of giving an *explanation* about mediation. A similar compulsion attends the meeting with the mediator for the purpose of determining *suitability* for mediation in respect of an application for Legal Aid for legal representation. Finally, it is important to remember that the other usual routes into mediation remain available – self-referral, referral from other agencies, solicitors, health visitors, etc.

Public funding for family mediation: Part III Legal Aid for mediation in family matters

Until now, Legal Aid in divorce cases has been available only for legal advice and representation. The new proposals make public funding for mediation, in the form of Legal Aid, available for the first time. Part III of the Family Law Act 1996, amending the Legal Aid Act 1988, provides for Legal Aid for mediation in family matters to those who are financially eligible. Public funding for family mediation is thus made available for the first time.

A 'mediator' is defined as 'a person with whom the [Legal Aid] Board contracts for the provision of mediation by any person' (Family Law Act, s.26(3)). It is the mediator who determines suitability for mediation in respect of the dispute, parties and all the circumstances (Family Law Act 1996, s.27(3)).

Any contract entered into by the Board must require the mediator to comply with a code of practice which must also require the mediator to make arrangements designed to ensure the voluntariness of participation in mediation, the identification of the fear of violence or other harm, the review of the possibility of reconciliation, and that each party is informed about the availability of independent legal advice (Family Law Act, s.27(7)).

Under the code, such arrangements must also ensure that the parties are encouraged to consider the welfare, wishes and feelings of each child, and that there are opportunities for the consultation of the child in mediation (Family Law Act, s.27(8)).

The details of the terms and conditions for the payment for mediation – liability to make contributions, the amount of such contributions, the statutory charge, etc. – are to be covered by regulations yet to be published (Family Law Act, s.28). How the litigation concept of 'property recovered or preserved', to which the statutory charge now applies, can be imported into mediation remains to be seen.

The White Paper (1995) and the Green Paper (1995) on Legal Aid reform set out the likely form of funding as block-funded grants in the form of franchises to local mediation providers. Such franchises will have to be underpinned by quality standards relating to good professional practice and quality-assured standards of provision and delivery. These government proposals are based on the kind of service provision provided by National Family Mediation's 68 services. These already form the basis of an expanded nationwide network of services. As non-profitmaking services, they already have the advantages of clear structures of supervision and accountability and independent mediation facilities geared to families, providing intake sessions and screening for domestic violence. For mediation services to meet the demands of the new divorce law, the growth and expansion of services is essential. This cannot occur without planned, co-ordinated and properly-funded support from government if standards are not to be lowered and imbalances are not to arise between demand for mediation and the supply of mediators. This investment in development must therefore be recognized, notwithstanding that the government's main objective of these proposals is to reduce the costs of matrimonial proceedings to the Treasury (£332 million, or one third of the net civil Legal Aid budget, 1994/95).

A major concern about 'backdoor' compulsion into mediation for those on Legal Aid was centred on clause 26 of the Family Law Bill, which contained a presumption in favour of mediation over legal representation for the purposes of determining civil Legal Aid, except in certain prescribed circumstances, such as domestic violence or where a mediator determines a case is unsuitable. The Family Law Act 1996 now removes this presumption, though before a person is granted Legal Aid for legal representation, a meeting with a mediator in order to determine suitability for mediation, with particular reference to any fear of violence, must take place (Family Law Act, s.29(3F)). If mediation does appear suitable, the purpose of the meeting is also to help the person applying for representation to decide whether to apply for mediation instead (Family Law Act, s.29(3F)(b)).

The White Paper (1995) and the Green Paper (1995) are unequivocal in affirming that independent legal advice and assistance should be available at an early stage, and during and after mediation, wherever necessary. State funding for such advice and assistance should be available for eligible clients.

Relying on research findings (Walker et al., 1994), the White Paper states that with quality assurance mechanisms in place, it will not be necessary for lawyers to 'shadow' mediation or unpick mediated agreements (White Paper, 1995, para.6.21). On the other hand, the White Paper, because it envisages less need for arms'-length negotiations between lawyers, limits access to legal representation. This will be confined to cases where it is necessary – for example, where there is domestic violence, where the legal technicalities of the case require it, or where matters are unresolved in mediation.

Marriage guidance and counselling

Alongside mediation and legal services, counselling and marriage guidance services are encouraged in the divorce reform proposals to assist couples with marital problems to seek help as early as possible. The White Paper (1995) set up an Interdisciplinary Working Group on Marriage chaired by the Lord Chancellor's Department, to integrate policy and resources on marriage and divorce and to consult with researchers and service-providers. Responsibility for funding marriage guidance organizations and research organizations has been transferred from the Home Office to the Lord Chancellor's Department. While funding for counselling remains outside the remit of Legal Aid (because such issues are not justiciable), a free meeting with a marriage counsellor for those who would qualify for Legal Aid on a non-contributory basis, is now incorporated in the Family Law Act (s.23). Every party attending an Information Meeting will be encouraged to attend such a meeting, which will be paid for from sources outside the Legal Aid Fund. This free counselling meeting will also be available to individuals or couples moving from mediation to counselling during the period for reflection and consideration.

Pensions

The Pensions Act 1995 amends the Matrimonial Causes Act 1973 in four respects:

- There is a specific duty on the court to take into account pension rights when considering financial provision on divorce under section 25 of the Matrimonial Causes Act 1973.
- The court now has power to direct trustees or managers of a pension scheme to make a payment of a Deferred Lump Sum or Maintenance Order on behalf of the scheme member to the party without pension rights when the appropriate benefits under the scheme become due. The court also has power to order the scheme member to commute all

or part of the benefits which he/she has or is likely to have under the scheme, within the permitted Inland Revenue rules.

- The powers of the court to make Lump Sum and Deferred Lump Sum Orders are extended to the making of orders relating to lump sums payable on death under a pension scheme, including the nomination (where that power exists) of death benefit to the former spouse of the scheme member. In making such an order, the court can override the discretion of trustees or managers.
- It removes the reference to 'foreseeable future' in section 25 of the Matrimonial Causes Act 1973 so far as pension benefits are concerned.

The Family Law Act 1996 (s.16) now amends section 25B of the Matrimonial Causes Act 1973 (clause 15) and provides the court with the power to divide the pension assets on divorce, creating pension rights for the party who lacks them. This is unlikely to be brought into effect before the year 2000.

Pilot projects

The government is proposing to test and monitor the new arrangements for information and mediation services through a 'major comprehensive pilot project' before full implementation. In response to Part III of the Family Law Act 1966 which requires the Legal Aid Board (LAB) to secure the provision and availability of publicly funded family mediation services for clients eligible for Legal Aid, the LAB has published proposals for piloting the contracting of quality assured family mediation services (LAB, 1996).

The broad aim of the family mediation pilot project is 'to enable LAB to ensure that arrangements are in place to meet the demand for mediation services created by the Family Law Act 1996' (LAB, 1996, p.3). The LAB recognizes the problems of the current limited provision of family mediation services and the limited number both of fully trained and accredited mediators and of qualified supervisors. This aim will be achieved therefore 'by facilitating the development and expansion of the most effective arrangements to provide publicly funded and quality assured family mediation services for eligible clients throughout England and Wales' (LAB, 1996, p.3).

The objectives of the pilot project are to determine:

a) the relative benefits and cost-effectiveness of contracting for the provision of publicly funded and quality assured family mediation services through different supplier arrangements;
b) the most effective quality assurance and contracting arrangements for the delivery of publicly funded mediation services;
c) the level of quality assured legal advice necessary to support publicly funded family mediation and the most cost-effective arrangements for providing it;

d) the relative cost/benefits, for both the assisted persons and the taxpayer, of the provision of publicly funded mediation and the supporting legal advice compared to current legal aid arrangements (LAB, 1996, p.3).

In particular, the pilot is intended to identify:

- the best ways of providing high-quality, objective information;
- estimates of volume of demand for family mediation;
- the implications of state funding for family mediation;
- the most effective mechanisms for determining quality assurance and the evaluation of family mediation services;
- the most effective provision arrangements, and the development and expansion of these to create adequate provision of quality-assessed, cost-effective mediation services to meet the demand created by the Family Law Act.

The implementation plan proposed for the pilot project is structured to evolve over four overlapping phases commencing in September 1996 and culminating in early 2000. Phase I, following the initial consultation and preparation stages, is intended to start in early summer 1997. Subject to demand, increasing numbers of selected 'suppliers', meeting minimum franchise quality and contract requirements, will become progressively incorporated into the pilot project in ways that are intended to test the different arrangements most effectively and 'to ensure the most rapid and controlled expansion' (LAB, 1996, p.3). A final Code of Practice and Family Mediation Franchise Specification is to be published by early 1999. By Phase IV, contracting arrangements (three-year contracts) will be in operation with potential suppliers. Extensive marketing, audits, consultation and research evaluation will be conducted throughout the pilot project.

In addition, the pilot will be designed to address a number of other issues to determine the relative advantages of different arrangements, and any important interdependencies or effects of these arrangements. One of these issues will be the relationship between different types of clients and success rates – according to social group, age, education, ethnic origin, religion, and so on. This provides an important opportunity to ensure that there is recognition that for the provision of mediation to be efficacious, it must be available to all members of the community.

Given the careful design required in order to relate to a representative population of divorcees nationally and the range and number of questions to be considered, it is unlikely that the pilot project will be completed in less than three to four years (Family Policy Studies Centre, 1996).

Domestic violence: Part IV of the Family Law Act 1996

This is an amended version of the Family Homes and Domestic Violence Bill 1995, amended specifically to make a distinction between cohabiting and married victims of domestic violence. The original bill was perceived by some MPs as undermining marriage by according cohabiting couples equal status to married couples in cases of abuse. As it happens, existing law enables an abusive partner, whether married or cohabiting, to be excluded from the family home. Although unmarried victims of domestic violence will enjoy lesser protection under the bill than their married counterparts, the quality and quantity of personal and housing protection for adults, married or not, is improved and expanded. For example, Occupation Orders reduce the threat of homelessness, and Non-molestation Orders can apply to 'associated persons' as well as partners, married or cohabiting. 'Associated persons' can be ex-partners (married or cohabitees), relatives and non-related members of the same household (Family Law Act, s.62(3)). The Act increases powers of arrest attached to injunctions, 'unless satisfied that in all the circumstances of the case the applicant or child will be adequately protected without such a power of arrest' (Family Law Act, s.47(2)). The risk of violence to children is reduced, and their interests are given greater consideration in Magistrates' Courts, as well as County and High Court proceedings.

Ancillary relief

The matrimonial home

The court has extensive discretionary powers to make financial and property orders ancillary to divorce, nullity or judicial separation (the principal relief). All orders can be made in favour of either party to the marriage, and while the spouses are treated by the court on the basis of complete equality, this does not mean that there will be equal provision. Ancillary relief orders fall into two categories – those orders relating to income (periodical payments) and those relating to the transfer of capital assets (Cretney and Masson, 1997).

In proceedings for divorce or judicial separation, the court has very wide powers to do what it thinks just in relation to the ownership and occupation of the family home (Matrimonial Causes Act, ss.23, 24 and 25). This may extend to the transfer of ownership rights from one spouse to the other. It is nearly always a 'purely theoretical exercise' to determine the strict property rights of the spouses in these proceedings (*Fielding* v. *Fielding* 1978), though the court will be reluctant to interfere with joint ownership. The primary objective of the court will be to consider how the asset can best be used as a home (*Browne* v. *Pritchard* 1975). Each case is dealt with on its own facts, which means that the court needs to adopt the greatest flexibility in coming to its decisions.

Where the parties are not married or where the litigation does not fall within section 26(1) of the Matrimonial Causes Act (petitions for divorce, nullity or judicial separation), the power to vary title is unavailable. The court must therefore determine the legal and beneficial interests of the parties in accordance with the rules of property law.

So far as the occupation of the home is concerned, consideration should be given to the impact of any injunction that may be in operation. An injunction may either exclude a spouse (whether owner or non-owner) from the family home or part of it, or a specified area in which the home is situated, or it may require a spouse to allow the other to enter or remain in the home or part of it (Domestic Violence and Matrimonial Proceedings Act 1976, s.1). An injunction may also be granted restraining one spouse from molesting the other or any child living with the applicant. The court may also exercise these powers in favour of an unmarried cohabitee (see also Family Law Act, part IV).

Physical violence, or the threat of it, eviction (actual, attempted or threatened) and conduct making it impossible or intolerable for a spouse or the children to remain in the home, all come within the ambit of section 1 of the Domestic Violence and Matrimonial Proceedings Act 1976, which gives the court the power to suspend or restrict rights of occupancy, usually for a short period.

The disposition of the matrimonial home is a matter of profound practical significance in disputes over children. As it is in the material interests of children that they have accommodation, the issue of residence and the issue of the matrimonial home are inextricably connected. Since 1973, the practice of the courts has been to allow the custodial parent (now 'the parent with residence') the use of the matrimonial home by granting him or her occupation and, where appropriate, ownership rights. This applies whether the home is owner-occupied or is rented privately or from the local authority. In practice, therefore, fairness between the spouses *vis-à-vis* their property rights may be incompatible with the need to secure a home for the children. This accounts in part for the claim by some men that their lot is worse as a result of divorce than that of their former wives, who, as mothers, are the main carers of the children. Economic realities also account for the fact that Maintenance Orders are mainly made against husbands.

Ancillary relief reform

The unacceptably high cost of ancillary relief applications has caused considerable concern among all members of the legal profession. As a result, the Lord Chancellor's Department set up the Ancillary Relief Working Party, which has drafted New Rules intended to remedy the problems of expense and waste. Frequently, costs can be out of all proportion to the assets, and settlement, because it so often occurs at the door of the court, increases legal costs and wastes public resources.

The objectives of the reform are:

● to achieve more settlements cost-effectively, by controlling disclosure and isolating relevant facts;
● to concentrate on costs at the outset of the case, and to keep the parties publicly informed at every stage;
● to assist the courts better to control the pace and content of litigation, in order to achieve the just resolution of disputes promptly, economically and in accordance with the needs of the clients and their children;
● to ensure uniformity in practice and procedure in courts in different parts of the country;
● 'to interlock effectively' with the new procedures of divorce reform (Lord Chancellor's Department, 1995, p.2).

One of the new means of achieving these objectives is the introduction of the Financial Dispute Resolution (FDR) Appointment (Rule 8), a forum for the District Judge 'to explore, guide and direct the parties and their advisers through discussion of the issues in an informal setting' (Lord Chancellor's Department, p.4). It is recognized that this is a new kind of alternative dispute-resolution process, 'neither arbitration, adjudication or mediation', for which the District Judges will require special training (Lord Chancellor's Department, p.4). The FDR Appointment is not, it is stated, a 'head-banging' process, but 'a genuine opportunity to resolve any contentious issues in an atmosphere conducive to settlement with all the known facts and information available' (Lord Chancellor's Department, p.4).

Other proceedings

The mediator must be aware of the implications of proceedings other than those related to divorce that may affect the parties or the children – for example, wardship proceedings (where the High Court exercises its inherent jurisdiction with respect to children), injunctive proceedings (for example, Exclusion and Non-molestation Orders), and applications under the Children Act 1989 in the case of unmarried parents.

Legal advice and legal information

Mediators should not give legal (or any other) *advice*, but they can give legal *information*. The differences are set out below.

Legal advice involves applying the relevant law to the facts of the case and giving a legal opinion on those facts. In other words, legal advice involves interpreting the particular circumstances of the case in the light of the relevant law. Legal advice therefore includes evaluation and the recommendation of a particular course (or courses) of action – 'This is what you ought to do.' The giving of legal advice, because it involves a partisan relationship with the client (that is, a relationship of loyalty), is also inseparable from a relationship of representation (Riskin, 1984; Ryan, 1986).

Legal information involves setting out information as a *resource*, without recommending which course of action or which option to choose. The information could include statutory definitions, criteria used by the court, court procedures, grounds for divorce, tax consequences, legal rules and legal perspectives. This is more complex than it sounds, as subtle judgements are often required to explain the application of the law in general in setting out options, risks and benefits. A lawyer giving legal information does *not* represent either party, and remains impartial.

Informed consent protects both the disputants, the lawyers and the mediators. When a lawyer acts as a consultant or a mediator, it must be made clear to the parties that no representation of either party is involved. This is important, particularly where legal information is given by a lawyer to *both* parties. What is important is the nature of the relationship with the party, and the objective of that relationship. This must be clarified explicitly with the parties, and their consent must be obtained – again explicitly (Riskin, 1984). It is also important that the parties' legal interests are protected – by their own solicitors.

Solicitors

The growing interest in family mediation among solicitors comes at a time when there is official consensus about its nature and benefits and its relationship to legal process (Conciliation Project Unit, 1989; Roberts, 1992, 1993a, 1993b, 1995b). The Court of Appeal landmark decision on privilege in family mediation (*Re D*. 1993) was also significant in officially confirming understanding about the institutional location of mediation. Their lordships stated explicitly that mediation did *not* form part of the legal process, thereby affirming unambiguously the independence of mediation from legal process. It is in being a true and viable alternative to the legal system that the benefits of mediation lie. Where alternative processes have become adjuncts to an adversarial legal system, they have usually been co-opted to subserve overriding diversionary and cost-saving purposes, often without the protection of due process or a lessening of court control. Other dangers to the mediation process lie in attempts by lawyers to regain control over domains of dispute-resolution traditionally perceived as theirs. During the early development of family mediation in the UK, the Law Society was instrumental in seeking to confine dispute-resolution to the sphere of legal activity, and therefore the control of lawyers. This profoundly influenced and distorted the terms in which family mediation (or 'conciliation', as it was called) was then perceived – as a form of welfare activity primarily concerned with issues concerning children. This early way of thinking was reinforced by the professional ideology of the early mediators, many of whom came from professional backgrounds involved with child protection and welfare, such as social work, counselling and family therapy.

In the UK now, as witnessed in the USA over a decade ago, when 'legal professionals tumble[d] over each other in their enthusiasm for non-legal dispute resolution alternatives', the dangers of lawyers dominating the development of alternatives must be heeded. 'The relentless force of law in modern American society can be measured by its domination, and virtual annihilation, of alternative forms of dispute settlement' (Auerbach, 1983, pp.15 and 139).

Solicitors as mediators

Solicitors have historically claimed for themselves a partisan, advisory and representative role, and have come to be associated with it by the public. In acting as a mediator, the solicitor must adopt a role that is essentially different – that of impartial, non-directive facilitator of other people's own negotiations. As active, dominant, specialist advisers and champions, some solicitors have understandable difficulty in transforming to a role that is completely different.

There is nevertheless no reason why, with careful selection for personal aptitude, training and experience, a solicitor should not also act as a mediator, bringing valuable legal information into the process. A number of lawyer mediators already work in both the independent, non-profitmaking sector and the private sector of provision of family mediation. Here, these lawyer mediators offer their services outside their legal practice, having to make clear to the parties the capacity in which they are acting in accordance with the NFM and FMA Joint Code of Practice (NFM and FMA, 1993, para.2.5). However, worrying pressures are also being exerted towards confusing the separate roles and functions of lawyers and mediators, diluting and damaging both. Examples of this trend are set out below:

- Notwithstanding the creation, by the main mediation providers, of an independent professional body to establish standards and monitor and regulate professional practice (the UK College of Family Mediators), the Law Society of England and Wales (which is not a professional mediation body) seems bent upon determining its own professional mediation standards for solicitors. This could be damaging to the carefully-nurtured development over many years of mediation as a distinct and autonomous professional activity.

- The Law Society has authorized the practice of mediation by solicitors as part of their legal practice, provided the parties to the dispute are sufficiently informed as to the solicitor's role (Law Society, 1993, ch.22, principle 11.01).

- The Law Society has adopted the terminology 'solicitor-mediator'. This creates the same confusion of incompatible roles as does 'barrister-mediator' or 'judge-mediator'. If, as is understandable, the Law Society would want to highlight the value of the kind of substantive knowledge the mediator (who is also qualified as a solicitor) brings to the process, the role-neutral term 'lawyer mediator' could usefully serve that purpose.

- The definition of mediation used by the Law Society, while identifying most of the essential features of the process, does not make clear the crucial point that in mediation, it is *the parties* who are the negotiators, assisted in *their* negotiations by the mediator. This is a serious omission in a report for solicitors, given this fundamental departure from traditional practice, under which it is the solicitors themselves who are the negotiators (Brown, 1991).

Some solicitors endorse their practice of what they call 'evaluative' mediation. This is a directive form of intervention which involves an assessing and evaluative role for the intervener – assessing information about the parties and their quarrel, identifying and evaluating the options available to them, and persuading the parties to adopt a course of action which the *intervener* considers, in the light of his/her professional expertise, to be the best in the circumstances, on the basis of an evaluation of the merits of the case and of what the court might decide. In 'evaluative' mediation, therefore, the 'mediator' proffers him/herself as an authoritative specialist adviser who determines the outcome on the basis of knowing better than the parties what is best for them.

Other pressures, such as increased formalization, over-reliance on documentation and the elevation of the importance of legal (compared to mediatory) expertise, can lead to the mediation process becoming an alternative form *of* legal process, rather than an alternative *to* legal process (Effron, 1989).

Solicitors as consultants in mediation

Where expertise that is not already within the ken of the parties is required in mediation (such as legal, tax or welfare rights information), this may be introduced into the process in two main ways – either via the mediator him/herself (for example, a lawyer mediator), or via a consultant outside the process, providing the necessary expertise either to the mediator or to the parties. Research endorses the efficacy of both models, and confirms that the occasional presence of a lawyer neither causes difficulty to clients nor disrupts the flow of negotiations. Clients appreciated the contribution of this legal expertise (Walker et al., 1994).

Solicitors as solicitors-within-mediation

While it is widely accepted that parties in mediation should have independent legal advice available to them outside the process, the presence of the parties' solicitors during mediation is not the practice in the UK, nor does it appear to be a popular notion (McCarthy and Walker, 1996a). It is difficult to see how such a presence could be compatible with the chief objective and benefit of mediation – that the parties retain control over their own decision-making (see Chapter 11, note 3).

Solicitors as advisers

Mediation is not a substitute for legal advice, nor is it an alternative to legal representation. Mediators consider it important that the parties have resort, before and during mediation, to their own independent legal advisers, especially where financial and property issues are being decided (McCarthy and Walker, 1996a). Solicitors are also needed after mediation is completed, to provide advice on the merits of the agreement and to draft assistance in converting the Memorandum of Understanding (the record of decisions reached in mediation) into a legally enforceable agreement or a Consent Order. The Green Paper (1995) recommends provision of Legal Aid for these purposes, but denies the need for solicitors or other legal advisers 'to "shadow" the mediation process throughout, or to go over ground already covered or, except in rare cases, to unpick understandings reached in mediation' (Green Paper, 1995, para.9.13).

Research has shown that the thoroughness of discovery and disclosure of assets in all-issues mediation makes it extremely unlikely that mediated agreements will need to be unpicked by solicitors. Findings showed that clients valued the partisan support they received from their solicitors during and after mediation, and the reassurance they received about the decisions they were taking, especially the protection against unfavourable settlements (Walker et al., 1994).

It is not uncommon that negotiations between solicitors, and even litigation, over financial and property matters are going on in parallel with mediation efforts over children. The attitude of solicitors to mediation, the course of prevailing negotiations between solicitors, the way information is or is not communicated by lawyers to their clients, the imminence of hearing dates: all these legal influences affect the environment within which mediation is taking place.

Solicitors and mediators need to understand and respect each other's area of expertise and mode of intervention. Interdisciplinary co-operation, particularly over referrals, is necessary. The parties should be informed of their legal rights, and mediators should urge those who are unrepresented to consult solicitors. Similarly, solicitors should refer suitable cases to mediation. However, the mediator should not take over from the parties their responsibility to inform their solicitors of the progress or outcome of mediation. This could appear as if the professionals were assuming control and undermining the parties' authority. The mediator needs to hear what the dispute is about from the parties themselves, not from their solicitors. The mediator can help the parties to be clear about what has or has not been agreed (in writing, where appropriate), so that they can communicate information directly and unambiguously to their own solicitors, who may then translate any agreement reached through mediation into a formal Consent Order – again, if this is preferred by the parties.

The impact of litigation and adjudication

Although the disadvantages of litigation (cost, delay, further conflict, etc.) must be clearly understood by the parties in assessing their options, these should not be used by the mediator to pressure couples into agreement. It may well be that an adjudicated decision based on a full assessment of all the facts would be the best solution to a genuinely irreconcilable conflict of interest, for example in some disputes over children. If mediation in such a case fails and the parties choose to litigate, this does not necessarily mean they do not have their children's best interests at heart, or that they are being 'selfish'. On the contrary, their decision to seek an adjudicated decision may be precisely because they do care about the welfare of their children but differ fundamentally as to how to promote this. The benefits of adjudication in appropriate cases must be recognized. These include cases, for example, where an immediate decision is necessary in the interests of either of the parties and their children, where there are serious disparities of power and resources, or where an issue of public importance requires an authoritative ruling. The Law Commission (Law Com.192, 1990, para.7.24), endorsing

mediation as 'an important element in developing a new and more constructive approach to the problems of marital breakdown and divorce', nevertheless did not fudge the adjudicative responsibility:

> There are also dangers in relying too heavily upon conciliation or mediation
> instead of more traditional methods of negotiation and adjudication. These
> include exploitation of the weaker partner by the stronger, which requires con-
> siderable skill and professionalism for the conciliator to counteract while remain-
> ing true to the neutral role required; considerable potential for delay, which is
> damaging both to the children and often to the interests of one of the adults
> involved; and the temptation for the court to postpone deciding some very diffi-
> cult and painful cases which ought to be decided quickly. It is important that,
> whatever encouragement is given by the system to alternative methods of dispute
> resolution, the courts are not deterred from performing their function of determin-
> ing issues which require to be determined (para.5.34).

Referrals

Referrals to out-of-court mediation services come from many sources,
including Citizens' Advice Bureaux, Relate and self-referrals. The majority of
referrals, however, are from legal sources – solicitors, county court judges,
the magistrates' courts and the divorce court welfare service. Where referrals
are from the court or court welfare service, the mediator has a special responsibility to ensure that the parties know their attendance is a voluntary matter.
Although the court has no power to order a person to attend an out-of-court
service, a recommendation may be interpreted as an order (Davis and
Roberts, 1988). With voluntariness an essential characteristic of mediation, it
is important that people do not feel coerced. Research suggests that such
pressure reduces the chances of agreement, and that those agreements that
are reached are unlikely to last (Davis and Roberts, 1988).

Some American commentators have distinguished between coercion (of a
mild kind) into mediation, which might be acceptable (as part of the process
of educating the parties), and coercion within the process, which they regard
as unacceptable (for example, McCrory, 1985). While it is doubtful whether
many of those ordered into mediation would experience any lifting of
pressure once involved, it can be argued that there are those for whom the
compulsory attempt at mediation might prove a valuable face-saving device.

The legal position of parents

Both parents of a legitimate child are treated by law as each having parental
responsibility and its accompanying bundle of rights, duties, powers and

authority in respect of their child (Children Act, s.3). Until legal proceedings are initiated, therefore, parents have considerable power in relation to their children. But once the court is invoked, as in divorce or in proceedings relating to the care and upbringing of a child, then the court has the widest powers to make any order it thinks fit, and the welfare of the child becomes the paramount consideration (Children Act, s.1). As there is no agreed definition of what constitutes the best interests of the child, the chief value of the welfare principle lies in the moral and social ideal that it represents – that dependent and vulnerable children need to be protected from harm and given every opportunity to become happy and successful adults (King, 1987). Although in practice this principle may be used to legitimize the subjective values and prejudices that underlie the decisions of the court, it does at least require that the decision-makers attempt to look at the issues from the child's point of view (Children Act, s.1(3)(a)).

While in divorce proceedings the court has the widest powers to make such orders as it thinks fit in respect of any child of the family, it must be recognized that the intervention of the court, however powerful, is a relatively brief affair.

The legal status of mediated agreements

While couples are living together, there is a presumption that the domestic arrangements they make are not intended to give rise to legally enforceable obligations (*Balfour* v. *Balfour* 1919). No such presumption operates once they have separated or are about to separate (Bromley and Lowe, 1992). In those circumstances, it is their intention to create legal relations that is decisive, and that becomes a matter of fact to be inferred from all the evidence (*Merritt* v. *Merritt* 1970).

As far as children are concerned, in one way, the intention of the parties is of less importance, as the court always retains ultimate authority to intervene, and with the widest discretion (Matrimonial Causes Act, s.42, as amended by the Children Act, s.10). Nevertheless, the court will be reluctant to alter the agreed arrangements made by the parties if these are fair and satisfactory (*Beales* v. *Beales* 1972). An agreement that is written down is not more binding than an oral agreement, though as a record it could be of evidentiary importance. Mediators should make clear to the parties that the court must consider whether or not to exercise its powers regarding the arrangements made for the children before it will grant a decree absolute (Matrimonial Causes Act, s.41, as amended by the Children Act, schedule 12, 31).

As far as privately-agreed financial and property arrangements are concerned, the court will usually be prepared to impute to them an intention to create legal relations (Cretney and Masson, 1997). This applies whether or not the agreement is in writing. Maintenance agreements in writing are legally binding, and therefore enforceable. Their legal status is governed by statute (Matrimonial Causes Act, ss.34–6), and the definition of a maintenance agreement is wide, including agreements about the matrimonial home, its contents and the education of the children.

The parties must be aware that they can never achieve finality in their financial arrangements by making a private agreement. This will always be open to review. In the first place, it is against public policy for any agreement to fetter or to oust the jurisdiction of the court in matrimonial proceedings relating to financial provision or property adjustment. Any agreement that might restrict the right of either party to apply to court for financial provision is void (*Jessel* v. *Jessel* 1979). Furthermore, either party has the statutory right to apply to court to vary a subsisting maintenance agreement if there has been a change in circumstance or if the agreement does not make proper financial provision for any child of the family (Matrimonial Causes Act, s.35(2)). If these conditions are met, the courts have extensive powers of intervention. There are also other, more rarely employed means of reviewing private agreements, for example an agreement may be attacked as unconscionable. It should also be noted that once a financial agreement is embodied in a Consent Order, its legal effect derives from the court order, and no longer from the agreement.

Notwithstanding these powers, the court is reluctant to interfere with freely-negotiated agreements on financial matters made by the parties with full knowledge and proper advice unless there is 'some clear and compelling reason', such as duress or failure to disclose (Cretney and Masson, 1997, p.403).

At the conclusion of mediation, where a record is drawn up, whether a Parenting Plan or a Memorandum of Understanding (following all-issues mediation), this will set out all the matters settled (and, where appropriate, the reasons for decisions reached), accompanied by all the documents required for full disclosure of assets and income. Even where there is no written record, agreement over contact or residence may not easily be separated from agreement over maintenance or the family home. Because the legal implications of these arrangements are far-reaching, mediators need to be vigilant in urging the parties to check their agreements with their legal advisers.

Rule 261, Family Proceedings Rules: Full disclosure

Where the parties make a private agreement that includes any financial or property arrangements, and where that private agreement is to be embodied in a Consent Order under sections 23, 24, 24A and 27 of the Matrimonial Causes Act 1973, the court requires that there be full and frank disclosure (rule 76A, revised by rule 9 of the Matrimonial Causes (Amendment No.2) Rules 1985). This is an important protection against dishonesty by both parties and non-disclosure by one party, and is of particular value where only one party is legally represented. Most practising mediators are required by their code of practice to ensure that the parties make their decisions based upon sufficient information and knowledge. They must inform each party of the need to give full and frank disclosure of all material relevant to the issues being mediated, and assist them, where necessary, in identifying the relevant information and any supporting documentation. Mediators must make clear that they do not verify the information. The parties may obtain independent legal advice as to the adequacy of the information disclosed (NFM and FMA , 1993, ss.2–4). Research confirms that discovery and disclosure of assets were undertaken carefully in the NFM services offering mediation on all issues (Walker et al., 1994).

The decisions of the court

One important aspect of the legal environment of private decision-making is the kind of decisions that the courts are likely to make in similar circumstances. It would obviously be helpful if there was certainty in the law, or at least if the legal rules involved were reasonably capable of being ascertained. Unfortunately, as far as financial and children's cases are concerned, there is a lamentable uncertainty (for example, *Richards* v. *Richards* 1984; *Camm* v. *Camm* 1983; *Robinson* v. *Robinson* 1983; *Re G.* 1994; *Re M.* 1994).

However, it is possible, broadly speaking, to discern some of the principles that underlie decisions of the court, and which should therefore inform the legal backcloth against which solicitors as well as private individuals negotiate. But these 'legal endowments' (Mnookin and Kornhauser, 1979) do not necessarily influence the bargaining positions within these negotiations (Menkel-Meadow, 1993a).

Richards (1981) has identified four broad principles influencing decisions of the court, based on a study of reported cases and surveys of divorce cases. These are set out below.

The status quo

As far as decisions over the care and upbringing of children are concerned, it is very unusual for the court to change the child's place of residence. In most cases, the court confirms the *de facto* situation – it accepts the arrangements made by the parties (Eekelaar et al., 1977). The status quo is therefore rarely altered, both in uncontested and contested cases. This judicial reluctance to interfere recognizes that what is best for the child is the minimum of disruption of the child's emotional, social and educational life. In effect, it is also an acknowledgement of the limited effect of legal proceedings in such complex social and psychological circumstances.

What this highlights for mediators is the fact that the initial arrangements relating to children, made informally after separation, have important long-term legal implications. These arrangements are likely to persist and become the status quo confirmed by the court.

Mother or father as 'custodial' parent

On the whole, the courts do not favour either sex as the more suitable parent (Eekelaar et al., 1977). In pursuit of the objective of minimum disruption to the existing emotional and social ties of the child, the paramountcy of the status quo usually prevails. As all decisions are at the discretion of each judge, there are bound to be variations in the significance attached to the age or sex of the child, or to other considerations. Although, in practice, mothers frequently end up with care of their children following divorce, a preference for maternal care is no longer adhered to as a matter of principle (Maidment, 1984). It is because women are in the main the chief child-carers in marriage that they are likely to continue being so on divorce. Although a father may intend to press for residence initially, he is often influenced against pursuing his claim by the belief that he is unlikely to succeed. This clearly illustrates the way prevailing court decisions can affect the bargaining positions of the parties.

Parental responsibility

Within marriage, parents share parental responsibility and have equal rights in relation to children (Children Act 1989, s.3). This situation continues after divorce, whether or not a Residence or Contact Order is made. Parental responsibility may not be surrendered or transferred; some or all of it may be delegated, but it always remains intact (unless removed by adoption). This means that a parent with parental responsibility will always be responsible for ensuring adequate arrangements for the care of the child. If a Care Order is made, the local authority shares parental responsibility with those who have it already.

Prior to the Children Act 1989, a Joint Custody Order enabled both parties to retain their right to be consulted on major decisions affecting the child's upbringing, while recognizing that the child would live with only one parent (Cretney and Masson, 1997).

However, the significance of a Joint Custody Order lay, not in conferring any additional legal rights on the absent parent, but in its symbolic value in affirming for that parent a continuing commitment to and involvement in the upbringing of the child. The advantage of a Joint Custody Order was therefore psychological. Neither parent 'won'. The advantage from the child's point of view was the affirmation that both parents stood equally in relation to him/her. One possible legal disadvantage of the Joint Custody Order, particularly for the parent with care and control, was that independent action by either parent was limited to where no disapproval has been signified by the other (Children Act 1975, s.85(3)). In the absence of a Joint Custody Order, however, the rights of each parent were equal and exercisable without the other (Guardianship Act 1973, s.1). This meant that separate, equal rights allowed greater freedom of action than a Joint Custody Order (Maidment, 1984). Situations where no custody order was granted therefore usually proved to be the least problematic, both legally and psychologically. Parental responsibility similarly gives each parent the authority to act independently of the other in relation to the children (unless a court orders otherwise).

Where parents are unmarried, the mother has parental responsibility automatically. The father does not have parental responsibility unless he acquires it, either by an agreement with the mother made in a prescribed form ('a parental responsibility agreement'), or by application to court (Children Act 1989, s.4(1)) or on being appointed guardian. The essence of the granting by the court of a Parental Responsibility Order is the granting of status given to the father by fatherhood (*Re S*. 1995). The court will give express consideration to the father's degree of commitment shown to the child, the degree of attachment existing between father and child and the reasons for applying for the order (*Re H*. 1991). If the father fulfils these requirements, then, *prima facie*, it is in the child's interests that such an order be made (*Re G. (A Minor)* 1994).

The courts are reluctant to make Shared Residence Orders. All decisions depend on the individual facts, but a recent decision of the Court of Appeal indicates that such an order should only be made where it can be clearly demonstrated that there is a positive benefit to the child in making such a 'non-conventional' order (*A*. v. *A*. 1994).

Contact

Prior to the Children Act 1989

In about one-third to half of divorces, no Access Orders were made (Eekelaar et al., 1977). This is because they were not asked for, and the courts did not make Access Orders unless requested to. Only rarely was access denied to the then non-custodial parent (as in the case of *Wright* v. *Wright* 1980, where the father would use access visits to indoctrinate the child with Jehovah's Witness beliefs and possibly cause emotional disturbance). Sometimes, the court ordered conditions to be attached to access, for example that it be supervised by friends or unbiased relatives, or that the child should not be brought in contact with a named person.

After the Children Act 1989

The principle of continuing contact is generally upheld by the courts. This means that the court regards it as important that the child's contact with both parents is preserved – a principle enshrined not only in the Children Act 1989, but also in the UN Convention on the Rights of the Child (article 9) (*Re R.* 1993). Contact with a parent is regarded as a fundamental right of the child, save in exceptional circumstances (*Re W.* 1994). There must be cogent reasons why a child should be denied contact with both parents (*Re H.* 1992).

Despite the importance that the courts attach to preserving links with the non-resident parent, the legal system can do little if parents fail to exercise their right to contact, or if a parent obstructs contact, psychologically or practically. The courts are reluctant to enforce an order for contact if it has been flouted.

Notes

1 Matrimonial Causes Act 1973, s.1(2)(b): 'that the respondent has behaved in such a way that the petitioner cannot reasonably be expected to live with the respondent'. The test is objective – not 'Has the respondent behaved reasonably?', but given that the respondent has behaved in a certain way, can the petitioner 'reasonably be expected to live with the respondent' (Cretney and Masson, 1990, p.108).

2 For the purposes of this Act, 'the court' means the High Court, a county court or a magistrates' court (Children Act 1989, s.92(7)).

3 '"A specific issues order" means an order giving directions for the purpose of determining a specific question which has arisen, or which may arise, in connection with any aspect of parental responsibility for a child ... "A prohibited steps order" means an order that no step which could be taken by a parent in meeting his parental responsibility for a child, and which is of a kind specified in the order, shall be taken by any person without the consent of the court' (Children Act 1989, s.8(1)).

4 Conflict and disputes

The mair they talk, I'm kent the better,
E'en let them clash.
(Robert Burns, 'A Poet's Welcome to his Love-begotten Daughter')

The primary focus of the mediator is on disputes. These are the specific, identifiable issues which divide the parties and which need to be distinguished from the wider conflict that is also associated with family breakdown. The settlement of a dispute is achieved when the parties find a mutually acceptable basis for disposing of the issues over which they are in disagreement, even against a background of continuing conflict (Cormick, 1982). This may be compared with the resolution of conflict, which is achieved when the basic differences of value or fact or inequalities of power that divide the parties are removed. Broadly speaking, conflict in this domain is of three kinds.

Interpersonal conflict usually occurs between the two adults who are separating, and is associated with powerful, usually negative, feelings about each other, such as anger, resentment, betrayal, and so on. Conflict often spreads. Children may take sides in the matrimonial battle, involuntarily or from choice. New partners and grandparents may become embroiled as well. One basic cause of interpersonal conflict (and also an inevitable consequence) is poor communication between the parties. Misunderstanding, mistrust and hostility are frequent concomitants of broken lines of communication.

Conflict of interest may exist independently of interpersonal conflict. For example, there may be a genuine conflict of interest over residence or property. On the other hand, lawyers necessarily transform all issues and the objectives of their clients into established categories of legal conflicts of interest, simplifying them in the process, the better to gain control (Mather and Yngvesson, 1981). This and the competitive strategies of an adversarial legal system may exacerbate interpersonal conflict between the parties.

One conflict of interest not easily acknowledged is that between the parties and their own children. As former partners, both parties may want a 'clean break' and an end to contact with one another so that they may start new lives afresh. This wish will clash in most cases with the preferences and needs of their own children, for whom the continuation of a loving relationship with both parents requires their continuing contact (Richards, 1981). The decision of the parties to divorce is itself imposed on the children of the family, regardless of their views or needs (Mitchell, 1985).

Structural conflict – this includes the social-economic conflict of interest between men and women (Bottomley, 1984). In most cases, family break-down exposes the structural dependence of women in marriage, as far as work opportunities, wages and the division of labour within the home are concerned. The single-parent household, composed in the main of separated and divorced women caring for children on their own, bears in full the adverse consequences of women's economic dependence on men within marriage (Smart, 1984). These households, the majority of which are dependent on state benefits for at least a period of time, constitute the poorest, most disadvantaged section of our community (Maclean, 1991). Although the Finer Committee recommended the Guaranteed Maintenance Allowance in 1974, there is still no coherent policy of income maintenance. Not only has the Child Support Act 1991 failed to improve the financial position of lone mothers on means-tested benefits, but the high level of child care and housing costs associated with coming off Income Support, means that the UK has a low and declining proportion of lone mothers in employment, com-pared with other countries (Joseph Rowntree Foundation, 1996a, 1996b).

Conflict associated with family breakdown has many causes, some of which have been outlined briefly. Individual shortcomings, difficulties in getting along with others, stress, changes in circumstances, ill-health, poverty, isolation, belligerent legal advisers and an alienating and expensive legal system may, in the most unfortunate situations, combine to place people under impossible pressures. In this context, it may be helpful to emphasize four general points relating to family conflict.

In the first place, it would be misleading to associate conflict exclusively with separating or divorcing families. With little or no research on the sub-ject, practically nothing is known about conflict in intact families. It is usually when families break up that private conflict becomes public, perhaps for the first time, and the stresses and strains, insensitivities and inequalities of ordinary family life become manifest.

Secondly, attitudes to conflict, and the emotional and behavioural cues signalling conflict, differ according to culture and ethnicity. In some cultures, for example, direct confrontation is regarded as exacerbating conflict, and therefore best avoided. In other cultures, on the other hand, confrontation is seen as desirable (Goldstein, 1986).

Thirdly, the positive benefits of conflict must be acknowledged. Conflict can signal constructive ways of bringing about change and of re-ordering lives. At least the potential for positive change is greater where there is anger than where there is the helplessness and hopelessness of depression.

Finally, there are limits to the impact of outside intervention of any kind. The healing effect of time itself, plus people's own efforts in overcoming their difficulties, must not be underestimated.

Disputes

A dispute may be defined as a sense of grievance over a specific issue, which is communicated as a contested claim to the person regarded as responsible or blameworthy (Roberts, 1983b, p.7). The complex evolutionary processes by which experiences of injustice and conflict become grievances, and grievances become disputes – the 'naming', 'blaming' and 'claiming' stages that characterize the emergence and transformation of disputes – have been identified by Felstiner et al. (1980).

Disputes can be about many things (Caplan, P,1995):

- material goods – for example, rights to land and property;
- the right to make decisions;
- social relations – for example, marital relations;
- the need to work out 'existential predicaments' such as the meaning of love, beneath the ostensible reasons, – for example, land, sexual jealousy (Caplan, P, 1995, p.2);
- ways of grouping people together, even in the short term;
- the need to highlight important differences.

Anthropologists have identified the importance of the dimension of time for understanding disputes. The relevance of the past has also been highlighted for family mediators (Grillo, 1991). That certain structural relations can give rise to 'chronic eruptions' of dispute, even if each episode is settled, reflects the longer history of which each episode is part. The story goes on in 'the still-to-be experienced futures' of the individual protagonists and the larger social group (Falk Moore, 1995, p.32).

The focus of family mediation in the UK has been primarily upon issues over children following separation or divorce – residence and contact disputes in the main – for example, which parent is to have the day-to-day care of the child, and how, when and for how long the non-resident parent can have contact with the child. Financial, property as well as children issues are also being mediated, although these represent only about 20 per cent of mediated cases (NFM, 1994b). Disputes can also occur over the divorce itself (whether there should be a divorce, who should petition, on what 'grounds', and so on). Since the Children Act 1989, a wider range of family issues is being mediated, some involving grandparents, step-parents, and more recently local authorities, in public law (child protection) cases. Family disputes generate intense emotional reactions, though disputes of any kind, particularly between individuals, have a high emotional content as well. While recognizing that those disputes brought to mediation may well have deep and tangled emotional (as well as social and economic) roots, the mediator does not reinterpret issues in ways that give underlying conflict greater significance than the 'surface' disputes defined as problematic by the parties themselves.

Disputes over contact

In most cases, parents make their own arrangements over contact. This fundamental fact has crucial legal as well as social and psychological implications, and yet there is practically no information available about either this process of voluntary negotiation or what factors contribute to the making of such successful arrangements.

Murch (1980) has described how access problems are often symptomatic of a fundamental dilemma that faces divorcing parents – how to disengage from a broken marriage while still being an adequate parent with a part to play in the children's future. Thus separation of spousal and parenting roles involves the recognition that the kinship relationship between the parties as parents, created by the very existence of their children, can never be sundered (Bohannan, 1971). But although the kinship relationship is not altered, the way that it is carried out is (Simpson, 1994), and this requires the working out of contact arrangements, both by negotiation between the parties (in order that joint decisions can be made) and by their co-operation, however meagre, over the practical ways and means of carrying out those decisions.

Yet in the aftermath of the breakdown of personal relationships, conditions for direct negotiation could not be more difficult, and the potential for conflict is enormous (Kressel, 1985). It is not surprising, therefore, that findings suggest that access has generated more contention than custody, largely because access is a continuing source of friction, requiring the parties to collaborate over arrangements for their children over many years (James and Wilson 1984; Kressel, 1985). It also generates great anxiety, particularly of loss or the threat of loss (Murch, 1980), and it has been found that the course of access reflects very accurately the success or otherwise of the reorganization of the post-separation household and the adjustment of its members, most especially the children (Wallerstein and Kelly, 1980; Murch, 1980).

Contact and the law

Section 8 of the Children Act 1989 governs the orders that the court may make concerning contact, to resolve specific areas of dispute, rather than to confer rights. A Contact Order 'means an order requiring the person with whom a child lives, or is to live, to allow the child to visit or stay with the person named in the order or for that person and the child otherwise to have contact with each other' (Children Act 1989, s.8(1)). Contact Orders are wider in scope than Access Orders, and may cover arrangements other than physical contact, such as letters. The emphasis has also shifted from the adult to the child. The Contact Order is more child-centred than an Access Order, in that it allows the *child* to visit, stay or have other contact with the person named in the order, rather than the other way round. There may also be more than one Contact Order made out to any person. The Contact Order is a positive order, *requiring* contact to be allowed.

Another difference of note is the emergence of contact as a legal entity in its own right. Under section 42 of the Matrimonial Causes Act 1973, which used to govern the orders the court made over access, access appeared to be of little juristic importance. It warranted no separate mention, subsumed as it was under the definition of 'custody' (Matrimonial Causes Act, s.52). Judges continue to have the widest possible discretion in the making of Contact Orders, governed by the same welfare principle that used to inform the making of decisions over custody (Guardianship of Minors Act 1971, s.1) and which now informs any decision relating to the upbringing of children or the administration of a child's property (Children Act 1989, s.1).

In about 45 per cent of divorces, the court made no order for access at all, leaving arrangements to the parents themselves (Eekelaar et al., 1977). Where the court did make an Access Order (and there was wide variation between individual courts), 'reasonable' access was the rule, rather than the exception. Reasonable access, premised as it was on the principle of parental competence, left to the parents responsibility for making whatever arrangements were suitable to themselves (Wilkinson, 1981). Where conflict made this coordination impossible, access might be defined by the court and conditions and details laid down, such as location, frequency and duration. Occasionally, the court exercised a supervisory function, with access overseen by the court welfare service or, where facilities were more suitable, by a local authority social services department nominated by the court. Also, a child might be made subject to a Supervision Order where this was thought to be in his/her interests.

Most access disputes that were brought to the attention of the court were 'settled' either by solicitors or court welfare officers. Contested access cases rarely reached the hearing stage, and those that did were some of the most difficult to come before the court (Eekelaar et al., 1977). Long delays were common, in some cases a year passing before the hearing (Eekelaar, 1978). Section 1(2) of the Children Act 1989 now states:

> In any proceedings in which any question with respect to the upbringing of a child arises, the court shall have regard to the general principle that any delay in determining the question is likely to prejudice the welfare of the child.

Courts have a proactive duty to ensure that section 1(2) of the Children Act is not contravened (*Re A.B.* 1995).

Whatever the court orders, however, the implementation of contact depends ultimately on the willingness and ability of the parents themselves to make contact work – a fact seldom appreciated by those threatening legal action over contact. Although the court has powers of enforcement (the imposition of a fine or imprisonment of up to two years for contempt of court) and has threatened an obstructing parent with the removal of custody, in practice, little can be done if a parent is determined to thwart a court order and make contact difficult or impossible. In *Re D. (A Minor)* (1993), the Court of Appeal held that implacable hostility *may* be a cogent reason for departing from the general principle that a child should grow up to know both his/her parents, and certainly would be a reason if the mother's implacable hostility put the child at serious risk of harm.

In most disputes over contact, however, English case law reveals a strong presumption in favour of contact with the non-resident parent taking place. Coincidentally, in line with recent social research findings, contact is believed by the courts to be in the interests of children, and will be denied only in exceptional circumstances. This presumption was also extended to illegitimate children (*S. v. O.* 1978). As stated earlier, an unmarried father does not have parental responsibility automatically, unlike an unmarried mother, unless he acquires it either by an agreement with the mother, or by an application to the court, or by being appointed guardian (Children Act 1989, s.4).

Whether contact is regarded by the court as a basic parental right (as in *S. v. S.* 1962) or as a basic right of the child (as in *Re W.* 1994), the outcome should not be affected, as the welfare principle applies either way. In the majority of cases, the arrangements which the parents make over contact are accepted by the court at the Children's Appointment (Matrimonial Causes Act s.41). But as the petitioner will want no restriction on obtaining the decree absolute, as the respondent is not required to be present at the Children's Appointment and seldom is, and because of constraints of time and a reluctance by the court to disturb the status quo, difficulties over contact will seldom surface.

Contact and social research findings

Research findings stress the importance of stability and security through continuity of the child's relationship with both its parents after divorce, and the importance of contact as the means of implementing this (Walczak with Burns, 1984; Wallerstein and Kelly, 1980; Benians, 1976, 1980). At the same time, research findings in the UK and the USA reveal that regular contact is actually exercised in a minority of cases, and that within a short time, separation results in the virtual end of the relationship of the child with one of the parents and the wider family, usually the father, with significant effects on the child's social development and capacity to form and sustain relationships with others (Richards, 1994a).

The broad, current consensus of professional opinion, sociological, psychological and medical, that emphasizes the importance of the successful management of contact – 'the single most important factor in reducing to a minimum the emotional upheavals for children' (Benians, 1980, p.378) – is subject to two caveats. Firstly, the research of psychiatrists is biased towards the disturbed cases, which are the ones that come to their attention. Secondly, there are so many variables that affect children on separation, such as the age of the child, experiences before and after separation, the circumstances of separation itself, the quality of relationships, the impact of domestic violence[1], poverty and class, to mention a few, that in the light of existing knowledge, generalized conclusions should be regarded with great caution.

Contact and parents

Mediators should never presume that the parties know that they can and may make their own decisions over contact. In spite of the fact that in the majority of cases contact arrangements are left to parents to sort out for themselves, it is not uncommon for them to express surprise on two counts:

- that they are 'allowed' to make their own arrangements (rather than that these be determined for them by solicitors or courts);
- that these arrangements do not have to conform to some fixed standard pattern of what contact ought to be like, but may vary in accordance with the wishes and particular circumstances of those involved.

Even though one of the advantages of mediation is the scope that it provides for educating the parties regarding their rights and powers of self-determination, it is not uncommon for one or both parties to try to cast the mediator in the role of arbitrator, in an attempt to abdicate decision-making responsibility. The mediator must resist any temptation to assume parental responsibility. However helpless and confused the parties may feel, and however intractable the problem may appear, their active participation is essential to its resolution.

Contact and mediators

Until the late 1980s, the bulk of the work of British mediators concerned disputes over children, mainly contact disputes. As already noted, the limitations of the legal process for tackling the complex personal, economic and social facets that are often part of any dispute over contact, plus the fact that ultimately, the couple themselves must work together if contact is to take place, make mediation a particularly appropriate method of dispute settlement for contact disputes.

It would be fair to say that most mediators share the pro-contact presumption of the court, where this is consonant with the child's welfare and happiness. Most parents, too, in voluntarily resorting to mediation, establish their own concern over the issue of contact. It is not for the mediators to decide that a quarrel over children is really a quarrel about finance, or vice versa, or an excuse to act out interpersonal emotional issues. As one mother frankly put it: 'We are using the children to fight about the children.' This is not to deny the intermeshing of issues, or the fact that the settlement of one dispute, say over contact, may lead to co-operation over other issues such as maintenance or the family home. Research findings (McCarthy and Walker, 1996b) show that those couples who used all-issues mediation were more likely to reach agreement than those who used mediation only for sorting out children issues. In the latter cases, there was more likely to be continuing disagreement over contact arrangements and other issues relating to children, such as religious upbringing, education and health care.

Mediators may be tempted to refer to social research findings on divorce and its consequences for children, both to endorse their concern about the damage that might be inflicted on children by parental conflict, and to back up suggestions they might make as to how to mitigate this. Great caution must be exercised. In the first place, it is not the function of the mediator to give expert advice. Secondly, there are problems involved in offering expertise in matters of child care that must be acknowledged. As already noted, research findings are inconclusive, changing and conflicting (for example, Goldstein et al., 1973, on the central right of the custodial parent to determine access). Then there are the difficulties of extrapolating from general findings to the particular case. The dangers that research findings may be used (intentionally or not) to pressurize parents psychologically should not be underestimated. For example, parents may be made to feel guilt or fear if told that unless certain courses of action are or are not followed, they may be putting their children 'at risk' (of emotional disturbance, delinquency, or whatever).

The sort of information that the mediator can usefully proffer to people working out their own arrangements is of a neutral kind and related to their particular circumstances: for example, where a couple who have a relationship fraught with conflict want a flexible arrangement requiring continuous negotiation over every contact visit, the potential disadvantages of this should be pointed out, compared to the advantages of a predetermined and predictable arrangement that avoids occasions for confrontation. For a co-operative couple, on the other hand, such flexibility may be less of a problem.

Contact disputes may erupt at any time, even many years after divorce. However, the sooner a satisfactory regime of contact with the non-resident parent is established, the better, both because the arrangements (or absence of arrangements) set up are the ones likely to continue, and because at least one of the harmful effects of separation may be mitigated – the loss of contact between children and one of their parents. The longer the delay, the more difficult it is to renew a broken relationship (Mitchell, 1985).

Typical contact disputes

Some typical disputes over contact are set out below, but it should always be remembered that although there are recurring patterns, no two families are the same, and the unique and special circumstances of each predicament should never be ignored. Having said that, it should be mentioned that couples also take comfort in knowing that they are not alone, and that their disputes and difficulties are commonly experienced by others who are separating or divorcing.

- The resident parent reports that the child does not want to see the non-resident parent, who is demanding contact. The resident parent may or may not agree with the child's stand. Either way, the resident parent says he/she is not prepared to force the child into contact against its will. The non-resident parent blames the other parent for 'brainwashing' the child, and for not encouraging the child to keep in contact sufficiently.
- The resident parent opposes contact, not in principle, but because of the failure of the non-resident parent to abide by certain conditions, such as reliability, punctuality, and so on. Contact involving overnight stays is often opposed, because the resident parent does not want the child exposed to 'immorality' – namely the presence of a new partner in the non-resident parent's home or bed.
- The resident mother believes the father is using contact as a means of 'getting at' her. The demand for contact is viewed as an interference, preventing her from leading her own life. Years of past neglect or lack of interest in the children are cited as proof that the father does not

really care about the children. The father may admit taking his children for granted in the past, but is now seeking to remedy that situation.

- Contact may be denied in retaliation for the non-payment of maintenance. It is claimed that if the non-resident parent really cared about his children, he would contribute more to their material well-being.
- The resident parent wants to decrease or discontinue contact, because the children are disturbed or distressed before and/or after contact visits.

In most cases, the resident parent is the mother, but it would be wrong to regard disputes over contact only in terms of mothers exploiting their powerful position as parents with the care of children in order to obstruct the fathers' contact with their children. Most resident parents accept that contact is desirable, but there are frequently valid obstacles and genuine differences of view about terms and conditions that obstruct unproblematic contact, regardless of the gender of the resident parent.[2] Some resident parents are anxious to improve the quality and circumstances of contact and to effect an *increase* in contact between child and absent parent, both for the child's sake and to gain some respite from the unrelieved grind of child care. A sharing of discipline may be positively welcomed, particularly as children get older.

Emotional tensions surrounding contact visits may also aggravate disputes. The contact visit may provide the only opportunity former spouses have of pursuing private quarrels. The presence of an ex-partner on the doorstep may trigger off a row. For children, contact may be the equivalent of moving from one hostile camp to the other. The conflict between the adults and the conflict of loyalties that this imposes on the children may make contact a dreaded rather than a happy event. Contact may be a reminder to children of their broken family, so that transitions to and from visits may be painful and the cause of distress, rather than the visits themselves.

Another issue that frequently emerges in negotiations over contact relates to the social and economic context of the specific dispute. Until reckoned with, it may constitute a major obstacle to agreement (Davis and Roberts, 1988). Many women bringing up children on their own demand recognition from the fathers of the important job they are doing and of its difficulties. What is wanted is an explicit acknowledgement from the father of the mother's part in bringing up their children alone in tough, often unremitting circumstances. It is a task not to be taken for granted by the father, associated as he often is with good times, holidays and treats. This recognition must not be confused with a demand for pity or sympathy, nor necessarily with a demand for more material support.

Similarly, non-resident fathers often need explicit reassurance from mothers that they will not lose their children, and that nothing will be done to jeopardize their relationship with them. This anxiety is particularly acute when stepfathers are in daily contact with their children, or there is talk of changing surnames, or even adoption. The strength of feeling on this issue is expressed by one non-resident custodial father following a mediation session at which he agreed not to see one of his children:

> I think the biggest thing that came across, other than the two main agreements, was that she [the resident mother] was made to be aware of the fact that I am the children's father and nothing she or anybody else can do can change that, and she shouldn't try to.

Notes

1 In situations of domestic violence, findings show that the welfare of children may not be best served by children having direct contact with fathers who continue to behave abusively towards their ex-partners and/or their children (Hester *et al*, 1996).

2 Simpson (1994) highlights the relationship between level of contact and class. The maintenance of continuing ties after divorce depends on resources – the support of family and friends and crucially, material resources (e.g. money for maintenance, travel, gifts, socializing etc).

5 Negotiation and mediation

In negotiation there are two distinct though interconnected processes going on simultaneously: a repetitive, cyclical one and a developmental one. A simple analogy is a moving automobile. There is the cyclical turning of the wheels ... that enables the vehicle to move and there is the actual movement of the vehicle from one place to another. (P.H. Gulliver, 1979, *Disputes and Negotiations: A Cross-cultural Perspective*, p.82)

The process of negotiation

Unless the investigator has some theories about the agreement process in negotiation, about why and in what ways the parties do (or do not) reach agreement, it is difficult to see how he can analyze the contribution of the mediator to the resolution of conflict. (Stevens, 1963, p.123)

The nature of the negotiation process as essentially a process of communication and learning through a series of exchanges of information has been mentioned earlier (see Chapter 1). This process is not in itself either haphazard or chaotic. If it were, negotiations would be doomed to failure. Whatever the differences in the society, the kind or complexity of the dispute, the length of time needed to reach a settlement, or the framework, the process itself generates an internal structure of its own, a 'succession of stages' that are common to all negotiations, even though no two instances are the same (Stevens, 1963, p.10). This intrinsic structure that emerges from and is shaped by the process of negotiation also manifests itself in the rules the parties themselves create, and in the mutual understanding that is a product of the process. The role of the mediator is understandable only as part of this process.

An invaluable processual analysis of negotiation is described by Stevens

(1963) and Gulliver (1977, 1979). It is derived from their empirical research in the sphere of labour relations in the USA and in dispute-resolution processes in East Africa, respectively. This is an analysis of great relevance to mediation in family disputes as well. Gulliver (1977, 1979) has highlighted two concepts that are fundamental to an understanding of mediation and the role of the mediator:

- Mediation serves a negotiation process.
- The role of the mediator is understandable only within an understanding of that process.

Gulliver (1977) has described the negotiation process realized through mediation as 'the gradual creation of order and of co-ordination between the parties'. The mediator orchestrates this process, in which the parties begin with a degree of assumed knowledge, but also, both consciously and unconsciously, with a considerable degree of uncertainty and downright ignorance. That knowledge is tested and altered and refined in the process of interaction. Exchanges of this kind proceed through a series of 'overlapping phases', by means of which progressive and orderly movement towards settlement becomes possible. Each party is engaged in learning – about the other, about him/herself, about the children, and about the possibilities and impossibilities of their common situation and possible outcomes. Through a process of improved communication and understanding, the parties have the opportunity to learn not only more about all the circumstances, pressures, feelings, perceptions, attitudes and needs that attend the particular dispute, but also how to negotiate. This involves learning how to listen and understand more fully the other's perceptions and interests, how to act rationally and communicate effectively, and how to be open to persuasion rather than coercion or bullying. The wheels of information exchange and learning that the mediator activates motivate the negotiation process through its developmental progress towards settlement.

These interlocking developmental and cyclical processes reflect the reality of 'a general overall trend from relative ignorance, uncertainty and antagonism towards increased understanding, greater certainty and coordination' (Gulliver, 1979, p.173). What propels this whole process is the basic contradiction between the parties' antagonism (the dispute itself) and their simultaneous need for joint action.

A developmental analysis of negotiation

The staged process outlined below follows Gulliver (1977, 1979) closely. When a disagreement is precipitated by a crisis into a dispute, one party, or perhaps both, seeks to gain the involvement of others, and the issue then enters the public or semi-public domain (Gulliver, 1977). Six overlapping phases then follow:

1 searching for an arena;
2 defining the agenda;
3 exploring the field;
4 narrowing differences;
5 bargaining;
6 ritualizing the outcome.

Searching for an arena

The arena must be acceptable to both parties, although one may be resistant initially. The arena covers not only the geographical or social location, but also who is involved and the ground rules.

Defining the agenda

The search for an arena is also part of the attempt to define the dispute. One party may not know what it is that is in dispute, or the issue may have to be clarified and distinguished from other issues or emotional implications.

Exploring the field

In this relatively early phase, the emphasis will be on the differences between the parties. The messages passing between them are intended not to influence or shift the other, but to explore the dimensions of the field within which further negotiations are to occur. Initial maximal claims and demands are likely to be set, and extreme assertions expressed. The atmosphere is likely to be of competition, even hostility.

Narrowing differences

There is a progressive shift in orientation from difference and animosity towards co-ordination and even co-operation. This may be accomplished by resort to one or more of several strategies – for example, by dealing with the less difficult issues first, or dealing with each issue separately. If this phase goes well, there should be a resolution of some items, and the clarification and isolation of any remaining differences.

Bargaining

This may follow on those items which have been most difficult to resolve, though they may not be the most important objectively. This is when 'I give in on this if you give in on that' may occur. Sometimes an outcome is reached with an unexpected and arbitrary suddenness, when 'agreement *per se* has become more important than the particular point of agreement' (Gulliver, 1979, p.168).

Ritualizing the outcome

If all goes well and agreement is reached, there is a ritualization of that agreement. This means that the outcome is marked in some way, according to culture – for example, by shaking hands or by drawing up and signing a document. 'The negotiations have been concluded and there may be a good deal of amity. On the other hand, a persisting antagonism and a number of disagreements may remain; the parties may be bitter rivals still. For the moment, however, there is agreement, whether limited or broad, and a mutuality in the achievement of an outcome' (Gulliver, 1979, p.169).

The stages of mediation follow these stages of the negotiation process – a process of discovery and clarification, the essence of which is learning through a series of exchanges of information. The process must be experienced by the parties themselves as negotiators, participating in a dynamic process of exploration of each other and themselves. This leads finally to the convergence of a joint decision acceptable to both parties, the end of the dispute, and the end of negotiations. It is the mediator's job to understand and manage this negotiation process between the parties.

The phases outlined in Gulliver's model have a psychological and social as well as a logical coherence. For example, at an early phase, when maximum claims and demands are likely to be made and antagonism will be greatest, the parties are furthest apart in every sense. Intense emotion and harsh language will characterize this distance, for anxiety and insecurity are acute. With the articulation of resentment, the exchange of information and the increase of learning, stress diminishes. Yet this distance between the parties is necessary if subsequent movement is to be apparent.

Real-life mediated negotiations are often more complex and variable than is suggested by these analytically distinct phases. Breakdown can occur at any stage. But without a regular pattern of expectations, adjustments and behaviour, negotiations would fail. Without an understanding of this pattern by the mediator, negotiations could be prolonged or damaged if, through ignorance, hurry or inexperience, short cuts were attempted.

One feature of the mediation process unavailable to judges is its 'procedural flexibility' (McCrory, 1981, p.56). This enables the parties themselves to determine the parameters of their exchanges, freeing them from legal formalities or prohibitions, so that they may include those aspects of the dispute that they deem to be pertinent – for example, the emotional ramifications of the dispute, and private ethical attitudes to fault and fairness.

The procedural flexibility of mediation also allows the requirements of full and accurate disclosure necessary for the mediation of financial and property matters to be accommodated. Procedural steps can be inserted at every stage of the process for dealing with the income (gathering, verifying, displaying and sharing), the assets (identifying, understanding and valuing), the options (collating, identifying gaps, dividing, etc.) and the outcome (integrating the package, drawing up a Memorandum of Understanding).

The framework of mediation

'For of Mediation one is tempted to say that it is all process and no structure' (Fuller, 1971, p.307).

What this observation serves to highlight is the difference between the processes involved in mediation and those involved in adjudication. The latter is characterized by institutional rules, formal procedures and clearly demarcated roles and authority (judges, barristers, clerks, and so on). It is within this formal pattern of due process that any dispute is dealt with.

As we have seen above, no such institutional framework occurs in negotiation processes. The parties seek to sort out their dispute by voluntary exchanges, negotiation and decision-making. But where the parties cannot manage this on their own and so resort to mediation, some structural changes are inevitable.

Firstly, a simple bilateral process is obviously transformed into one involving a third party. Secondly, the very presence of this third party imposes the rudiments of a framework upon the encounter – for example, who is to participate and where, the time to be made available, and so on. Mediated negotiations require this minimum of rules at least, although cross-culturally, mediation processes differ greatly in the way they are organized, the degree of formality (a lack of formality by no means indicating a lack of control), the rigidity of the framework and the number of rules imposed upon the disputants (Roberts, 1983b).

This framework within which mediatory processes occur serves two main purposes:

- It enables the parties to negotiate together in a way that would not have been possible on their own. Ground rules – for example, the right of the mediator to intervene if things get out of hand – embody the values that underpin mediation (such as mutual respect, equity of exchange, and so on) and make rational communication possible.
- The framework is designed to secure fairness. Rules of procedure make possible equal opportunities for full and confidential expression – for

example, the separate meeting with the mediator within the session, and the guarantee that both parties will be able to state their positions without interruption.

The interwoven nature of structure and process is a conspicuous characteristic of mediation – the structure encompassing the process, and the process itself informing the structure.

Models of mediation: Structural variations of mediation sessions

There are a variety of structural arrangements or models that can be used to frame the mediation process. Some examples of these are examined below.

Single or plural meetings

Some agencies (such as the out-of-court South-East London Family Mediation Bureau) offer mediation on children issues in a single session. The intention is to focus effort on reaching an agreement on at least one issue in a single negotiating session lasting up to two-and-a-half hours. A second or even a third session may be organized if the couple wish to renegotiate an agreement or when warranted by the circumstances – for example, when some trial arrangement is being tested out and needs reviewing, when there are several issues in dispute, or when very entrenched parties need more time to make the movement that is necessary for an agreement to be reached. On the whole, however, the parties start out knowing there are clearly-defined time constraints, and that they are not embarking on a protracted counselling-type relationship with the mediator. This single meeting is particularly suitable for the single-issue dispute such as contact or residence, when the limitation of time and the concentration of focus combine to direct energies and attention onto the settlement of immediate and specific issues. Research has shown that the outcome of the first meeting is usually replicated on subsequent meetings (Davis and Roberts, 1988).

It can be argued that the single mediation session places the parties under too much pressure, and that agreements so reached will be superficial and unlikely to be adhered to. There is no evidence to support this criticism in relation to out-of-court mediation, although there is research evidence suggesting that where settlement-seeking takes place in the course of court proceedings, the pressures do undermine the parties' authority (Davis and Bader, 1985) (see also Chapter 2).

Joint or separate sessions

A joint session involves the presence of both disputants at the same mediation meeting. When the meeting involves the mediator and one party only, this is a separate session, and may take place as an early phase within a longer joint session (what Americans refer to as a 'caucus').

There are powerful arguments as to why mediation is best conducted in the presence of both parties. Joint meetings enable the mediator 'to observe the parties in their direct relationships with each other', and thereby to gain a clearer understanding of the issues in dispute (ACAS, no date, paras 38 and 39). One of the main advantages of mediation in disputes involving children is the opportunity it provides to increase mutual understanding and to facilitate communication and continuing negotiation between the parties. The couple must manage the many adjustments that are inevitably part of the process of maintaining contact through their children over the years. They must be able to negotiate together. If they will not agree even to be in the room together, doubt must be cast on the appropriateness of mediation in these circumstances.

Within the joint session, the parties must have an opportunity to express their viewpoint to the mediator in the absence of their former partner. This vital protection should be available not only at the first meeting, but at the outset of any subsequent session. It gives the mediator a fuller understanding of the situation and how each party sees it, and gives the couple the safety and freedom to state their views and feelings fully. This separate time with each party is not a substitute for pre-mediation screening for unsuitability for mediation.

Shuttle mediation

This refers to the way the mediator may function as a go-between, shuttling between the two parties, who remain physically (and possibly temporarily) apart. The mediator may act as a simple conduit, passing messages back and forth, or may negotiate actively on behalf of those disputants who obviously cannot negotiate directly. Shuttle mediation is commonly used in international disputes, and occasionally in community, environmental and labour relations disputes.

There are three main purposes behind the use of shuttle mediation:

- It aims to avoid confrontation, both for the parties and for the mediator, where the level of conflict is high.
- It allows the parties to disclose confidential information to the mediator that they do not want revealed to one another (see Chapter 9, p.134).
- It gives the mediator the opportunity to discuss matters that would be uncomfortable to raise if the parties were together (Folberg and Taylor, 1984).

In disputes following family breakdown, the disadvantages of shuttle mediation outweigh the advantages, except in special circumstances such as illness,
extreme stress or intimidation, where it may be of value as a prelude to joint
negotiation. A vulnerable party may feel safer initially communicating at a
distance, but it is fair to say that if the level of conflict, anxiety or fear is that
high, mediation is probably not appropriate anyway.

Some disadvantages of shuttle mediation:

- The mediator lays him/herself open to charges of partiality. Alliances
  may more easily arise, or be perceived to arise, between the mediator
  and one party. The mediator is placed in the well nigh impossible
  position of having to act as spokesperson for each party, and yet not to
  take sides. In the absence of both parties, the mediator cannot demonstrate the impartiality that is central to the mediatory role.
- The mediator does all the negotiating. The parties are not only denied
  the information derived from direct experience of each other, but they
  do not learn how to negotiate together.
- The power of the mediator and possibilities of manipulating the mediation process are increased. The mediator may find it tempting to
  exceed the messenger role, especially when negotiations are going
  badly, as is likely when the parties cannot or will not meet directly
  together in the first place. The mediator's total control over communication gives opportunities to control the substance of that communication, for example by changing an emphasis, omitting or reframing
  statements, and so on. Misunderstandings, many of which cause or
  exacerbate conflict, are often compounded or created in communications between third parties (solicitors' letters, for example). While the
  role of a mediator in shuttle mediation differs from that of a solicitor,
  who represents the interests of one party only, the problems arising
  from third-party communications remain the same. Unless everything
  is out in the open, and seen to be so, the task of the mediator in improving communication is seriously hampered.
- The protection of confidential information is problematic. Disputants
  have no means of knowing whether private information imparted in
  confidence to the mediator remains protected, especially if the subject
  crops up spontaneously anyway, such as the intention to move house,
  change job, end the relationship with a new partner, and so on. This
  could lead to a loss of trust in the mediator, and so undermine his/her
  efforts.

Co-mediation

This occurs when two mediators, ideally one male and one female, mediate together in a particular case (see Chapter 11, p.168). Co-mediation by two members of the same sex should always be avoided because of the risk of perceived bias, and of being outnumbered three to one by the opposite sex. Although it may appear to be more expensive and requires careful planning and time for preparation, there are distinct advantages in using two mediators in certain cases – for example, where there are a number of parties, or where there is high conflict or there are particularly difficult circumstances.

The advantages of co-mediation are:

- Impartiality is enhanced if neither the male nor female viewpoint prevails, or is perceived to prevail.
- Co-mediators can set an example to the disputants of how to negotiate. Of particular value to the disputants is the way the mediators overcome their own (occasional) disagreements. Courteous and considerate behaviour by the mediators sets the tone for relations between the parties.
- Co-mediators can share the demanding task of mediating, especially in the longer, single sessions. They can monitor each other's contributions, offsetting weaknesses, reinforcing messages and providing complementary skills, information and approaches, particularly if they have different professional backgrounds, for example law and psychology or social work.

In addition to gender bias and imbalance, the disadvantages of co-mediation include:

- Problems of authority, status, control and territory between the two mediators, particularly when they have different professional backgrounds.
- Conflicting styles and approaches which can result in confusion over strategies, timing and the division of labour or a power struggle between the workers.
- An increase in the risks of exerting pressure on the parties for or against certain options and outcomes.
- One mediator dominating, setting a bad example to the parties.

6 The mediator

... the primary function of the mediator ... is not to propose rules to the parties and to secure their acceptance of them, but to induce the mutual trust and understanding that will enable the parties to work out their own rules. The creation of rules is a process that cannot itself be rule-bound; it must be guided be a sense of shared responsibility and a realization that the adversary aspects of the operation are part of a larger collaborative undertaking. (Lon L. Fuller, 1971, 'Mediation – Its Forms and Functions', p.326.)

In this chapter, the role and functions, the attributes and the ethical responsibilities of the mediator are outlined. Some of the inherent tensions in the mediatory role are also pointed out.

The role and functions of the mediator

The main functions of the mediator are those of catalyst and facilitator. A large body of work exists to illustrate the complex and subtle ways in which the mediator, notwithstanding these minimal functions, is acknowledged to exercise influence within the process (Deutsch, 1973; Gulliver, 1979; Pruitt, 1981; Rubin and Brown, 1975; Stulberg, 1981; for further discussion on this subject, see Roberts, 1992b, 1994).

The mediator as catalyst

Succinctly stated, the mediator's presence affects how the parties interact. His presence should lend constructive posture to the discussions rather than cause further misunderstanding and polarization, although there are no guarantees that the latter will not result. (Stulberg, 1981, p.94)

Merely by being there, the mediator alters the relationship between the disputing parties and exerts an influence. This happens in the following ways:

- The mediator brings about an interaction that would not have been possible otherwise.
- The presence of the mediator is a reminder that the issues in dispute are there to be confronted. In identifying these, the parties may find it necessary to justify and explain their respective positions and demands, and therefore have to think them through.
- The mere presence of the mediator generates pressures towards co-ordination, even co-operation. Schelling gives two vivid examples of this aspect of the mediator's role:

> The bystander who jumps into an intersection and begins to direct traffic at an impromptu traffic jam is conceded the power to discriminate among cars by being able to offer a sufficient increase in efficiency to benefit even the cars most discriminated against; his directions have only the power of suggestion, but co-ordination requires the common acceptance of some source of suggestion. Similarly the participants of a square dance may all be thoroughly dissatisfied with the particular dances being called, but as long as the caller has the microphone, nobody can dance anything else. (Schelling, 1960, p.144).

Expectations of reasonableness, open communication and mutual respect can actually bring these behaviours about. People want to look good in the eyes of third parties, and so behave towards each other with restraint and minimal courtesy (Rubin and Brown, 1975; Pruitt, 1981). In setting up norms of 'rational interaction', the mediator fulfils an important function. At the very least, with fair rules, the parties in conflict are helped 'to fight fairly' (Deutsch, 1973).

The mediator as facilitator

The mediator's main function is to facilitate the negotiating process between the parties. The more relevant and accurate the information that passes between them, the greater will be their understanding of the facts, feelings, expectations and values that give rise to and colour the issues that divide them. This shared knowledge of the pressures that affect both parties, and of the implications both of reaching and of not reaching an agreement, may lead to a modification of preferences and goals. This improved understanding is produced by the process of negotiation itself (Fuller, 1971). But the mediator contributes to this process by facilitating the parties' communication, learning and decision-making.

Stulberg (1981) analyses the main facilitator functions in the following terms:

- *educator* – the mediator explains and informs, about aspirations, reasons, constraints, meanings, and so on;
- *translator* – the mediator conveys each party's proposals 'in a language that is both faithful to the desired objectives of the party and formulated to insure the highest degree of receptivity by the listener' (Stulberg, 1981, p.94);
- *'agent of reality'* – the mediator points out the feasibilities, practicalities and crucially, the possible consequences of proposals.

These main functions are supplemented by many others (see Chapter 7). What is necessary now is to examine the specific attributes required of the mediator, in order that he/she may fulfil these functions most effectively.

The attributes of the mediator

The attributes of the good mediator, both personal qualities and qualifications, are clearly elucidated in Goethe's description of his character Mittler, in his evolutionary progress as a mediator:

> This singular gentleman was in earlier years a minister of religion. Unflagging in his office, he had distinguished himself by his capacity for settling and silencing all disputes, domestic and communal, first between individual people, then between landowners, and then between whole parishes. There were no divorces and the local judiciary was not pestered by a single suit or contention during the whole period of his incumbency. He recognized early on how essential a knowledge of law was to him, he threw himself into a study of this science, and he soon felt a match for the best lawyers. The sphere of his activities expanded wondrously and he was on the point of being called to the Residenz so that he might complete from on high what he had begun among the lowly when he won a big prize in a lottery. He bought a modest estate, farmed it out and made it into the central point of his life, with the firm intention, or rather according to his fixed habit and inclination, never to enter any house where there was not a dispute to settle or difficulties to put right. People superstitious about the significance of names say it was the name Mittler, which means mediator, which compelled him to adopt this oddest of vocations.[1]

Of great importance are Mittler's knowledge relating to the matter in dispute, his skills in analysis and problem-solving, his awareness of the moral dimension to the problem, and his wisdom and compassion in his relations with people. What emerges is a combination of attributes, intellectual, moral and personal,[2] that goes towards making the practice of mediation both a science and an art.

Very little has been written about the qualities of the mediator. One reason for this is the weight that has long been attached to the personal rather than the processual aspects of the role. Personal qualities, often elusive and idiosyncratic, are not easily susceptible to analysis. The most useful approach to an understanding of what qualities make up the ideal mediator is to adopt the perspectives of the parties to the dispute. In one such study (Landsberger, 1956), based on the parties' evaluation of what was required of the good mediator, the following preferred qualities emerged:

- originality of ideas;
- sense of appropriate humour;
- ability to act unobtrusively;
- the mediator as 'one of us';
- the mediator as respected authority (that is, personal prestige);
- willingness to be a vigorous 'salesperson' when the situation requires it;
- control over feelings;
- attitudes towards and persistence and patient effort invested in the work of mediating;
- ability to understand quickly the complexities of a dispute;
- accumulated knowledge (of labour relations, in this study).

Raiffa's (1982) list of the qualities of a good mediator, quoting from the experience of the well-known American mediator William Simkin, includes most of the above, as well as physical endurance, faith in voluntarism (in contrast to dictation), the hide of a rhino and the wisdom of Solomon. Stulberg (1981) further includes the capacity to appreciate the dynamics of the environment in which the dispute is occurring, and intelligence, manifested in both 'process' (communication) skills and 'content' knowledge (depending on the kind of dispute involved). Such knowledge equips the mediator to ask penetrating questions, to be aware of subtle nuances and of when artificial constraints are being erected, but it should not be used 'for the purpose of serving as an expert who advises the parties as to the "right answers"' (Stulberg, 1981, p.96).

Impartiality

The white line down the center of the road is a mediator and very likely it can err substantially towards one side or the other before the disadvantaged side finds advantage in denying its authority. (Schelling, 1960, p.144)

Maintaining an intermediate position between the disputants is one of the most essential of the attributes of the good mediator. The mediator must prevent head-on collision between forces advancing in opposite directions, in an unobtrusive, minimal yet authoritative way, providing protection and/or support to one or the other party whenever necessary.

The mediator must always be above suspicion that he/she is biased for or against one or other party. Impartiality is central to the trust both parties must have in the mediator if his/her intervention is to be effective. This depends on skill and knowledge, as well as on the personal integrity and commitment of the mediator (ACAS, no date, para.15). Impartiality therefore constitutes a fundamental principle of practice, an essential attribute of the mediator, a duty and a skill.

Impartiality *vis-à-vis* the parties must be distinguished from the separate issue of *neutrality* (McCrory, 1985). There are three main problems in confusing neutrality with impartiality. The first is one of accuracy: the mediator is not neutral, inevitably having his/her own views, values and interests. Secondly, claims to mediator neutrality overstate what is possible, laying mediators open to legitimate challenge. Thirdly, claims to neutrality could be dangerous if neutrality is asserted in situations of inequality (Haynes, 1980).

The impartiality of the mediator may be protected in the following ways.

The mediator must make absolutely clear at the outset, his/her commitment to impartiality in the decision-making process.

The mediator must give due weight to each party's point of view. This is best secured by giving each party a separate opportunity at an early stage in the session to express their perspective in the absence of the other, and by making sure in the subsequent joint gathering that each point of view is heard and understood by both. The right of each party to hold a different, even conflicting, position on the issue will often have to be affirmed. At the same time, the mediator must recognize and challenge self-righteous claims about motives and behaviour based on biased perceptions of benevolence and legitimacy – 'I am right/good; you are wrong/bad' (Deutsch, 1973).

The mediator should not pronounce on the merits of either party's position or express a preference for any given outcome, but where it is appropriate to voice an opinion, to proffer guidance or to make a suggestion, this must be done tentatively and openly so that the risk of imposing views or insinuating assumptions is avoided. Another risk damaging to impartiality is where the mediator's own views may be seen to coincide with those of one of the parties – for example, on the need for regularity in the contact arrangement or in favour of contact with an absent father.

An even-handed approach is not incompatible with the mediator pointing to the consequences on each other and their children of the parties' respective behaviour, especially to the negative effects. It is the way this is done that is important. However, the making of judgements, moral or psychological, is incompatible with the mediator's task of managing the quarrel impartially. The mediator must accept the validity of a variety of child-rearing practices, religious and moral beliefs and lifestyles, and must not allow private attitudes or feelings to intrude, for example by disapproving or approving of lax or authoritarian approaches to child-rearing.

An impartial stance does not mean that the mediator cannot give support to either party at different moments in the negotiation process. Whatever the objective facts, each party is likely to perceive themselves as the more vulnerable one. The purpose of the mediator's understanding of these feelings is to enhance reciprocal understanding in the parties themselves.

The use of co-workers of different genders is one way of safeguarding impartiality in certain circumstances. This can prevent any one perspective predominating or being perceived as such, or alliances being formed along or across gender lines (see Chapters 7 and 8).

The structural framework or model governing the mediation session may enhance or diminish the protection of impartiality, for example joint meetings. Where the parties are not expected to meet together, but negotiate separately through the mediator shuttling in between, impartiality cannot be seen to operate, and the mediator may lay him/herself open to charges of partiality (see above). The structural arrangements play a vital part in preventing the occurrence of 'negative positioning' of one party, as identified in North American research (Cobb and Rifkin, 1990, 1991).

Ethical responsibilities

The major ethical responsibilities of the mediator are set out below. These are more likely to be fulfilled if mediators constantly bear in mind the nature of their intervention – as 'outsiders involving themselves in the affairs of others' (Cormick, 1982, p.264). These responsibilities can only be fulfilled if the mediator earns trust by practising with integrity and competence (Davis and Gadlin, 1988).

The mediator's first responsibility is to protect the right of the parties to be the architects of their own agreement.

The mediator has a responsibility to those parties not actually present at the negotiating table but who are affected by any agreement reached there. 'The greater the impact of the issues in dispute on parties not at the table, the more critical the responsibility of the mediator' (Cormick, 1977). This does not amount to the mediator representing the interests of those unrepresented at the table. However, the mediator must ensure not only that the parties consider the impact on others of any agreement they make, but also the impact of others on the agreement.

A premise underpinning mediation in family disputes is that parents love their children and are best able to make decisions for them (Folberg, 1984). The mediator is neither the advocate of the child nor the social worker for the child. It is the parents' role to protect the interests of their child (Folberg, 1984, p.205). The task of the mediator is to assist the parents in fulfilling that role, and to ensure that in making joint decisions, they consult and give due weight to their children's views wherever possible, and consider all the likely consequences of alternative arrangements, especially on their children. While most mediators will be very concerned about the needs of children as the innocent victims of separation and divorce, they must be careful, in expressing their concern, not thereby to imply a lesser concern in the parents themselves. The mediator therefore has a responsibility to assist the parties to protect the interests of their children. (See also Chapter 10 on children and the mediation process.)

The mediator has a responsibility to ensure that the parties' participation in the negotiation process is fair and equal. Imbalances in bargaining power must be recognized. Where duress occurs, mediation should cease. (See Chapters 7 and 9 for a fuller discussion of this topic.)

Mediators have a responsibility to ensure that they understand and respond appropriately to the impact of cultural difference on mediation. One approach to this emphasizes the need for mediators to share the cultural and ethical norms of the disputants, and therefore to come from the same cultural background and community, exploring and adapting indigenous forms of mediation where appropriate. Another approach argues that with training, a single group of mediators can work with a variety of cultural groups. A third approach recommends the combination of the two, recognizing that further research is necessary (for discussion on this subject, see Goldstein, 1986; Gale, 1994; Shah-Kazemi, 1996).

Mediators have a responsibility to understand the nature of their authority and power (see pages 164–70 for a discussion on the safeguards necessary to minimize the potential for the abuse of power by the mediator). They need to recognize their potential to influence or manipulate the course of the negotiation process as well as the substantive issues in discussion (see, for example, Dingwall, 1988; for a debate on this research, see Roberts, 1992b, 1994, and Dingwall and Greatbatch, 1993, 1995). This means that they need to acknowledge their own interests and values, however altruistic (for example, in protecting children or the weaker party), and the ways in which these might be insinuated, for example by emphasizing some issues or in rephrasing or ignoring others. The giving of information by the mediator, which is acceptable, must be distinguished from the giving of advice. The latter involves recommending strategic courses of action or making tactical suggestions in the light of the law, decisions of the court and the particular circumstances. The giving of information, on the other hand, is supposed to be neutral, involving an explanation or clarification only of rights, resources, terms, and so on (see pages 64–5).

Central tensions in the mediator's role

> The process of mediation and the role of the mediator in particular is shaped by the strategies adopted to cope with this tension between the need to settle and the lack of power to do so. (Silbey and Merry, 1986, p.7).

This tension between the need to settle and the lack of power to do so is what Silbey and Merry call 'the mediator's dilemma' – the dilemma of how to settle a case without imposing a decision. The closer the link with the court, where pressures towards settlement are greatest, the greater the tension (see, for example, Davis and Bader, 1985). Although only one of the three agencies studied by Silbey and Merry was officially affiliated to the court, the other two were court-linked. A repertoire of strategies were employed by the mediators in their attempt to resolve this tension, for example in the way the mediators presented themselves and their programme (for instance, laying claim to power based on expert knowledge or legal authority), and in their control over the mediation process.

Kressel (1985, p.203) highlights the inherent tension of the mediator's role, which derives from three principal and interrelated sources. He describes these as:

- the 'lofty and at times contradictory and ambiguous demands of the role itself';
- the intermediate position the mediator occupies between the two parties;
- the objectively difficult circumstances in which the negotiations typically occur.

The mediator is expected to maintain a calm, disinterested, creative and rational presence in the midst of the parties' stress and distress. At the same time, the mediator is also exposed to great stress. Saposnek (1983) gives a number of examples of situations that impose emotionally demanding pressures on the mediator. These are inevitable when the work involves couples in open conflict, but even apparently co-operative couples must be approached with scepticism, for why then are they in need of a mediator? Working with limited information under time constraints is, for example, like 'stepping lightly across a minefield. If [the mediator] accidentally steps in the wrong place the entire process can blow up in his face' (Saposnek, 1983, p.27).

Finally, there exists a fundamental tension between the directive control the mediator may need to exert to prevent destructive emotional exchanges overwhelming rational discussion, and the party control that is the chief objective of the mediation process. This requires of the mediator an unobtrusive and minimal style of intervention. Managing this tension effectively and creatively presents mediators with one of their central challenges.

Notes

1 Extract from J.W. von Goethe (1809), *Elective Affinities*, translated by R.J. Hollingdale (Harmondsworth: Penguin Classics, 1971), copyright © R.J. Hollingdale, 1971, pp.31–4. Reproduced by permission of Penguin Books Ltd.
2 National Family Mediation has a mandatory selection procedure for all its trainee mediators, centred not on the prior professional qualifications of the candidate, but on the primary requirement of *aptitude* for mediation. Based on a specification of identified essential and desirable personal attributes (intellectual, interpersonal, ethical and personal and motivational) relevant to effective practice of mediation, the selection procedure is designed to elicit a range of personal attributes resulting in the creation of a profile of each candidate's strengths and weaknesses. This procedure, comprised of several specific selection exercises and procedures and conducted by a panel of trained selectors, is an open opportunity for candidates to demonstrate potential personal suitability as mediators, rather than being a competition between candidates. As a consequence of this selection approach, mediators in NFM represent a wide range of professional backgrounds.

7 The session and the strategies

Perhaps they were both right. All misconceptions are themselves data which have the minimal truth of existing in at least one mind: Truth, my work has taught me, is not something static, a mountain top that statements approximate like successive assaults of frostbitten climbers. Rather, truth is constantly being formed from the solidification of illusions. (John Updike, 1965, *Of the Farm*, p.120)

The conduct of the session

Although, as we have seen in Chapter 5, the mediation session may be framed by a variety of organizational arrangements, there are some features that are essential if the framework is to fulfil its purpose, and address, through the structure of the session, the central issues of party authority for decision-making, mediator power and bias, and the protection of a fair process. These include:

1 gathering individual pre-mediation intake information, and screening the parties for unsuitability;
2 an introductory joint meeting;
3 an opportunity (however brief) for each party to see the mediator on their own;
4 the summing up by the mediator of the issues as propounded by the parties.

These are vital preliminaries to direct negotiation between the parties, which constitutes the major content of the session.

The first session

This first mediation session should start with a joint meeting between both parties and the mediator. Initially, the mediator should explain or clarify the purpose of the meeting, the framework designed to achieve this (for example, the organization of the session, the number of sessions if more than one, and so on), the ground rules and the terms of participation (for example, voluntariness, confidentiality and its child protection exception, and so on). As mediation is a new and probably unfamiliar process to many resorting to it, it is crucial that at this stage mediators give time to describing its characteristics carefully and unambiguously so that the parties understand what they are embarking upon, ensuring that their consent to participate is fully informed.

At this stage, mediators must also ask the parties' permission in advance to intervene if exchanges show signs of getting out of hand. This request constitutes:

- explicit recognition by the mediators of the existence of powerful underlying feelings (usually of hostility, bitterness, anger or hurt);
- legitimization of their possible eruption;
- authorization to curb them.

This request for *permission* to step in and stop possibly destructive exchanges is a way of establishing at the start that authority lies with the parties.

There are three main reasons why it is necessary for both parties to attend together. Firstly, the mediator must establish an even-handed relationship with both parties from the start. Furthermore, he or she must be seen to do so. Initial separate meetings could lay the mediator open to charges of bias or prior recruitment. Secondly, if the mediator's main objective is to launch the parties on a joint enterprise of negotiation and decision-making, they ought to begin the way they wish to continue – in direct contact, if not yet in direct communication. Thirdly, a joint meeting is the best means of achieving a clear understanding of the issues in dispute (ACAS, no date, para.38).

The separate interviews

These can occur as a second stage of the first session following the introductory joint meeting or be held at another time. The purpose of these interviews is to give each party an opportunity to state their views, objectives and any fears to the mediator on their own. This means that they can have their say free from fear of interruption or contradiction. It gives the mediator an opportunity to gain a clearer understanding of existing or future fears about safety issues and the issues in dispute. It is the common experience of mediators that a version of the dispute with which both parties apparently agree in the introductory joint session often turns out to be perceived quite differently by one party when interviewed alone. Research confirms the importance for each of the parties of separate time with the mediator(s) (Davis and Roberts, 1988; Walker et al., 1994).

The summing up by the mediator

After seeing each party on their own for as long as it takes them to state their position, the mediator should briefly sum up the issues and demands of each party to both of them together. The advantages of this are threefold:

- The parties are more likely to listen calmly to the mediator than to each other.
- The mediator is able to report the substance of the dispute and the accompanying strength of feeling (*that* the party feels strongly, *how* strongly they feel, and *what they feel strongly about*), but free of the angry tone, aggravating facial expressions and acrimonious language that could trigger off emotional recriminations and escalate the conflict.[1]
- Misunderstandings can be sorted out as early as possible.

Where communication has been difficult or non-existent, or has taken place only through solicitors, the potential for misunderstanding is enormous. It is not uncommon for parties to discover that much less divides them than they had imagined, once clear lines of communication are opened.

Practical considerations

Attention to certain details can contribute substantially to easing the tense atmosphere in which couples frequently meet

Separate waiting rooms

It is more than likely that the atmosphere between the parties will be strained at best, and hostile at worst. They need to be assured in advance that they will be meeting each other in a safe arena, and only in the presence of the mediator. The provision of separate waiting rooms is essential if such protection is to be ensured prior to the meeting. New partners and children will also be able to wait in peace.

Seating arrangements

As many practitioners have pointed out, the seating arrangements are very important (Coogler, 1978; Haynes, 1981a; Folberg and Taylor, 1984). These should encourage relaxed, informal and open exchanges. A circular arrangement around a low coffee table is helpful, with the mediator facing both parties. The mediator should not be distanced in status or place by sitting behind a high desk or table, or on a raised dais. The parties should not be placed opposite one another, or in any relation that might increase confrontation between them. If seated at right angles to one another, they can then choose to face each other if they so wish.

Refreshments

The timely arrival of a tray of tea or coffee can help to ease tension. At one agency which focuses on the single negotiating session (usually lasting up to two-and-a-half hours), tea is brought in after about an hour, at the stage in the negotiation process when differences may be being explored and when the distance between the parties is likely to be greatest. The impact is often dramatic. Anger may diminish if people pause, refresh themselves and feel they have been treated considerately.

The Coogler model

An increasing number of family mediation services are adopting (and adapting to their practice), the Coogler model of family mediation, first introduced into this country by Fred Gibbons, the Co-ordinator of the South-East London Family Mediation Bureau, in 1978. Devised by O.J. Coogler, a lawyer and psychotherapist and one of the founding fathers of family mediation in the USA, the Coogler model deploys structure to secure a fair process and outcome, with the mediator adopting a modest profile throughout (Coogler, 1978).

Coogler emphasized the importance of a clear structure, involving the integration of three structural components designed to protect the parties procedurally, ethically and psychologically:

- The procedural structure is designed to ensure an orderly process. There is advance agreement upon the 'rules' of procedure and the guidelines to be followed by the parties and the mediator.
- The value structure is designed to secure a fair process and ethical standards of exchange so that the outcome is fair and is perceived as fair by the parties.
- The psychological structure is designed to secure physical and emotional safety. This framework includes:

  - joint sessions only (though with separate time for each party included);
  - direct negotiation between the parties;
  - limiting the issues to those for which decisions are needed for settlement to be reached – these include the marriage, property, finance and children;

- dealing with one item at a time;
- using procedural methods for collecting and examining factual information;
- each party having their separate lawyer as adviser outside the process.

The strategies of the mediator

The strategies of mediators reflect their assumptions about:

- the nature and goals of the process in which they are engaged (see Chapter 5);
- the qualities of the 'ideal' mediator (see Chapter 6);
- the nature and function of conflict in family breakdown – whether conflict is regarded as a pathological phenomenon, or as a normal, even constructive, response to the need to re-order relationships (see Chapter 4).

In order to understand what is happening in mediation, there is a need to understand the complex interrelationship of the developmental stages of the process with the cyclical exchanges of information that propel those stages forward towards an outcome. The kind of information exchanged is related to the stage in the negotiation process. The same message may carry different information at a different stage.

Different strategies will be required at different stages. The intervention of the mediator is most needed (and most problematic) at the moments of transition in the negotiation process. For example, at an early stage, when uncertainty, insecurity, ignorance and hostility are at their most intense and when the shift of attitude required of the parties is greatest, a greater strength of intervention may be necessary from the mediator than at other, less critical stages in the process. Here, as already mentioned, lies one of the central challenges to the role of the mediator – how to control potentially destructive conflict effectively, and at the same time remain impartial and non-directive. The interventions of the mediator therefore have to be understood not only in terms of *what* they contain, but *how* and *when* they take place.

Given that strategy deployed by the mediator is highly dependent on its timing within the process, what may be appropriate at an early stage may be totally inappropriate at a later stage, and vice versa. An understanding of the meaning of the strategy can only occur within an understanding of the context of the process it serves.

Nor, of course, are the parties passive recipients of the mediator's interventions. The strategies of the parties themselves combine with those of the mediator in a dynamic and fluid situation of 'reciprocal influence' (Kressel and Pruitt, 1985, p.196). Whatever repertoire of strategies may be available to the mediator, he/she must recognize that their use will depend both on what the disputants will require or tolerate, and on what strategies they will seek to promote themselves – for example, in order to use the mediator as a scapegoat, or to win him/her over to the justice of their own cause (Gulliver, 1977).

For these reasons, there should obviously be consonance between the strategies a mediator seeks to deploy and the phase that negotiation has reached. This means that the timing as well as the degree of intervention is crucial. For example, for the mediator to emphasize a narrowing of differences at a stage when the parties have not yet fully explored the extent of their differences could be useless, or even harmful. Similarly, where the parties have begun to communicate together directly and constructively, this could be prejudiced were the mediator to adopt strongly interventionist strategies rather than minimal ones. The skill and judgement required for the effective deployment of strategies are best developed through the experience of the process itself (ACAS, no date, para.16).

The main constellations of strategies available to the mediator are set out below. These categories overlap, however, and are not so clearly distinguished in practice. Within the dynamics of the mediation session, many things are going on, often at the same time. Each interaction is unique and often unpredictable. This unpredictability has been described as one of the most challenging aspects of the entire mediation process (Saposnek, 1983).

Whatever strategies are employed by mediators, it is important to remember that they are working in two directions:

- to facilitate communication and learning between the parties (the more they understand of each other's predicament, the better their chances of co-ordination and agreement);
- to instruct the parties in the norms and methods of negotiation.

As already mentioned, mediation involves adherence to certain key values – mutual respect, shared responsibility and equity of exchange. The dignity and consideration which the parties are shown by the mediator sets an example and the tone for communication. Thereafter, by learning to negotiate, the parties learn to talk to one another. Communication between them is necessary if they are to work together as parents. Changes of mind and circumstance over time require that they must be able to renegotiate and modify their agreements themselves. The strategies demonstrated by the mediator should therefore become the present and future strategies of the parties.

The main strategies

Identifying the issues

One of the mediator's first tasks is to understand what the issues in dispute (or potential dispute) are about. This may be a relatively simple matter, or, especially in the early stages of separation, more complex, with many interrelated issues over, for example, the matrimonial home, residence, maintenance and contact.

The mediator needs to understand the issues as the parties see them: 'To understand disputes ... it is necessary to attend to the categories of meaning by which participants themselves comprehend their experience and orient themselves toward one another in their everyday lives' (Caplan, L, 1995, p.156, quoting Rosen, 1989, p. xiv). This will involve seeing each party on their own at an early stage within a joint negotiating session, so that they can feel free to describe matters in their own way. The mediator needs to listen very carefully, asking pertinent questions where necessary. The mediator has no permission to delve into the past history of the couple's relationship or into the details of the interpersonal relationships of the family. What is necessary is for the mediator to understand clearly how each party sees the dispute, bearing in mind that 'a significant portion of any dispute exists only in the minds of the disputants' (Felstiner et al., 1980). The mediator needs to understand the environment of the dispute as well (the relevant history, the pressures and the constraints that impinge on the settlement of the dispute), what the parties' respective objectives and interests are, and what they hope to achieve by resorting to mediation.

The mediator should help the parties to agree an agenda. It may make sense to postpone the sticky or more contentious issues until later, and to tackle the relatively less significant differences first. Single issue disputes – for example, over contact – are by no means the simplest to agree, nor are the more obdurate issues necessarily the more important (Gulliver, 1979). 'Graduality,' or the detailed, step-by-step progression on issues, was one of the secrets of success in the Norwegian mediation of disputes between the Israelis and the Palestinians.

Facilitating communication

Poor communication and mistrust characterize the relationship of many couples who turn to mediation. Perhaps that is why they look to the mediator for help. Stress and inadequate information impair their ability to see beyond their own hurt or anger or to place themselves in another's shoes (Deutsch, 1973). Mediation can provide the opportunity to open up channels of communication and to improve both the quantity and quality of the information exchanged. The mediator's control over the communication structure is one of the most important aspects of the mediation process (Stevens, 1963; Coogler, 1978). The mediator may act as a translator, stimulating communication and explaining the context and framework that give meaning to communication (Deutsch, 1973; Stulberg, 1981). Furthermore, mistrust may be diminished when two parties who have lost trust in each other find, in the impartiality and integrity of the mediator, someone they both can trust.

As already noted, the mediator needs to have a clear understanding of the dispute, including the respective attitudes, priorities and objectives of the parties, and the pressures each is under (ACAS, no date, para.14). This understanding must be translated to each party if their mutual understanding of one another's position is to be improved. Only then will movement from these positions be possible.

The effective facilitation of communication by the mediator involves not only increasing the flow of information between the parties, but also the careful monitoring of the accuracy and 'non-belligerence' of that information (Kressel, 1985). Too much information (in volume and complexity) may be as problematic as too little or conflicting information. For example, the parties' versions of the past are bound to differ. The mediator should therefore discourage the unproductive raking over of past quarrels, and should not be drawn into an arbitrating role over differences of fact or the merits of an issue. Instead, the validity of different, even conflicting, perceptions should be affirmed, and the parties encouraged rather to consider the present and future implications of their dispute.

One device for ending the futile exchange of accusations, usually about the other party's unreasonable or vindictive acts, is to get that party to rephrase an accusation as a question. Questions invite answers. Direct communication may be initiated. Alternatively, the mediator may encourage the parties to communicate through him/her where direct exchanges are proving destructive.

Haynes advocates the use of questions as the main form of intervention by the mediator. In this way, the parties 'own' the answers. Questions can promote a number of objectives in mediation. They can facilitate good information exchange (as above), provide clarification and insight, focus on core issues, encourage explanation, explore alternatives, stimulate new thinking, improve the climate of communication, and offset power imbalances. Silence, too, as well as conveying certain messages (uncertainty, non-compliance, acquiescence etc.) can be used as a powerful questioning technique.

Where information is inadequate or conflicting, the mediator may ask one or other party to restate their particular demand or point of view and to provide further information to support it. Alternatively, the mediator could attempt a restatement. For example: 'Am I right in saying that your view is ... ?' or 'If I understand you correctly, you are saying such and such?'

Restatement may be used to clarify as well as to emphasize important points and positive features, especially those relating to areas of interest shared by the couple. This does not mean that the differences between the parties should be underplayed or glossed over. Rather, the mediator must be alert to opportunities to draw attention to and encourage gestures of good-will or offers of co-operation (Coogler, 1978). These might arise, for example, when one party is not listening, or not apprehending the significance of what is being said by the other party, intentionally or otherwise. The other party may then be urged to repeat what he or she has just said, so that its import can be fully appreciated. The parties are halted in what might be a fruitless arguing past one another, and forced to listen to what is being said. They are re-routed into the same channel of communication, and more appropriate reactions are thereby stimulated.

A neutral forum free of stigma or coercion, the protection of confidentiality, the control and skill of the impartial mediator and the non-threatening framework of the session all make it possible for issues too highly charged for the parties to discuss on their own to be brought out into the open and talked about.

Opening up new perspectives

Common as well as conflicting interests characterize the relationship between adversaries (Schelling, 1960). One important way a mediator may contribute to settlement is to point out how the parties' own best interests may be served by getting them 'to consider their common interests as more essential than they did previously or their competing interests as less essential' (Eckhoff, 1969, p.171).

In disputes following family break-up, parents do not usually disagree with the mediator who stresses that certain interests – the interests of the children – are more important than who is right and who is wrong (Davis and Roberts, 1988). In most cases, the parents themselves affirm this. Whatever they may think of each other, the couple are presumed to be united in a shared love of their children. It is this intertwining of interests that constitutes the most powerful pressure towards collaboration in the mediation effort (Fuller, 1971).

However, a shared concern for the children does not eliminate differences of view over how the child's welfare may best be safeguarded. What the mediator can usefully point to is the dispute as a problem common to both parties. Together, they share a joint interest in reaching a mutually satis-factory agreement. Secondly, by focusing their attention on their child's perspective of events, the mediator enables the parties to move away from their interpersonal quarrelling. The mediator thereby ensures that the parents themselves fully consider and protect the interests of their own children (see Chapter 10).

One of the creative possibilities of mediation is 'the art of proposing the alternate solution' (Stevens, 1963, p.146). A fresh view from the mediator may reveal new perspectives and possibilities for solution inherent in the situation, which neither party has perceived. This calls for inventiveness, imagination and ingenuity. Often, the parties have lost perspective, particu-larly over time. Bogged down and embattled in conflict, they feel their predicament to be hopeless and endless. For example, they are often sur-prised to realize that contact over children will be a problem for them for only five years or so (depending, of course, on the age of their children). They can also begin to realize that they have a choice as to whether to continue in conflict or to try to reach some sort of accommodation, and can examine the consequences of this choice for their children and themselves.

One way of promoting new ideas for possible solutions is by orienting the parties to consider these themselves – for example, the mediator may ask questions that indicate fresh and practicable lines of thinking and acting. Each party could be invited to make their own suggestions or indicate what each thinks the other could do to help the situation.

Contact arrangements may take many forms, tailored to each family. There is no prototype of what contact should be like. Permutations are legion. As already noted, a flexible arrangement is more likely to work where there is a co-operative relationship between the parties. The necessary changes must be negotiated constantly, and a strained or acrimonious relationship would make this difficult or impossible. In these circumstances, a predetermined arrangement will be preferable, where negotiation, and therefore conflict between the parties, is kept to the minimum. The mediator needs to point out the possibilities and pitfalls of the parties making their own arrangements, as well as the consequences of court-imposed orders. As far as court-defined orders are concerned, the couple need to know that ultimately, they still have to co-operate together if contact is to work.

Schelling (1960, p.144) has highlighted the mediator's 'power to make a dramatic suggestion', especially where there is no apparent focal point for agreement. This may arise where the parties are so entrenched that they may be genuinely unable to see where common ground might lie, or even how to proceed at all (Gulliver, 1977). A suggestion coming from a disinterested third party might be more acceptable than if made by one of the parties, when it may be interpreted as a sign of weakness. The mediator may there-fore make it possible for concessions to be offered without loss of face. This opportunity for graceful retreat and face-saving is one of the most useful functions a mediator is able to provide (Rubin and Brown, 1975).

Another opportunity available to the mediator is to explain or interpret statements, feelings or acts positively but without misrepresentation. For example, a parent may cite past lack of interest in the child as a reason for opposing contact with the non-resident parent. It could be explained that this parent may well have come to realize that they had taken their children too much for granted in the past, and is seeking to remedy this. The separation itself may have brought about a genuine shift in their appreciation of the significance of their relationship with their children. Unexpected changes in the pattern of relationships between parents and children following separation or divorce are not uncommon, highlighting the fact that the quality of contact visits following divorce may be independent of the quality of relationships in the intact family prior to divorce (Wallerstein and Kelly, 1980, pp.104–5).

Controlling destructive exchanges

If the mediator's primary objective is to facilitate communication between the parties so that they may negotiate their own agreement, aggressive, irrational and excessively emotional exchanges cannot be tolerated. Presumably, the parties have resorted to mediation in order to avoid just such rows.

Some relatively brief opportunity to let off steam and express anger, hurt, bitterness, and so on is obviously necessary and helpful, especially for those who have had no previous chance to get things off their chest. For others, on the other hand, the mediation session could be yet another occasion for personal recrimination, which may therefore be totally unproductive. In any event, prolonged or too powerful an outpouring of emotion is not conducive to rational exchange.

The mediator needs to convey to the parties his/her recognition of the fraught climate in which they meet and his/her understanding and acceptance that stress is a normal (and temporary) response to circumstances of extreme emotional and physical upheaval. If the control of the mediator is clear and firm, the parties will feel safe to explore some of their potentially explosive differences. Yet the best control is that which is least noticeable (Coogler, 1978). If discussion of a particular topic is not only making no progress but leading to an escalation of hostility, the mediator should stop temporarily, if necessary, any further discussion of that topic. In the last resort, the mediation session itself may be suspended if emotions threaten to get out of hand. As mentioned earlier, the parties should have given advance permission for the mediator to intervene in the event of this being necessary. They should never leave the session worse off than when they arrived. That, rather than not reaching agreement, is failure in mediation.

Focusing on the relevant

In situations of high emotion, we have seen how the mediator needs to direct the parties away from potentially destructive exchanges. These are usually provoked by differences of view over past facts. As already mentioned, it is important to realize that there is nothing in the past over which to negotiate. The mediator must focus discussion on relevant and constructive issues – the specific dispute, priorities for the future, alternatives and options. The available alternative must be examined dispassionately, their various merits assessed, and their consequences compared and considered. By focusing attention on the immediate, the concrete and the practical, the parties can concentrate on what is feasible, and so begin to gain control. Furthermore, the children, as well as being the focus of dispute, provide, presently and for the future, the central reason for the exploration of collaborative rather than competitive strategems.

The need to concentrate on what is relevant may arise in situations when the information circulating is excessive or confusing. The mediator must ensure that the parties are talking about the same thing at the same time. It is very easy for them to become bogged down or side-tracked by petty yet disruptive red herrings, often without realizing it – for example, who said what when, whether a Chinese take-away was or was not bought, or whether a coat was sent with a child or not.

Balancing inequalities of bargaining power

One of the mediator's first tasks in setting out what mediation involves is to make clear the equal and joint efforts that are required of both parties. This recognition by each party of the right of the other to participate equally in the decision-making process is fundamental to participation in the process.

It is the responsibility of the mediator to ensure that this principle is realized in practice. In the first place, the parties must start off from positions of relative equality, but as Cormick (1982) emphasizes, the less equal the relative power of the parties, the greater the ethical responsibility of the mediator. If imbalances are gross, approaches other than mediation should be adopted – for example, legal representation, advice, guidance and support, counselling or treatment (see also Chapter 11).

Some of the ways in which the mediator can offset inequalities between the parties are described below.

Firstly, the mediator needs to ensure that inequalities are recognized by the parties themselves (Folberg, 1983). Rarely is this a simple matter, even in the least complicated contact dispute. For example, on the face of it, the non-resident parent (usually the father) is in the weaker bargaining position, presuming, that is, that he wants to increase his contact with his children. He has less contact with the children, and therefore less influence over them, and less power to determine the terms of contact. He may feel that he has lost everything – his marriage, his home and his children. The mother, with day-to-day care of the children, may suffer equal but different disadvantages, carrying the burden of responsibility for looking after the children single-handed, making ends meet, and trying to carve out some independent life for herself free of the emotional stress that contact with her former partner brings.

Secondly, the mediator must ensure that all the relevant information is in the hands of both parties. This means that information about the mediation process (including the limits of the mediator's role, and the ultimate right of the parties not to participate if they so wish) and the dispute and its ramifications must be available to the parties, as well as understood by them.

Thirdly, the mediator must see to it that both parties participate freely and fairly in the negotiations. There must therefore be equal opportunity for such participation. The mediator must prevent one party interrupting the other, one party talking for the other, or one party dominating discussion by force of personality, knowledge, greater articulacy or the exercise of moral or psychological pressure. This means that the mediator must be aware when and why one party is not speaking up, and when acquiescence does not signify genuine consent. The mediator must be alert to attempts at bullying (emotional and physical), threats or other intimidatory tactics, and must stop these at once, bringing the meeting to an end in the last resort.

Finally, if it turns out that an outcome is being consented to that is patently unfair, the mediator must say so, and recommend that the party in the more vulnerable position should not agree without taking legal advice or giving the matter further consideration.

The balance of power between the parties is affected by the mediation process itself, firstly in the expectations of equality of exchange, equity and mutual responsibility that it engenders, and secondly, in the improved capacity of the parties, as a result of mediation, to deal with one another on an equal (or more equal) basis in the future (see Chapter 11). The mediator also has an impact on the balance of bargaining power. Skill and integrity must be exercised in ensuring that differences of 'endowment' or ability in negotiation do not result in overreaching or duress.

Towards an agreement

The outcome of mediation should be the result of the parties' own and equal efforts at negotiation, and should be regarded by them as fair (as is practicable in all the circumstances) and in their children's interests. It is they who have to live with their agreement.

The agreement need not derive from any compromise, although many do. It may follow from the creation of an entirely new option, or (more rarely) one party may move to the position of the other. A process of pay-offs may take place. You give what is less valuable to you but more valuable to the receiver, and receive what you value but which is less valuable to the giver (Fuller, 1971).

Agreement may consist of deciding jointly that the continuance of the status quo is preferable to anything else that appears possible, or of being prepared to continue talking together in the future.

The mediator must ensure that when agreement appears to be reached, its details are examined carefully and comprehensively. Lack of clarity about wording and the practicalities of implementation may tip an agreement in principle into the immediate danger of disagreement over detail. Relief at attaining consensus should not inhibit the mediator from pointing out possible pitfalls or from slowing down finalization in order to check and clarify. A stable agreement must be founded on mutual satisfaction and mutual understanding.

Where the agreement is drafted in writing, such as the Memorandum of Understanding,[2] it must be expressed simply, clearly and unambiguously. On the balance to be struck between clarity and simplicity on the one hand and comprehensiveness on the other, Fuller (1971, p.230) has this to say:

> Now the forms of language, like rivers, have a certain inertia of their own; they cannot always be readily bent to accommodate every nuance of thought and a clause overloaded with qualifications may forfeit its meaning as a clear guidepost for human interaction. In the drafting of any complex agreement there is often an inescapable compromise between what can be simply expressed and what might be abstractly desirable. The mediational process plainly has a place in dealing with such problems.

The words chosen by the parties must be meaningful, not only to themselves, but also to third parties. Reasons for decisions can be explained, especially where these are unconventional or appear unfair. The mediator can provide that 'third party perspective' (Fuller, 1971, p.320). This will avoid future disagreement over what was agreed.

Special problems of strategy arising in mediation sessions

Overcoming transitions

Mediators have a part to play in all the different phases of negotiation.

Throughout, they maintain the momentum for negotiation by inspiring a belief in the possibility of agreement (Pruitt, 1981). But mediators are most needed – though their intervention is most problematic – where transitions between phases of negotiation have to be effected (Gulliver, 1977). As already mentioned, one of the most conspicuous of these transitions is from the phase of entrenched opposition, even hostility, to the phases when differences are narrowed and mistrust lessened. This is where the shift of attitude demanded of the parties is greatest, and is what Gulliver (1977, p.25) describes as 'the principal watershed in the whole process'. Here the stronger, more interventionist strategies of the mediator may be justified (for example, the making of direct suggestions orienting the parties' attention and efforts towards a common goal), and may be more acceptable to, even welcomed by, the parties. But such strategies remain problematic because, in these circumstances, the power of the mediator to influence the course of proceedings is most intrusive.

Deadlock

In certain circumstances, a state of deadlock may develop in the negotiations. This may be a prelude to their breakdown and a return to the status quo before mediation or the dispute may be pursued in other ways, such as litigation. In other circumstances, however, an impasse may be viewed positively as an indication of equality of power, and could, for that reason, produce movement towards a settlement (Pruitt, 1981). This is likely to arise in situations where the costs of disagreement (emotional as well as legal and financial) are so high as to be intolerable to all concerned, and where the continuing relationship between the parties is important and/or unavoidable to both. In such a case, any change must be for the better, with some settlement being of value, rather than nothing. In these circumstances, a strategy of minimal intervention by the mediator will be most efficacious, as the impetus for co-operation will be greatest.

Manipulation in mediation

Mediators need to face squarely the potential they have to affect the substance of communication by their control over the process of that communication (Silbey and Merry, 1986). Possibilities exist at every level of intervention (from the most minimal to the strongest) for the mediator to exert influence – in reformulating or rephrasing, in editing, in the kind of information and the way in which it is elicited, in stressing some matters and ignoring or obstructing others, and especially in making new suggestions. While this potentially presents the most creative of opportunities for the mediator, there are also serious risks. It is because the issue of party authority is central to mediation that the dangers of manipulation must be recognized and restricted. Some of these are set out below.

Dangers of the mediator adopting a directive role

A variety of strategies will be used by the mediator in any single negotiating session, depending on the stage reached, as well as on the needs of the parties. As already noted, more positive intervention may be necessary during transitional phases, when they will also be more tolerable to the parties. Intervention strategies may range from the most tentative, indirect and unobtrusive to the most directive and dominating. The risks of manipulation of the negotiation process by the mediator increase along the same continuum. The greater the strength and scope of intervention, the greater the opportunity for manipulation.

Mediators are not neutral (see Chapter 6). They have their own values and attitudes. Influenced by prevailing research findings, they are likely to adopt a strong pro-contact stance in the belief that it is better, on the whole, for children to have a continuing relationship with both parents after separation and divorce. In most cases, these values are shared by parents themselves. However, mediators should not brow-beat parents with research evidence or with warnings of emotional damage or of the harmful effects of litigation. This exertion of overt influence is incompatible with the facilitating role of the mediator.

Dangers in the adoption of family therapy techniques

Family therapy is in its nature manipulative (Walrond-Skinner, 1976, p.149; Nichols, 1989). Where family therapy approaches are adopted in mediation practice, there is a danger that covert attempts to manipulate the perceptions and preferences of the parties will occur. In reaching assessments, devising systemic hypotheses or making judgements – for example, that the parties do not always know what they want because they are too distressed, self-preoccupied or conflict-ridden to make rational judgements, the mediator uses private and subjective interpretations to define issues in his/her terms. The mediator's meanings then predominate, and in this way, control may be insidiously removed from where it rightfully belongs – with the parties. Even where the therapist disclaims diagnostic expertise and grants validity to each client's point of view[3], as Nichols observes (1989, p.423) '[D]uring therapy, however, the therapist's point of view is – to quote Orwell – "more equal" '. The greatest dangers of manipulation, and therefore of distortion of the mediation process, exist where family therapy techniques are used in the course of the court welfare practice of 'conciliation'. This results in the parties being subjected, unknowingly and involuntarily, both to the coercive pressures of the court and to the covert controls of 'treatment'. (For a more detailed exchange on this subject, see Roberts, 1992a; Haynes 1992, and Amundson and Fong, 1993.)

Manipulation by the parties

Just as the mediator needs to be aware of the considerable opportunities he/she has for manipulating the course and content of communication, so must he/she be aware of the possibilities of manipulation by the parties themselves (Gulliver, 1977). For example, one party, seeing the inevitability of giving way to the demands of the other, may, by accepting mediation, use the mediator as a scapegoat, a useful way of blaming someone else for the turn of events.

Mediation may also be used by one or both parties in pending proceedings, not in any genuine effort at decision-making, but in order to make a good impression in court – that they had tried to settle, but had failed.

Notes

1   Fuller (1971, p.321) alerts us to the difficulty of effecting this separation, 'especially since the depth with which a party feels about an issue is something that enters into the valuations that shape the final adjustment of diverse interests'.
2   For a detailed discussion on the requirements of the Memorandum of Understanding in all-issues mediation, see Haynes (1993, Chapter 7).
3   For example, the dialogical constructivist theoretical position has been adopted to counter ethical concerns about coercive and pathologizing clinical practice carried out under the guise of systemic 'neutrality' (Epstein and Loos, 1989).

8   When to mediate

Mediation is an educational device even more than it is a problem-solving device. Sure, it helps resolve problems but even when it fails to do that it can help, so long as it is done right, by assisting people to reach, to illuminate what is at issue, and to highlight underlying interests. (Patrick Phear quoted by A. Sarat in D.M. Kolb (ed.), 1994, *When Talk Works: Profiles of Mediators*, p.198).

Success in mediation

There is no absolute measure of success in mediation. An agreement that endures to the satisfaction of both parties and their children, as well as an improved capacity to negotiate together in the future, are obvious indices of success. Thoennes and Pearson (1985) have described success in mediation as a function of the pre-existing characteristics of the dispute and the disputants, as well as the degree to which the disputants perceive the mediators to have accomplished the primary tasks of mediation. For mediation to be successful, therefore, certain goals (identified by Thoennes and Pearson) must be accomplished:

- providing information about mediation;
- establishing ground rules;
- gaining an informed commitment from the parties;
- focusing on the full range of issues;
- maintaining control of pace;
- balancing power;
- opening communication;
- reducing tension and anger;
- ensuring that the parties feel responsible for and happy with the outcome.

Other researchers (Pruitt and Carnevale, 1993) cite the importance of rapport with and trust in the mediator as a significant predictor of agreement.

What is achievable therefore depends on a variety of factors, not least of which is the level of conflict characterizing the state of the relationship between the couple when mediation is initiated. The worse the state of the parties' relationship with one another, the dimmer the prospects of success. This is likely to be the case where there has been prior litigation, violence, a wide range of disputed issues, especially over children, and post-separation battles. Mediation is also unlikely to succeed where the motivation of one or both parties is low, where there is a refusal to accept the separation or divorce, and where there is a high level of continuing psychological attachment and a grave scarcity of financial resources – all these are 'situational determinants' of a poor prognosis of success (Kressel and Pruitt, 1985).

Even if mediation fails to secure either an agreement or an improvement in communication, the parties will have lost nothing by resorting to it. But mediation has failed if the parties emerge from it worse off in terms of conflict, mistrust and misunderstanding than when they started.

Mediation is more likely to succeed if both parties have reached a minimum 'threshold of trust' at the point of entry into mediation (Davis and Gadlin, 1988, p.55). These experienced practitioners have identified the inter-relatedness of 'gaining entry' and building trust, which has four dimensions:

1   trust in the mediator;
2   trust in the mediation process;
3   trust in one's own ability to negotiate;
4   trust in the other party.

As mediation progresses, trust grows, particularly trust in the process and in each party's competence as a negotiator. At the intake stage, however, mediators have to *earn* trust by, from the start, making no presumption that everyone understands what a mediator does, recognizing the 'legitimacy of scepticism' about mediation, and addressing, openly and frankly, any reservations about suitability or readiness for mediation (Davis and Gadlin, 1988, p.57).

It is also clear that mediation is likely to succeed when there is some specific issue in dispute over which a decision has to be made. Where there is generalized conflict or a range of problems, as above, it is likely to prove an unsuitable mode of intervention. Other circumstances may also render it inappropriate.

When mediation is unlikely to succeed

Unsuitability of referral

There must be an actual or anticipated dispute between the parties which cannot be reconciled by the normal (that is, everyday) processes of decision-making, if referral is to be appropriate. Other problems, for example in relationships, or over social and economic difficulties, should be referred elsewhere for help.

Unsuitability of dispute

The dispute must be capable of being negotiated. If the dispute consists of a fundamental divergence over facts or moral or legal norms, then legal processes of dispute-resolution will be more suitable. Family disputes are in most cases suitable for mediation because they involve the making of decisions relating to the future by two people bound together by an enduring common interest – their children.

Serious imbalances of bargaining power

There must be no substantial impairment of mental or physical capacity to negotiate, or other inequality between the parties that would render an unfair outcome unavoidable – for example, in most cases of domestic violence, in cases where one party may feel so guilty or defeated or so anxious to be free of the marriage that they may be prepared either to compromise their own interests or acquiesce in ways that they may later come to regret, and in cases where cultural norms deny women any decision-making authority.

Involuntary participation

Neither party must feel that they are participating in mediation against their will.

Criminal/child protection implications

Mediation in the private law is likely to be inappropriate where the issues to be decided are complicated by these factors.

Extreme conflict

Where conflict between the parties is so great that co-operation, however minimal, is out of the question, mediation will not succeed. There has to be some willingness, not necessarily to end conflict, but to set it momentarily aside, for any agreement on the specific interim or immediate issue to be possible.

Non-acceptance of the end of the relationship

Where one party uses mediation to try to cling on to the marriage, they will in all probability sabotage decision-making relating to its dissolution. (See also 'Abuse of mediation', below.)

Referral that is too early or too late

When emotions are intense and raw, as in the early stage of breakdown or when a commitment to litigating the dispute is already established (for example, when mediation is attempted within days of a court hearing), mediation is unlikely to be of use.

An unfavourable environment

Powerful third parties, such as combative lawyers unsympathetic to mediation, or unco-operative new partners, may fuel hostilities and jeopardize agreements.

Abuse of mediation

One or both of the parties may seek to use mediation for a variety of purposes that have nothing to do with its true objective of joint decision-making. They may, for example, participate in the belief that some strategic advantage may be obtained in subsequent litigation, or to 'have a go' at the other party, or to exert some ulterior pressure (for example, to effect a reconciliation or to impose their own wishes). Where either party demonstrates a lack of commitment – for example, by failing to keep appointments, produce the necessary information or abide by interim agreements – mediation may be found to be unsuitable.

Lack of clarity and competence

The mediator may fail to make clear to the parties what mediation is and what it involves, and mistaken expectations may therefore arise – for example, the mediator may be seen as an arbitrating figure whose function is to make a decision for the parties, as an adviser, or as some sort of counsellor who will be dealing with underlying relationship problems. The mediator may actually create misunderstanding if he/she uses confusing terminology such as 'solicitor mediator', as well as offering mediation as part of another activity such as legal practice, or worse, by attempting to combine in the same case the mediatory function with other forms of intervention such as therapy or the giving of expert advice. 'Evaluative' mediation, in confusing a mediatory with an advisory role for the intervenor, runs these risks (see page 67).

A failure to control destructive exchanges, so that the meeting ends in an emotional shambles, a lack of innovative thinking or a lack of intelligent understanding of what is going on are further examples of lack of competence on the part of the mediator.

At what stage mediation?

It is generally assumed that the earlier mediation is resorted to, the better the prospects of success, for relationships will not yet be worsened by litigation (*Practice Direction* [1982] 3 All ER 988, para.2; Booth Committee, 1985, para.3.12).

Advantages of early mediation

Mediation occurring soon after, or even before, a dispute manifests (for example, when a couple are planning to part or have only recently parted) can contain conflict or limit its damaging effects. The dispute will not yet have had time to develop a past, with its own history and associated pattern of behaviour (Felstiner and Williams, 1985). The parties need not be adversaries. At this early stage, the first question – whether the relationship is in fact at an end – is more likely to be resolved in favour of an attempt at reconciliation, with a consequent referral to the appropriate counselling agency.[1] If they both decide they want a divorce with the minimum of antagonism in sorting out their affairs, they share the same legal interests (Wishik, 1984). The potential for co-operation and agreement could be thwarted by the initiation of legal proceedings – for example, a divorce petition citing unreasonable behaviour, or by communication through lawyers' letters. Early on, there will be a wider choice of options – both short- and long-term – and before entrenched positions are adopted, there will be a greater willingness to consider them. Furthermore, decision-making control can be consolidated and preserved at a time when stress could lead to its abandonment.

Agreement on specific and immediate issues can defuse tension and prevent escalation of animosity. If, through early mediation, the parties acquire a better understanding of each other's perspectives and demands, as well as an improved capacity to negotiate, then future conflict may be reduced or aborted.

Disadvantages of early mediation

Decisions made early on have far-reaching consequences for all concerned – for example, where and with whom the children will live. The obstacles to calm, co-operative and reasoned exchanges must not be underestimated. In the first place, many interrelated issues will be unresolved – the relationship, the children's future, the home, finances, the division of the property, and so on. At the same time, the emotional, social and economic conditions will be fraught. Heightened feelings of anger, hurt and grief, as well as physical exhaustion resulting from changes and worry, all increase the difficulties of decision-making.

Research shows that couples referred to mediation after the granting of the decree absolute achieved higher agreement rates than were obtained by those resorting to mediation before divorce (Davis, 1981; Davis and Roberts, 1988). This is not surprising when only a single issue (contact) was disputed in most cases, and with the passage of time, the emotional temperature between the disputants was lowered.

Note

1   NFM statistics show a higher rate of reconciliation where the couples who came to mediation are not yet separated compared to when they are. Of those still living together, about 25 per cent decided to reconsider or reconcile. At present, however, 82 per cent of mediating couples are already separated, with one or both cohabiting in 42 per cent of cases (NFM, 1994b).

9 Confidentiality

... it is plain that the parties will not make admissions or conciliatory gestures, or dilute their claims, or venture out of their entrenched positions unless they can be confident that their concessions and admissions cannot be used as weapons against them if conciliation fails and full-blooded litigation follows. (Sir Thomas Bingham, *Re D. (Minors) (Conciliation: Privilege)*, [1993] 1 FLR 934, CA).

Confidentiality is integral to the relationship between the mediator and the parties, and as noted in Chapter 1 (page 7), is one of the four fundamental and universal characteristics of mediation (McCrory, 1981). It is the cornerstone of the relationship of trust that must exist between the mediator and the parties, and of the free and frank disclosure that is necessary if obstacles to settlement are to be overcome. It is crucial to the voluntariness of participation of the parties, and to the impartiality of the mediator. The parties must not feel that they might be disadvantaged by any disclosure that may be used in legal proceedings, or in any other way. They need to know they have nothing to lose by resorting to mediation.

Confidentiality between the mediator and the parties

Mediators have a duty to make clear to the parties at the outset that communications between them and the mediator are made in confidence, and that the mediator must not disclose any statements made or information received (to the court, solicitors, court welfare officers, social workers, doctors or anyone else) without their joint and express consent or an order of the court (NFM and FMA, 1993).

The risk of child abuse highlights the need to define the limits of confidentiality in mediation. Confidentiality is, of course, not absolute, as it is always subject to the requirement that the law of the land shall be complied with

(*Parry-Jones* v. *Law Society* 1968). The limits are those pertaining in all confidential or professional communications, whether between doctor and patient, priest and penitent, or journalist and informant. Therefore, the promise of confidentiality does not prevent the mediator from disclosing information in the exceptional circumstances where there is substantial risk to the life, health or safety of the parties, their children or anyone else.[1]

Mediators, when outlining the limits to confidentiality, refer specifically to dangers to children. There may be other equally applicable life or health-threatening risks associated with situations of great stress, such as suicide or physical violence between adults.

The problem for mediators is not whether confidentiality is absolute, nor whether its limits – implied, as they generally are, in the confidential relationships described above – should be spelt out. The question that arises is *how* this should be done without at the same time stigmatizing decision-making processes with inappropriate criminal/pathological overtones, or damaging the wholehearted commitment of the mediator to the principle of confidentiality by hedging it about with too many restrictions and reservations.

National Family Mediation sets out guidelines on what courses of action to adopt when a child protection issue arises in mediation (Child Protection Guidance and Procedure, 1996), where it appears that there is 'substantial danger, particularly to a child'. In the first instance, it advises that the parties themselves should be encouraged to seek help from an appropriate agency. The mediator should take action in accordance with local child protection guidelines, and should only report the matter to both solicitors or to the social services department or the court welfare service, if already involved, where neither party is willing to do this, and normally, after discussion with both parents.

Confidential information vouchsafed to the mediator by each of the parties is also problematic. Some mediators overcome this by stating in advance that all information disclosed separately must be able to be shared in the joint session. This is intended to prevent alliances being formed between the mediator and one party. Other mediators do allow separate confidential communication, on the basis that free and frank disclosure is necessary for constructive exchanges. Often, such confidential disclosures have little immediate bearing on the matter at hand, in which case there is no problem. There is a problem, however, when information imparted in confidence to the mediator by one party is central to subsequent joint discussion of the dispute. If that party cannot be persuaded to make the necessary disclosure to the other party, then it may be necessary to end the mediation session. This may be preferable to negotiations taking place fettered by the concealment of vital information, unbeknown to the mediator and one of the parties, which might occur if separate confidential communications were not allowed in the first place.[2]

All communications made in the course of mediation – whether between the parties themselves, or between the parties and the mediator(s), or between mediators or the parties' solicitors – are confidential, subject to certain exceptions, and will not be disclosed. In addition to the child protection exceptions already referred to, another exception relates to factual disclosures made in the course of mediation on financial or property issues. Factual data of this kind may be disclosed in any subsequent legal proceedings (NFM and FMA, 1993, paras 7.3 and 7.4).

Confidentiality of communications between the parties and third parties outside the process

While confidentiality can be promised by the mediator, confidentiality belongs to the parties, and it is a matter of their own discretion and their decision what information they impart to their solicitors or anyone else. These matters should all be clearly stated at the outset, as should the fact that the court will be very reluctant to allow confidential exchanges between the parties to be used as evidence in any subsequent proceedings (see below).

Confidentiality in relation to legal proceedings (privilege)

Mediation as an alternative to litigation nevertheless occurs within a legal framework. Legal proceedings may follow mediation or take place concurrently over other disputes (for example, finance). Agreements may break down, and litigation may be resorted to subsequently. Variation proceedings may follow changes of circumstance. Details of proposed arrangements for children must be provided before a decree absolute may be granted by the court (Matrimonial Causes Act 1973, s.41).

Public policy has always favoured the settlement of disputes – it is in the public interest that disputes be settled and litigation reduced to the minimum. The privilege of 'without prejudice' negotiation (that is, without prejudice to the legal rights of the maker of the statement) has long been a principle of English law. It attaches to statements and offers of compromise made by the parties and their legal advisers in negotiations for settling disputes. These disclosures may not be used in subsequent legal proceedings without the consent of both parties. The policy of the law has also been in favour of enlarging the cloak under which negotiations may be conducted without prejudice (Cross, 1985).

Over the years, the 'without prejudice' privilege was extended to cover new categories of cases. The privilege was accorded to confidential communications between a mediator and two parties, where the purpose of negotiations was designed to effect a reconciliation between them (for example, *Mole* v. *Mole* 1950; *Henley* v. *Henley* 1955; *Theodoropoulos* v. *Theodoropoulos* 1963; *Pais* v. *Pais* 1970). The protection derived from the activity engaged in, and not from, the office of the mediator involved (a clergyman in one instance, a probation officer in another). In the earlier case of *McTaggart* v. *McTaggart* [1948] 2 All ER 755, Lord Justice Denning stated:

> The rule as to without prejudice communications applies with especial force to negotiations for reconciliation. It applies whenever the dispute has got to such dimensions that litigation is imminent. In all cases where estrangement has reached the point where the parties consult a probation officer [the mediator in this case] litigation is imminent.

The public policy considerations behind this ruling were based on the interest of the state in preserving the stability of marriage.

In 1971, a Practice Direction on matrimonial conciliation issued by the President of the Family Division of the High Court (*Practice Direction* [1971] 1 All ER 894) provided that both reconciliation and conciliation negotiations should be legally privileged. *Practice Direction* [1982] 3 All ER 988 provided that discussions at 'conciliation appointments' before a registrar attended by a court welfare officer and at a private meeting with the court welfare officer be privileged. Conciliation that was not part of court proceedings was not covered by this Practice Direction. The critical issue of how the same officer could engage in the privileged communications of conciliation and at the same time engage in the non-privileged welfare investigation and report-writing was not addressed.

The Booth Committee, on the other hand, made clear the incompatibility of the same officer carrying out both conciliation and report-writing in the same case (Booth Committee, 1985, para.41.2). It also recommended that conciliation in court proceedings be absolutely privileged (Booth Committee, 1985, para.4.60). There is, in fact, no legislation – and until 1993, no case law – to clarify the issue of privilege in mediation where reconciliation is not an issue.

That is why the decision of the Court of Appeal in *Re D. (Minors)* is such a landmark. This case establishes for the first time that in mediation where reconciliation is not the purpose of the negotiations, discussions in relation to disputes involving children are privileged. The case establishes that statements made by either of the parties in the course of mediation cannot be disclosed in proceedings under the Children Act 1989, except in the rare case that such a statement clearly indicated that the maker had in the past caused or was likely to cause serious harm to the well-being of a child. Even within that narrow exception, the trial judge would admit the statement only if, in his/her judgment, the public interest in protecting the child's interest out-weighed the public interest in preserving confidentiality.

This Court of Appeal decision is significant in three further respects:

- The privilege of exchanges relating to the resolution of disputes over children exists as an independent head of privilege based on the *public interest*, both in sparing children unnecessary suffering by encouraging the settlement of issues concerning them, and in reducing the burden of the cost and delay of litigation.
- Their lordships stated explicitly that mediation did *not* form part of the legal process, though, as a matter of practice, it was becoming an important and valuable tool in the procedures of many family courts.
- The Master of the Rolls stated that the privilege belongs to the parties themselves, and that they may, if they so choose, waive it. In such cir-cumstances the implications are clear – the mediator may be compelled to testify. McCrory (1988) has argued for the removal of this limitation by the extension of privilege to matrimonial mediation on the basis of public interest immunity. This is founded on the principle that mediation serves an important public interest in promoting the reduc-tion of conflict and promoting co-operative decision-making, and that the privilege should attach therefore to the *mediation process* itself, immunity from disclosure being essential to the effectiveness of the process.

Notwithstanding this limitation, the judgment of the Court of Appeal in *Re D. (Minors)* (1993) is a valuable clarification of the legal position in relation to the confidential exchanges that occur in family mediation. The decision is confined to the circumstances of the case – that is, to matrimonial disputes over children in proceedings under the Children Act 1989. It may be assumed that the privilege of 'without prejudice' negotiations still attaches to mediated negotiations relating to finance and property issues.

This 'without prejudice' privilege is subject to three limitations when applied to mediation (Cross, 1985):

- The privilege belongs to the parties jointly, and not to the mediator or the process. It can therefore be waived by both parties, expressly or otherwise, in legal proceedings, and then the mediator could be com-pelled to testify.
- The cloak of the privilege does not cover statements that are not suffi-ciently related to the dispute which is the subject of negotiation.
- A binding agreement that results from privileged negotiations is not itself privileged. It is therefore important that the status of any

mediated agreement be clear to all concerned. In most cases, the parties will not intend their agreements to be legally binding in any event.

In practice, the court is unlikely to allow either party to make use of evidence derived from failed negotiations. Agreements are encouraged by the court, which will not wish either party to be disadvantaged by prior attempts to reach agreement. Although, for example, no privilege exists as a matter of law to protect confidential communications (except between lawyers and their clients and in proceedings under the Patents Act 1943), in practice, these are frequently protected. The judge has a discretion to disallow questions concerning them, and witnesses are not pressed to disclose confidential information (Cross and Wilkins, 1975).

Notes

1   The NFM and FMA (1993) *Joint Code of Practice* states: 'Where it appears to any mediator that a child is suffering or likely to suffer significant harm, the mediator must advise the participants to seek help from the appropriate agency' (para.8.3). 'Where it appears necessary or desirable in order to protect the child from significant harm, the mediator must in any event contact the appropriate agency' (para.8.4).
2   NFM and FMA (1993) covers this in para.5.7: 'if any relevant information emerges which a participant is not willing to have disclosed to the other, mediators must consider whether or not it is appropriate to continue'.

10 Children and the mediation process

Childhood is entitled to special care and assistance. (UN Convention on the Rights of the Child, 1989, Preamble)

Introduction

The place of children in the mediation process has generated much debate ever since family mediation was first introduced in the UK in the late 1970s. There has long been a consensus that mediation can enhance children's interests. The process and outcome benefits of mediation – collaborative approaches to decision-making, improved communication between parents, reduced misunderstanding and conflict, and parents retaining control over the fashioning and content of their own agreements – have recognized advantages for children. Research also highlights the negative consequences for children of the competitive, adversarial approaches of litigation and adjudication, which require the disputants (parents, in this case) to take up opposing stances in order to achieve their objectives (Lund, 1984; Wallerstein and Kelly, 1980; Maccoby and Mnookin, 1992; Cockett and Tripp, 1994).

Family mediation has long been identified with a greater concentration on the needs of children (Davis and Roberts, 1988). One of the special features of family disputes referred to earlier (see Chapter 2) is the continuing and interdependent relationship of the adult disputants, who, as parents, are bound together for ever through their children (Fuller, 1971). Children provide the common interest and the mutual inducement for collaborative effort. Children may be simultaneously the cause of dispute, the main casualties of dispute, *and*, as a result, the best reason for ending the dispute (Davis and Roberts, 1988). There is also a common view that mediation offers the 'best setting' for the voice of the child to be heard (Simpson, 1989). This is linked to the presumption, embodied in the UN Convention on the Rights of the Child

1989, the Children Act 1989 and the Family Law Act 1996, that greater aware-ness of and greater attention to the views and feelings of children both acknowledges their worth and significance and alleviates distress at the time of separation and divorce.

On the other hand, the vexed question of children's direct participation in the mediation process – whether, when and how this should take place – has excited controversy rather than consensus. Discussion on this issue in the 1980s was characterized by two features: a polarization of positions for and against the direct 'involvement' of children in mediation, and the import-ation into family mediation of the child-saving and paternalist aspects of social work and family therapy practice. There has always been a danger that the preoccupation of professionals regarding the issue of 'children's interests' could give rise to a conflict – not between the interests of parents and their children, but between parents and the various professionals who claim to know and represent the best interests of children (Berger and Berger, 1983). The fundamental issue at stake here is whether divorcing parents, like parents in intact families, should be trusted to make decisions about the future of their own children.

By the 1990s, the convergence of the long practice experience of family mediators, the clarification of the nature of the mediation process that had by then occurred, and a fresh climate of thinking about the 'voice' of the child in decision-making (for example, the UN Convention on the Rights of the Child 1989, and the Children Act 1989), resulted in a new appreciation of the distinctive and precise role of children in mediation (NFM, 1994a).

The discussions in the 1980s

Arguments in favour of 'involving' children

Those who argued in favour of the direct involvement of children in the mediation process did so on two counts. Firstly, the physical presence of the children was a reminder to the parties of their parental responsibilities (James and Wilson, 1986, p.191). Secondly, research findings suggested that parents' views of what their children thought might differ considerably from what the children themselves thought (Wallerstein and Kelly, 1980; Walczak with Burns, 1984; Mitchell, 1985). It was claimed that stress-induced inca-pacity and poor communication, especially in the immediate aftermath of separation, accounted for this discrepancy of perception. The presence of children was therefore necessary to give the parents firsthand information (Saposnek, 1983).

It was also argued that although children should not have a final say in the decisions that were made, they should be involved in the making of arrangements that affected them. This helped them to make happier adjustments following the disruption of their families (Walczak with Burns, 1984). The 'real' feelings of children, it was also claimed, could only be ascertained when children were seen 'within the context of their parenting rather than taken from it' (Howard and Shepherd, 1982, p.92).

Furthermore, those who advocated a 'family systems' approach to mediation required the presence of *all* family members as 'contributors to the interactional process', at least at some stage, so that the mediator 'maximizes her leverage as a result of her more comprehensive view of the functional rules of the family system' (Saposnek, 1983, p.120).

Arguments against the direct 'involvement' of children

Those who argued against children participating directly in the mediation process did so:

- because of the stressful effects on the children;
- because of the difficulties of children making informed judgements in times of crisis about future plans affecting them;
- because that was what most parents preferred;
- because the parents' decision-making authority might be undermined;
- because of the incompatible demands it placed on the role of the mediator.

The mediatory role might be distorted, certainly complicated, where the mediator interviewed children separately. The mediator was not a spokesperson for the child, yet when called upon to voice the views of the child, took on the role of child advocate, a role which was incompatible with the mediatory role.

Where great weight was attached by one or both parents to what the child said, as was likely where there was a clash of views between the parties as to what the child was saying, then the mediator, in acting as spokesperson for the child, could be forced into an arbitrating role. The mediator could become identified with the position of the child, and therefore with one of the parents. The impartiality of the mediator would inevitably be compromised, with the child's views taking precedence over both parents' views.

The mediator could be placed in an impossible position *vis-à-vis* the confidentiality of the information vouchsafed by a child. The mediator might hold information and yet be unable to use it. There could therefore be serious difficulties for the mediator, both in conveying and not conveying information revealed by a child.

Judges, it was argued, were reluctant to see children in disputes affecting them for two main reasons, both of which applied in mediation. Firstly, an unfair burden was placed upon the child to express a preference on an issue, knowing that his/her parents were in dispute over it. Secondly, where a decision would be reached (by the judge or, in mediation, by the parents) that was likely to be contrary to the wishes of the child, this also placed the child in an unfair position (Poulter, 1982).

Families, it was noted, made decisions in their own way. These decision-making processes of the autonomous, intact family should be encouraged to continue after separation and divorce. In that process, parents commonly impose decisions on their children. The decision to divorce is a stark example of this, and one which 'society sanctions through its non-intervention' (Maidment, 1984, p.273). Why, it was asked, if children's views are so important, are they accorded greater significance in relation to decisions over family breakdown than in relation to other decisions taken by intact families that also profoundly affect their future – for example, moving house or a mother's return to work (King, 1987)?

In conclusion, it was argued that the disadvantages of involving children directly or indirectly in the mediation process far outweighed any advantages. The boundaries between mediation and therapy might become dangerously blurred. The parents' authority might be undermined. The children might become embroiled in an anxious and unnatural situation, feeling obliged to make unfair choices and carry some of their parents' responsibility to improve conditions.

However, there were specific, relatively rare occasions when, it was argued, it might be appropriate to see the child – for example, when the child (particularly the older child) was creating obstacles to any agreement the parents might wish to make, or had access to information unavailable elsewhere. With both parents' consent, the child might be interviewed in order that these obstacles might better be understood and overcome – for example, when a child suddenly and for no apparent reason refused to see one parent. There were also occasions when one parent, voicing the child's point of view, was disbelieved by the other parent. This difficulty might arise when the parent with residence had to express his/her own position and act as the spokesperson for the children at the same time. The mediator could play a confirmatory role after seeing the child separately, validating the views of the child, and also enabling the non-resident parent to accept the message because it came from an impartial third party.

Arguments in favour of indirect 'involvement' of children

It was argued that children do have independent views which should be heard, but it is the parents who should talk to and listen to their children as far as possible. It is not appropriate for the mediator to decide at the outset that children have the right to be present at the discussions between their parents. This could undermine the adults' authority before they even start. Rather than take over these decisions and responsibilities, the mediator should encourage parents to fulfil these tasks themselves – assuming, of course, that they had not already done so.

Research showed that many parents were very concerned about the harmful effects of separation on their children, and positively welcomed the explicit focus on their needs that the mediator might provide (Davis and Roberts, 1988; Saposnek, 1983). There was no evidence to suggest that parents were less committed to their children's welfare than the mediator, and that without the intervention of the mediator they would tend to disregard their children's interests or treat them as 'inanimate objects' to be haggled over (for example, Parkinson, 1986, pp.116 and 161).

Children did not have to be present at the mediation session to have their views taken into consideration. As already noted, the mediator had an ethical responsibility to ensure that the needs of children were taken into account as part of the parents' examination of various options and their consequences, as should the needs of all those not at the negotiating table yet who were affected by the decisions made there (including grandparents and step-parents). The knowledge that their parents were actually talking together and taking responsibility was often reassuring to children. They might also be helped by the removal of the uncertainty that decision-making often achieved. Parents themselves often did not know what was or would be happening. This uncertainty itself inevitably contributed to the problematic communication between adults and their children in the post-separation period, as well as to the confusion of their children.

The wishes of children (certainly those under 16) were not conclusive. They could not be reliable judges of their own best long-term interests, and their expressed opinions and preferences at the time of the divorce crisis, however strongly felt, could not be decisive when arrangements over contact and residence were made (Wallerstein and Kelly, 1980). Some parents appeared only too happy to absolve themselves from decision-making responsibility and let the child decide. This frequently arose when a child was refusing to see the non-resident parent. The child should not be expected to shoulder such responsibility. There was a risk in such cases that the child might find him/herself ultimately alienated from both parents – cut off from the non-resident parent, as well as resentful in later years that the parent with residence had allowed this situation to come to pass.

Children could be pressurized or deliberately coached. In any event, they were usually most influenced by the parent with whom they were in closest contact. Where one parent (usually the parent with residence) insisted on the child being seen by the mediator, the possibility existed that the parent wanted their child's views elicited precisely because, at that moment, they coincided with their own views. But children's views do change. Mitchell

(1985), for example, has described how, when first interviewed, children expressed strong preferences for keeping their parents together even if they did not get on, rather than have them separate. Interviewed five to six years after divorce, only 6 out of 50 still thought their parents were wrong to have divorced. Family life was happier as a result of separation and divorce, but it had taken them a long time to appreciate this. Wallerstein and Kelly (1980, p.315) also found that many of those children with the most passionate convictions at the time of break-up came later to regret those statements with shame.

Developments in the 1990s

By the late 1980s, a productive interaction between researchers and practitioners in the field began to shed light for the first time on the delicate and complex role of children in mediation. For the first time, too, children's own views were canvassed (Garwood, 1989). For researchers, the very dilemmas of mediation practice in relation to children – for example, the multi-party consent requirements – both informed and complicated, even stymied, the research endeavour itself (Ogus et al., 1989; Simpson, 1989a). For practitioners, greater awareness of research, its value as well as its limitations, resulted in a more careful and focused approach (Davis and Roberts, 1988, 1989; Collinson and Gardner, 1990).

For example, practitioners no longer regarded the parents' right to determine their own decisions about their children as an abstract principle at odds with child welfare considerations. As far as their own children were concerned, parents might well be the true experts regarding the best arrangements for the children, knowing their children better than anyone else, and caring about their welfare. While in one research study the mediators' focus on children (encouraging the parents to adopt the *child's* perspective on the matter) was welcomed by parents, the mediators would limit themselves to the question: 'What is best for the child?' The answer remained a matter for negotiation between the parents, who were presumed to be the most competent judges of the issue. This did not mean the mediators had no useful specialist knowledge to offer, but there was greater recognition that this knowledge is, at best, tentative, that the general principle might not apply in the individual case, and that this expertise should not be paraded in such a way as to brow-beat parents. Disagreements over arrangements for children (residence and contact, in the main) did not arise simply from parents' own hurt, grief or bitterness – what might be termed their 'selfish' preoccupations with the past marital history. They might genuinely differ in their assessment of the children's interests. Furthermore, the mediators in this study no longer regarded a failure to reach agreement, or a preference for court adjudication, as an indication that parents did not have the best interests of their children at heart (Davis and Roberts, 1988).

The National Family Mediation report

In 1994, following a study of its services' practices in relation to children, NFM, supported by a grant from the Calouste Gulbenkian Foundation, published a definitive report on the subject, *Giving Children a Voice in Mediation*. The study yielded several specific findings:

- There was a continuum of views among mediators, ranging from those who were against direct inclusion of children, seeing mediation as an adult decision-making process, to those who were committed to their inclusion, either on the basis that it was the child's right to be included, or that it was in their best interests. The largest number of mediators were situated in the middle of this continuum, and whether reluctant or enthusiastic, adopted an approach of caution. The words 'only if appropriate' were frequently used.
- While most mediators and mediation services believed their primary concern was to protect the interests of children in divorce, it was rare for children to be directly involved. The average proportion of cases in which children were directly involved was 8 per cent, and there were only two services (out of 30 that responded) that saw children frequently. 'Apart from these exceptions, it is significant that those at the enthusiastic end of the continuum did not in fact appear to see children more frequently than those at the reluctant end' (NFM, 1994, p.12).
- There was no evidence to suggest that those most in favour of direct inclusion of children were more experienced or better trained than those who least favoured it. Those who were specifically trained *as mediators* to see children did not, in fact, see children more frequently.
- Most actual practice involved children being seen by mediators *outside* the mediation process and purpose.
- The language used to describe this practice was varied and unspecific – for example, 'working with' children; 'involving' children; 'seeing' children; 'including' children; children 'participating in', etc.
- All mediator respondents, despite strong differences of approach, were agreed that the decision-makers were the adults, not the mediator nor the children, and that an approach of caution in relation to children was appropriate (NFM, 1994a, p.20).

The policy question to be resolved was therefore this: 'How can children's perspectives best inform a process in which the parents are the ultimate decision-makers?' The concept of 'consultation' clarified language use, as well as providing the answer to the substantive question – children can be consulted as part of their parents' decision-making within mediation. This could take place in two ways:

- Indirect consultation by means of the *parents* themselves bringing their children's views into the process – this is the preferred form of consultation, because it encourages parents themselves to consider their children's views and perspectives fully.
- Direct consultation with children by the mediator within the process – this is of great assistance, particularly where the perspective of the child may be missing from discussions. Whether children should be consulted directly, how and at what stage, are matters to be agreed jointly by the mediator and the parties.

To implement its policy, NFM has since developed two training modules covering both the indirect and the direct consultation of children in mediation.

There is a view (for example, Richards, 1994b) that mediators should go further than giving children a voice in parental decision-making. Mediators should assist both in ensuring that the emotional needs of children are being met by others such as counsellors, and in educating parents in improving communication with their children.

There is no doubt that children will, on occasion, need specialist help in coping with the separation of their parents. Counselling, advice-giving, information, assessment and therapy should be available in these cases (Ross, 1986). But these forms of intervention, vital as they may be, should not be confused with mediation or be attempted at the same time by the same person. While every effort should, of course, be made to mitigate the unhappiness of loss and change, especially for children, misfortune in family life is, sadly, often unavoidable.

The UN Convention on the Rights of the Child

There is now near universal acceptance of the importance of the view that children are people, entitled to basic human rights. In 1989, the UN General Assembly adopted the UN Convention on the Rights of the Child, which was ratified by the UK government in 1991, and by September 1995, by 177 countries. In so doing, these countries made an explicit commitment to respecting and promoting children's rights. These embrace not only the survival, development and protection of children, but also their basic civil rights – the right of children to freedom of expression, religion, conscience, association, information, physical integrity, and to participation in decisions on matters that affect them.

Most pertinent to family decision-making, and therefore to family mediation, are articles 3, 5, 9 and 12, which are summarized briefly below:

- Article 3 sets out the principle that in all actions concerning children, the best interests of the child shall be a primary consideration.
- Article 5 sets out the state's duty to respect the responsibilities, rights and duties of parents and the wider family to provide appropriate direction and guidance appropriate to the child's evolving capacities.
- Article 9 sets out the child's right to live with his/her parents unless this is deemed incompatible with his/her interests, and the right to maintain contact on a regular basis with both parents if separated from one or both, except if it is contrary to the child's best interests.
- Article 12 states the child's right to express an opinion freely where capable, and to have that opinion taken into account in any matter or procedure affecting the child. The views of the child are to be given due weight, in accordance with the age and maturity of the child.

The Children Act 1989 recognizes the importance of respect for the child's perspective in family proceedings and in local authority decision-making, as does the European Convention on the Exercise of Children's Rights produced by the European Council in 1994. The Children (Scotland) Act 1995 goes further, and incorporates into primary legislation a specific provision requiring *all* those with parental responsibility:

> to have regard so far as practicable to the views (if he wishes to express them) of the child concerned, taking account of the child's age and maturity ... and without prejudice to the generality of this subsection a child twelve years of age or more shall be presumed to be of sufficient age and maturity to form a view. (s.6)

This Act therefore extends the obligation to take account of the views of the child into the private sphere of the family.

In addition to the rights of participation in decision-making embodied in the Children Act 1989, the House of Lords, in the 'Gillick' judgment, clarified the extent of parental authority in relation to decision-making on behalf of a child. Their Lordships' ruling (*Gillick* v. *West Norfolk and Wisbech AHA* [1986] AC 112) included the following:

> ... parental rights to control a child do not exist for the benefit of the parent. They exist for the benefit of the child and they are justified only in so far as they enable the parent to perform his duties towards the child, and towards other children in the family.

and:

> ...parental rights yield to the child's right to make his own decisions when he reaches a sufficient understanding and intelligence to be capable of making up his mind on the matter requiring a decision.

In *Re W.* (1993), the Gillick decision was redefined as extending only to the child's right to *give* consent, not to *refuse* treatment. Until a child reached the age of 18 years, a parallel right of consent continued to be vested in the parent, and would prevail if the child refused consent, irrespective of the competence of the child.

Striking the right balance between the rights and obligations of articles 3, 5, 9 and 12 – rights to care, protection, direction, guidance and consultation – is one of the many challenges involved in decision-making in separating and divorcing families. If children have the right both to express a view on matters of concern to them and to have those views taken seriously, then parents have a corresponding obligation to consult their children. This right of the child to participate in decision-making does not remove the ultimate authority of the adults to make the decisions in relation to the child, but it does significantly affect the process by means of which those decisions are made (Lansdown, 1995).

If striking the right balance within families is not without difficulty, then what of the difficulties of striking the right balance between families and professional interveners? The endorsement of private ordering and mediation in the Family Law Act 1996 has already precipitated warnings by children's rights advocates about the dangers of parental agreement for children. Such advocates urge the need for the greater welfare surveillance of family decision-making in divorce (Timms, 1995). Mediation is premised on the principle of party competence. There is no reason to presume that professionals care about children more or better than parents themselves. Nor is there any reason to presume that the implementation of article 12 in respect of divorce or separation requires there to be a professional involved, rather than a parent or parents, in non-contested or out-of-court decision-making. Is there not something of a paradox in the presumption of the competence of children by advocates of children's rights (that children will behave sensibly and reliably in participating in the making of serious decisions affecting them) and the concomitant denial of such a presumption of competence in relation to the parents of those children?

Furthermore, even where there may be an acknowledged conflict of interest between a child and parent(s), it is arguable that the interests of children are necessarily safeguarded by their separate legal representation by social workers in adversarial legal proceedings. Those who argue for a new, expanded role for guardians ad litem in private law proceedings seek to deny the fundamental difference between private and public law proceedings involving children (Timms, 1995). Unlike child protection public law cases, parental competence is not, by definition, legally challenged in private law proceedings. It has long been recognized that the costs of such professional intervention are great in terms of the risks of undermining family autonomy, stability, privacy and competence, with concomitant increased conflict and serious effects on children (Freeman, 1983). The parental role in child-rearing needs to be reinforced and strengthened, not undermined and weakened (Freeman, 1983).

Mediation and children: New areas of development

Child abduction and mediation

In response to the rising numbers of children being abducted by their parents and taken abroad without their consent and that of the other parent, the Parliamentary Working Party on Child Abduction was set up in 1990. Administered by Reunite, the National Council for Abducted Children, the All Party Group of MPs on Child Abduction and the specialist subgroups (prevention and mediation, law, Scotland and diplomacy) published a report entitled *Home and Away: Child Abduction in the Nineties* (PWPCA, 1993). Prior to the report, little information about child abduction had been available.

The prevention and mediation subgroup made a number of recommendations, one of which was that mediation could have a role to play at different stages in the developing dispute that escalates into an abduction. In particular, it recommended a pilot study to test the demand for and feasibility of mediation projects along the lines of the successful USA Child Find Project. This free telephone mediation scheme was set up with two clearly-defined goals: the return of the child to the pre-abduction position, and the parties' agreement on a forum in which to resolve their differences. One unexpected finding was the preventive value of the project. A large number of parents *contemplating* abduction contacted the mediators, even though the scheme was not aimed at them.

Adoption and mediation

An innovative mediation service involving the complex and controversial area of contact in the adoption of older children with histories of neglect or abuse has been initiated and provided by the Post Adoption Centre (1995, p.3):

Mediation seeks to return decision-making processes back to the people at the centre of adoption, whilst taking very careful account of child protection issues. Mediation is a process that can potentially promote a broader view of the concept of parenting in adoption by emphasising the mutuality of the relationship between the relinquishing parent and adoptive parent. Both are parents supported in co-operating directly, and there is a move away from having their relationship fragmented and defined by the intervention of outside agencies.

Mediation can involve birth parents (once plans to rehabilitate the child with birth parents have been abandoned) and social services departments in developing care plans. Birth parents engaged and involved in the preparation of the Care Plan are less likely to contest the adoption order later on. Mediation can also take place between the prospective adopters and the birth parents over contact arrangements. A number of difficult and important concerns must be addressed. For example, those issues which are or are not negotiable must be clarified at the outset. Intrinsic power inequalities (the birth parent starts off from a disadvantageous position *vis-à-vis* the adoptive parent, whose position is endorsed by the law) must be recognized and offset. Child safety parameters must be established, and reviewed in the light of changing circumstances.

There are already strong indications that an independent mediation service is proving to be effective in a difficult and conflict-ridden area of adoption practice. While the Post Adoption Centre originally developed mediation as a way of facilitating post-adoption contact, what has emerged is the need for such a service at a much earlier point in the adoption process, particularly at the court stage. With increasing numbers of referrals, practice findings are providing a valuable fund of learning in this pioneering field.

Child protection and mediation

North American studies (for example, Mayer, 1989) testify to the advantages of mediation as an alternative to litigation and adjudication in public law cases. NFM services are beginning to have such cases referred to them. Mediatory approaches are already operating in review and complaints proceedings under the Children Act 1989 (s.26). King and Trowell (1992) use case histories to point out the deleterious effects for the children (in many cases) of using the legal system as the only or the main forum for protecting children and promoting their welfare.

NFM and the Tavistock Clinic are therefore collaborating in a joint project funded by the Department of Health, aimed at identifying the knowledge and skills applicable for alternative dispute-resolution in child protection and child welfare cases within public law, applying these to a pilot case study and preparing a specialist training module.

Homeless young people and mediation

'Alone in London', an organization assisting young people alienated from their families, has set up a mediation service to try to re-establish communication and resolve disputes between those aged under 26 years and their families. With family breakdown a major cause of homelessness, their Family Mediating Service aims to prevent a young person running away or being ejected from their home, as well as to re-establish positive contact with family members where there is already homelessness or a young person is in care.

11 Fairness

Perhaps that is what love is – the momentary or prolonged refusal to think of another person in terms of power. (Phyllis Rose, 1985, *Parallel Lives*, p.16).

The very advantages of mediation over the adversarial legal system also create potential risks (Folberg and Taylor, 1984). Mediation is held in private. No legal representatives are present (certainly not in out-of-court agencies). Procedures are informal and flexible. The safeguards of due process do not apply. There is always a danger that the more powerful interests will prevail over the weaker. Therefore, fairness is a matter of central importance in mediation. The parties must feel that they have been treated fairly and that any agreement they reach is fair, or as fair as is practicable in all the circumstances, not only to them, but to their children and whoever else is affected by their arrangements. Given that, in mediation, the issue of party authority for decision-making is so central and delicate, it is also only in the independence of mediation from other forms of intervention that the essential ethical and professional principles that fully safeguard the interests of a fair process can be realised (see Chapter 2). In addition, a range of safeguards is necessary – procedural, structural and professional.

Justice and the law: Fairness and mediation

Justice is symbolized in Western culture by a blind goddess holding the sword of state power in one hand, and in the other, balancing the scales of justice exactly. This symbol of justice embodies three principles:

- Justice is *bestowed* by a third party – an official, state-sanctioned judicial authority.

- That third party must be strictly impartial.
- Impartiality is achieved by means of the application of consistent rules to each case.

Access to justice has traditionally meant equal, adequate and ready access to legal services and the courts. Access to justice, now that alternative dispute-resolution processes are available, also includes access to a choice in relation to the dispute-resolution process most appropriate to the type of case (Labour Party, 1995).

Justice – understood as impartial, rule-determined, consistent, third-party decision-making – therefore does not apply to mediation, where authority for decision-making lies with the parties themselves. Justice involves a finding. For example, in relation to marital breakdown, it has traditionally been taken to mean the accurate allocation of blameworthiness.

In mediation, on the other hand, fairness is determined by the parties themselves, and involves personal norms (including ethical and psychological aspects) as well as legal norms. There must be a fair process, as well as a fair outcome. One of the advantages of mediation is its procedural flexibility, which provides the opportunity for powerful concerns about fault and fairness to be addressed. This frequently necessitates consideration of the particular historical context of the dispute. Fairness, when it is equated with formal equality, excludes this context by discounting concerns about the past or disallowing their expression. For fairness to operate in mediation, this context may well be relevant.

The future as well as the past is relevant in considering fairness. When do the parties determine fairness – at the time the outcome is reached, or subsequently? The settlement of the family arrangements is, as noted earlier (see Chapter 4), not a 'closed episode', but part of 'the flow of time' (Falk Moore, 1995, p.31).

It must be remembered both that the intervention of the mediator within this dimension of time is limited and modest, and that the value and effectiveness of mediation lies as much in an improved understanding and an improved capacity to negotiate together in the future, as it does in the reaching of specific agreements.

A family systems approach and fairness

For mediation to have value, it must be fair to *all* parties concerned. Respect for the interests and objectives of each party and for those affected by any agreement, notably children, is not easily reconciled with the family systems approach, which analyses the family in terms of functional needs and services. It is an approach that claims to be value-free, yet can imply, at the same time, that all family members are responsible for the ills of the family (Grillo, 1991). Advocates of the family systems approach to mediation have this to say about fairness:

> 'Fairness' is another of those unfortunate concepts that appears so obviously to be a 'good thing' that seldom is its appropriateness in a particular context questioned. At the risk therefore of appearing to support unfairness we nevertheless wish to question this notion . . . [Fairness] represents a (perhaps legalistic?) distortion of the way in which relationships actually work . . . [R]elationships are not fair or unfair, they are what they are. (Howard and Shepherd, 1987, p.17).

Such an approach confuses what is with what ought to be, which is precisely what 'fairness' reminds us about. It ignores the ethical implications of situations in which the interests and rights of individual family members may be in direct conflict, or where there are significant disparities of power between the parties. Systemic levelling, through the application of techniques such as positive connotation, often 'flies in the face of common conceptions of justice' (Walrond-Skinner, 1987, p.3). As some systems thinkers themselves describe it, 'the positive connotation [as an intervention technique] is not related to truthfulness, but to the strategy of being therapeutic' (Campbell et al., 1989, p.46).

Reframing techniques elevate reinterpretation over action for change. Such techniques are designed to challenge the parties' different values, and can not only devalue what the parties regard as significant, but can also collude with and perpetuate unfairness by denying relevance to objective circumstances, such as the political, economic or gender factors of a dispute. One of the mediator's primary ethical responsibilities is to ensure that where these factors (or others) significantly affect the respective balance of power between the parties, this imbalance is recognized explicitly and duress prevented – if necessary, by ceasing mediation.

Bargaining power

There is no precise definition of 'bargaining power'. This is because there is no simple construction of the issue of power inequality, just as there is no single truth about relationships (Lukes, 1974). There is, rather, as Seidenberg (1973, p.97) puts it, a 'repertory of truths'. The richness and irreducibility of personal relationships is exemplified in Phyllis Rose's view of marriage as a shared imaginative construct, a 'subjectivist fiction', as well as the primary political experience of those adults involved:

> Whatever the balance, every marriage is based upon some understanding,

articulated or not, about the relative importance, the priority of desires, between its two partners. Marriages go bad not when love fades – love can modulate into affection without driving two people apart – but when this understanding about the balance of power breaks down, when the weaker member feels exploited or the stronger feels unrewarded for his or her strength. (Rose, 1985, p.15)

Unhappiness in marriage may therefore occur when 'two versions of reality rather than two people [are] in conflict' (Rose, 1985, p.15). This realm of personal power relations is, for the most part, inaccessible to outsiders, and may even be, if not unperceived by the parties themselves, unacknowledged by them.

The picture is further complicated, as Gilligan (1982) suggests, by the different perspectives that women and men can bring to relationships and to moral problems. Speaking different languages yet employing a common moral vocabulary, they are likely to mistranslate and misunderstand one another, thereby limiting the possibilities for co-operation. It is argued that women, for example, will tend to associate power with the capacity and strength to nurture, while for men, power is associated with assertion and aggression. Other feminists (for example, Williams, 1989) criticize what they view as gender-constructed dichotomies, denying such differences exist, or arguing that differences result from socialization, rather than innate and therefore inevitable differences between the sexes. Any examination of bargaining power must nevertheless take into account the tension between the complementary ethics that might motivate individual women and men – an ethic of care and responsibility, and an ethic of rights and self-advancement, respectively.

A consideration of what factors make up any assessment of bargaining power must include the following:

- financial and material circumstances;
- the legal 'endowments' – for example, legal rulings in relation to children and property (Mnookin, 1984);
- emotional and social vulnerability;
- *de facto* care and control of the children;
- the presence of new partners;
- readiness and ability to negotiate;
- personal attributes;
- access to legal and other advice and support, including access to Legal Aid;
- the family history (violence as a feature of family life, for example).

Furthermore, the perceptions of each party of their predicament must be taken into account. It is not uncommon for each party to feel they are the more vulnerable, and to see their former partner as all-powerful, whatever the objective circumstances. Bargaining power therefore involves a complex and subtle interplay of forces, objective and subjective, perceived or other-wise. Nor are situations static. The decision to separate may bring about a radical shift in the balance of power, for example, in relation to the children. Rarely are the disadvantages or advantages stacked all one way, nor should it be assumed that, where one party has superior 'endowments' of one sort or another, that power will necessarily be used, let alone exploited.

Feminist fears about mediation

Fears about mediation damaging women's interests were resurrected once again as the Family Law Bill 1995 made its way through parliament (Roberts, 1996). Feminist lawyers (for example, Bottomley, 1984, 1985) first voiced these theoretical concerns in the UK over a decade ago. Mediation, it was argued, was disadvantageous to women because:

- Individual women face their former partners as unequals.
- Women face a mediator whose dominant social values, it is claimed, are oppressive to women. The focus on children is seen as a denial of rights for women, as distinct from their children and their mothering role. Furthermore, the presumptions of many mediators in favour of access and joint custody (the terms then in use) served, it was claimed, to perpetuate the dominant role of the father in the reconstructed family.
- Women as a group suffer fundamental power inequalities in the family, and these are ignored. Mediation 'privatizes' family disputes, which are therefore concealed instead of emerging in the 'public sphere of formal justice' (Bottomley, 1985, p.180). Consensus masks and there-fore perpetuates the conflict that characterizes the power inequalities of relationships within the family.

Similar fears are being raised again:

> They [women] are more likely in this situation to be inarticulate and ill-informed about their rights, more likely to be timid, suffering from depression and possibly in fear of their husbands. Women mediators, it is said (and most of them are women) are more likely to side with the husband's account of affairs than the wife's. The husband is more likely to be able to afford legal advice in the back-ground, to have some experience of negotiation and to know his rights. Most seri-ously of all, it is not the job of the mediator, who may have no legal training at all, to inform the couple of their rights under the law. (Deech, 1995, p.12).

These views form part of a feminist critique of mediation underpinned by two assumptions: firstly, that women do not know what they want and cannot speak for themselves, and secondly, that where women do make certain demands – for example, for co-operation with their former partners, for maintenance or for increased contact for their children with their fathers – these are mistaken, reactionary or contradictory. While these views are unsubstantiated by empirical evidence, they do raise important issues of bias, fairness and power that mediators must recognize, and have indeed addressed in their writing, training and practice over many years.

One of the difficulties with this critique of mediation is its oversimplification of issues that are, in fact, complex, multi-faceted and interdependent. One also needs to bear in mind the complex and highly problematic nature of the circumstances that characterize the divorce process, and the complexity and interrelated nature of the disputes that frequently attend divorce. Usually, there is no one cause of difficulty, but numerous obstacles and sources of tension. In addition, it is important to recognize and acknowledge the uncertainty, the ambivalence, the inconsistency and the ignorance that often characterize situations, as well as perceptions, at times of conflict and change. Disputes also concern many interconnected issues, which are themselves affected by multiple variables and attributes.

Mediation as an alternative to other dispute-resolution processes

While it is important to raise questions about fairness in mediation, the same questions should also be raised in connection with all methods of dispute-resolution – whether private negotiations, solicitor negotiations, door-of-the-court settlements by barristers or adjudication: 'No dispute resolution mechanism is devoid of problems concerning fair outcomes, and none of the alternatives is best for every dispute' (Folberg and Taylor, 1984, p.247). Private negotiations between parties lack the checks of due process or third-party presence. Such negotiations may be coerced by the expense and uncertainty of litigation (Wishik, 1984). Most family disputes following matrimonial breakdown are negotiated by lawyers, with only a minority reaching the stage of adjudication. But neither bilateral lawyer negotiations nor adjudication avoid the problems of power differentials. If anything, new inequalities may be created – for example, of unequal resources, choice of lawyer or idiosyncratic judgements. Guilt and the extent of the non-mutuality of the decision to divorce are important determinants of both the dispute and its processing (Ingleby, 1992; Mather et al., 1995). Guilt – and this is an issue unrelated to gender – is a prime cause of unwillingness to claim legal entitlements (Mather et al., 1995).

North American research shows that 'in divorce, lawyers and clients negotiate power but they do so on uneven terms' (Felstiner and Sarat, 1992, p.1,497). Divorcing clients are typically the weaker parties, their situations characterized by personal crisis, vulnerability and inadequate resources, with critical issues in their lives at stake. Other North American studies into divorce negotiations between lawyers reveal imbalances of power so far as the clients' interests are concerned (Menkel-Meadow, 1993a; see also Chapter 3).

It is acknowledged that court intervention is likely to be most appropriate 'in a setting where conflict occurs among unequal strangers, when a court can, at least in theory, rectify an imbalance by extending the formalities of equal protection to weaker parties' (Auerbach, 1983, p.120). Research also exposes the fact that this ideal of equal justice is incompatible with the social and economic realities of unequal wealth, power and opportunity: 'The austere neutrality of law is constantly eroded by the special protection that its form and substance provide to privileged members of society' (Auerbach, 1983, pp.143–4).

Furthermore, the law is acknowledged to be patriarchal in its assumptions, and the legal profession is male-dominated (Smart, 1984). Lord Woolf's general indictment (Woolf Report, 1995) of a civil justice system where exploitation by the stronger party of the weaker party is endemic, is just as applicable in family proceedings, where imbalances in gender power are unlikely to be considered, let alone pointed out by predominantly male lawyers to women clients. In fact, the experience of legal proceedings of many people (men and women) is of being caught up in a process over which they have no control. People experience their disputes as being taken over and transformed by legal professionals, leaving them feeling impotent and irrelevant (Christie, 1977; Auerbach, 1983; Davis and Roberts, 1988). Ingleby (1994) speculates that the conflict between what the client wants and what the client is entitled to might account for these feelings of alienation and loss of control.

Disparity of bargaining power is not, of itself, a ground for the court setting aside a private agreement if there has been no unfair exploitation of superior bargaining strength and both parties have had the benefit of professional advice (*Edgar* v. *Edgar*, 1980). The parties are not required to be represented in matrimonial proceedings, nor is the respondent required to attend the Children's Appointment. Any bias shown to women in relation to decisions over children gives priority to them, it is argued, not as women, but as mothers (Smart, 1984).

Research evidence

The field of alternative dispute-resolution, and of mediation in particular, has been the subject of research to an unusually large extent since the early 1980s.

It is fair to say that there is no empirical evidence in the UK or elsewhere to substantiate the allegations that women are disadvantaged by mediation. On the contrary, there is a growing body of research showing high levels of satisfaction among women in relation to both the process and outcomes of mediation. The main research studies that attempt a gender analysis of their findings are set out below. Initial findings of consumer research in the UK suggest that:

- Fairness matters very much to both parties.
- Women do not regard themselves as disadvantaged by mediation. In fact, some felt 'empowered' by their experience of the process. Women in particular regarded the agreements they reached as fair.
- Social and economic aspects of the dispute were not ignored in mediation. On the contrary, women themselves exposed these topics for discussion. They demanded express acknowledgement of their predicament from their former partners.
- The explicit focus on children's needs by the mediator (also reflecting the values of the court in disputes involving children) was positively welcomed by the majority of the couples (both men and women), according as it did with their own priorities. (Davis and Roberts, 1988b)

In their Californian study, Kelly and Duryee (1992) found few differences of significance between men and women in their perceptions of the mediator, the process and the outcome. Where there were differences, they found that women rated the mediation experience more favourably than men because they benefited both from the opportunity the process provided to express their views and be heard, and from the increased confidence to stand up for themselves in relation to their ex-spouses. They also benefited from the opportunity mediation provided to put their anger aside and focus on the children.

The major Australian research report (Bordow and Gibson, 1994) also dispels several myths about mediation, finding, in summary, that 'separated couples come to mediation with the hope of reaching a fair and mutually satisfactory agreement and most did just that' (Bordow and Gibson, 1994, p.11). More specifically, the research data does not support the notion that women feel disadvantaged in the mediation process. On the contrary, women felt they had equal influence over the terms of their agreements, and reported increased confidence in their ability to stand up for themselves and handle future disagreements with their ex-spouses.

This research finds that in most respects, women's perceptions of the mediation process and outcomes (on all issues – financial, property and children) are as favourable as, and sometimes better than, those expressed by their partners. Where significant gender differences occurred, 'women felt more empowered by the mediation process and reported feeling more confident about their ability to stand up for themselves' (Bordow and Gibson, 1994, p.144). The most positive finding was the high level of client satisfaction with all aspects of the mediation service, and this was largely independent of whether or not agreement was reached. This confirms the earlier North American findings of Pearson and Thoennes (1989) and Emery et al. (1991),[1] and is confirmed in the UK by the research of Walker et al. (1994). In particular, both men and women who went through mediation were satisfied that their rights were protected (Emery et al., 1991). The North American research of Maccoby and Mnookin (1992) and Pearson (1993) was unable to detect negative financial consequences for women in mediation. More specifically, there was no ground for the fear that in mediation, fathers commonly persuade mothers to accept less financial support by using custody as a bargaining chip, or that women bargain away important and needed property in order to gain custody and avoid excessive visitation. The only difference Pearson found in relation to the dispute-resolution forum concerned legal fees and respondent satisfaction with the agreement, both of which were more favourable for the mediation group. Agreements were perceived to be fair, even among those who might be viewed objectively as the 'losing party' (Pearson, 1993, p.284).

Bohmer and Ray's Georgia and New York comparative study (1994), designed to evaluate the relative benefits of mediation for women and children compared to other methods of dispute-resolution, also found that women who chose mediation do not lose out in terms of outcome. The use of child support guidelines and the professional training of mediators were significant variables. In the UK, the bulk of the evidence also offers no support for feminist fears (Davis and Roberts, 1988; Walker et al., 1994; McCarthy and Walker, 1996b).

Finally, Grillo's important North American work (1991) highlights several dangers for women in mediation (mandatory and voluntary) when essential safeguards are abandoned and context is insufficiently addressed. For example, *mandatory* mediation requires women and men to speak in a setting they have not chosen, and in some mediation practices, reference to 'the past' is disallowed. This denies women the opportunity for the expression of fault and anger, therefore excluding powerful aspects of the historical context that makes up the dispute (see above). Grillo also warns of the dangers for either spouse of a family systems approach to mediation, where each takes on the burden of the other's irresponsibility and every family member becomes equally responsible for everything. Grillo (1991, p.1,550) states: 'Although this article cautions against mediation's dangers I should emphasise at this juncture that mediation is the work I most like to do'.

Research conclusions

All these findings suggest that mediation does not have the detrimental effects for women that have been feared (or hoped for). As a process, mediation is not inherently good or bad for women's interests (Menkel-Meadow, 1985). It all depends on the skill and competence of the mediator, and on the necessary screening, structural and procedural safeguards being in place.

As a process of consensual, joint decision-making, mediation requires high practice standards and high standards of provision and delivery. This means:

- the proper selection, training, supervision and accreditation of mediators;
- quality assurance procedures (including quality control mechanisms, quality audit and quality assessment);
- an independent and neutral environment for the provision of mediation, free of stigma, coercion or confusion with other professional interventions;
- pre-mediation screening out of unsuitable cases (for example, domestic violence or other serious imbalances of power or incapacity);
- rigorous adherence to the principles of mediation (voluntariness of participation in particular);
- equal access to full and accurate information necessary for informed decision-making (legal, tax, welfare rights, etc.);
- independent legal or other advice and review, where necessary.

These are set out in more detail below, under 'Safeguarding a fair process'.

The limits of mediation

It must be acknowledged that mediation should not be criticized for failing to remedy those ills which it cannot and never set out to solve in the first place (Felstiner and Williams, 1985). But social and economic inequalities (as well as deep-seated emotional problems) do, of course, exist, and their impact on disputes must be recognized – for example, the division of labour in the family; limited job opportunities, especially for women; unequal rates of pay, and so on. In the majority of cases, women with children – especially older women with dependent children, for whom remarriage is not easy – do suffer economic deprivation on divorce, even if they have jobs (Eekelaar and Maclean, 1986). But while inequalities exist and cannot easily be legislated or negotiated away, it is misleading to define these simply in terms of a battle between men and women (Smart, 1982). Solutions to economic disadvantage and other inequities lie outside mediation, in reforms to tax, welfare, housing, child care and employment provision.

Fault and mediation

One of the advantages of mediation is the opportunity it affords for the expression of personal (that is, non-legal) norms of fairness. These may be of great importance to the parties in arriving at an agreement that they deem fair and therefore acceptable, although these norms may have no legal validity – for example, the relevance of emotional vulnerability, or the accommodation of individual ethical standards of fault and responsibility (Folberg and Taylor, 1984). Unfairness may have to be accepted as a fact of life by one party if the children's needs, especially their need of a home, are to be satisfied.

The Family Law Act 1996 removes the need to establish irretrievable breakdown by means of any fault-based facts such as adultery or unreasonable behaviour. It is acknowledged that fault-based allegations create conflict, and that, in any event, the court is too blunt an instrument for allocating blameworthiness in this complex and sensitive area of family life. The White Paper (1995) on divorce reform, in arguing for the removal of fault as a legal construct, recognizes none the less that fault remains a powerful issue in marriage breakdown, but an issue that the couple *themselves* have to deal with. Mediation is seen as the proper forum for couples to address fault directly together:

> Such a process requires each party to accept that the marriage is over before proceeding to address the future of a life apart. In this way, *the couple* have to deal with issues of fault, acknowledge that the marriage has broken down irretrievably, and take responsibility for the consequences. (White Paper, 1995, para.2.18; emphasis added)

Mediators are accustomed to seeing couples at a bitter time in the divorce and separation process. Often, one of the first decisions to be made is whether or not the marriage is over. Feelings of injustice are often related to a belief that some moral obligation has been violated. The resolution of the dispute then requires acknowledgement of these powerful feelings of fault or blame, of being wronged as a 'good' mother and wife, or as a 'good' father and husband; or, in the aftermath of separation or divorce, acknowledgment of its almost inevitable inequitable impact on one or both parents' life, whether as struggling lone parent or as absentee one:

> It is as if there are certain magic words, varying from person to person, that when spoken sincerely by a spouse, are able to alleviate the other's sense of moral

injustice. The moral aspect addressed in this way can serve as a catalyst in the negotiations of the issue. (Folberg and Milne, 1988, p.52)

There is frequent disagreement over whether and why the relationship has ended. While the focus of mediation is on making future arrangements, there is unlikely to be progress in that direction unless there is first an opportunity for the parties to address powerful ethical and emotional concerns about fault and fairness. These may include grievances not only about past actions and responsibility for the breakdown, but also concerns about the present and the future, such as responsibility for the economic and social inequities arising from the family breakdown. It is the common experience of mediators that what the parties want in these circumstances is not necessarily judgement by a third party on who is right and who is wrong, but rather the opportunity to have their views heard and acknowledged, not by the *mediator* but by their *former partner*.

Safeguarding a fair process

Mediators need constantly to bear in mind, and address in practice, the vital questions raised about their authority and power:

- How can the authority of the mediator be exercised in ways that serve the essential objectives of the process and protect its fundamental characteristics and principles?
- When does the exercise of that authority cease to serve those objectives, becoming instead an abuse of power with the mediator exerting unacceptable pressures upon one or both of the parties who then act (or fail to act) in ways they would not otherwise have done?

These questions are part of a larger question – of how mediation can emerge as an independent activity, distinct both from the practice of therapy, social work and counselling on the one hand, and from legal process on the other; distinct, in particular, from attempts to refurbish court process and adjudication. One of the chief tasks of training is to assist trainee mediators to distinguish mediation clearly from those forms of intervention that may appear, at first sight, to be similar, such as settlement-seeking by court welfare officers and judges, conciliatory negotiations by lawyers, interventions into family functioning by family therapists, welfare interventions of social workers, and the personal and interpersonal focus of counsellors and psychotherapists.

Given that mediation is, by its nature, a private and informal process, and that the issue of authority in mediation is so fundamental, it is argued here that it is only by its independence from these other forms of intervention that the essential professional and ethical principles that give mediation its unique value and that fully safeguard the interests of an efficacious and fair process can be realized.

It is necessary to ensure that the safeguards to protect fairness in mediation are in place. There are several ways in which fairness may be safeguarded (though not necessarily guaranteed) in mediation.

The principle of voluntariness

The voluntariness of participation in mediation is one of mediation's four fundamental characteristics (see page 7). This is a vital safeguard against pressurization or coercion or inappropriate referral (for example, in cases of violence or incapacity). Voluntariness must be an explicit tenet of mediation practice at the outset (especially when referrals to mediation come from the court or the court welfare service, and are likely to be experienced as ordered by the court[2]) and throughout the process.[3]

The parties usually know one another, and so are in a position to make a choice as to whether or not they are prepared to attempt a mediated solution.

The skill and integrity of the mediator

Reliance on party control does not absolve the mediator from the ethical responsibility to ensure that both parties participate actively and freely in discussion and reach a mutually acceptable outcome. Attempts at bullying or overreaching must be prevented by the mediator as far as possible. Furthermore, 'some things cannot and should not be compromised' (Folberg and Taylor, 1984, p.247). If necessary, the mediator should bring the session to an end rather than countenancing any unfairness.

Where a situation of manifest inequality occurs, resort to mediation could be inappropriate or even unethical. One such example is when the capacity of one or other party to think or plan clearly and rationally is seriously impaired, as in cases of clinical depression or other mental disorder, or incapacitation through drink or drugs. Another is when fear or intimidation characterizes and distorts relationships – for example, where there is or has been violence.

The mediator needs to understand the situation of each party, so that imbalances, where these exist and are not recognized, or are recognized insufficiently, may be pointed out and talked about (for a discussion of useful interventions for power-balancing, see Kelly, 1995). Open discussion is necessary if each party is to make a proper evaluation of their own position, consider all the relevant factors and practicable alternatives, and so reach reasoned, consensual decisions. Imbalances in negotiating skill must also be taken into account – for example, where one party is less articulate, slower to grasp what is happening, or lacking in confidence. An understanding of the situation of each party requires, in addition to an understanding of gender inequality, an awareness and understanding of cultural dynamics – the specific cultural, religious and regional perspectives and responses of different communities in relation to attitudes to conflict and disputes (Shah-Kazemi, 1996).

Structural and procedural protections

These are necessary both to offset the kinds of inequalities that can arise – for example, from a failure to structure sessions fairly – and to enhance the control of the parties and of women in particular (Kelly and Duryee, 1992). The framework of the mediation session should be designed to achieve fairness. The separate opportunity for each party to talk alone to the mediator at an early stage of every session is one important structural safeguard that should in no circumstances be dispensed with if full and free disclosure is to be protected.

The research of Cobb and Rifkin (1990) at five dispute-resolution programmes in western Massachusetts, covering a range of civil, criminal and family disputes, has found that the order in which the disputants state the issue, and the ways in which they do so, can mirror the adversarial mode. The first disputant can 'negatively position' the second disputant. The research suggests that people may not have equal access to the mediation process, nor may they be able to participate fully or equally as a result of the structural arrangements of the session.

The Coogler model of structured mediation adopted and adapted by some independent family mediation services expressly addresses the issues of party autonomy, mediator power and the protection of a fair process by means of structure (see Chapter 7). Coogler's (1978) emphasis is on the importance of a clear structure, composed of the integration of three structural components, designed to protect the parties procedurally, ethically and emotionally.

Screening for domestic violence

In the light of the Family Law Act 1996, which endorses mediation both as a voluntary process and as the preferred approach to settling family disputes following divorce and separation, increasing numbers of couples are likely to be encouraged to use mediation. This creates two risks:

● That people will experience being pressured into mediation.
● That cases that are inappropriate for mediation, such as cases of domestic violence, will be referred to mediation.

National Family Mediation has responded to these developments and recent research (for example, Hester and Radford, 1992, 1996; Hester and Pearson, 1993; Pagelow, 1990) by making an unequivocal statement of policy and recommending best practice guidelines to address the issue of domestic violence in relation to mediation. The policy states that good practice:

> requires that each participant makes a fully informed and voluntary decision to enter mediation. This requires that each participant is sufficiently informed and has sufficient time to make the decision to attempt mediation after all safety issues including screening for domestic violence, have been fully considered. (NFM, 1996a)

In order to fulfil this policy, it is recommended that all services *must* routinely screen for domestic violence *before* mediation starts, and that if mediation does take place, procedures must be in place to ensure client protection, child protection and mediator safety, so that continuing attention is paid throughout mediation to the possible existence of domestic violence. The definition of domestic violence adopted in the policy is comprehensive:

> The most important factor in domestic violence is the *impact* of the behaviour as experienced by each/any of the individuals involved. Domestic violence is behaviour that seeks to secure power and control for the abuser and to undermine the safety, security, self-esteem and autonomy of the abused person. Domestic violence contains elements of the use of any or all of physical, sexual, psychological, emotional, verbal or economic intimidation, oppression or coercion. (NFM, 1996a; emphasis added)

What distinguishes this approach and the definition of domestic violence upon which it rests, is the pre-eminence that it attaches to the meanings and experiences of the individuals concerned. This is in contrast to an approach that involves the making of a diagnostic judgement on the part of the professional based on a typology of domestic violence profiles (for example, Johnston, 1993). The beauty of NFM's policy, on the other hand, is that it accords both with thinking in the recent literature in the field (for example, Astor, 1994) *and* with the basic precepts of mediation.

The practical implication of this definition for those who undertake screening (intake worker or mediator) means that in reaching a decision about whether or not to proceed (and the mediator, ultimately, has the final say), priority must be given to the individual's *perception* of violence, rather than making any judgement about levels of severity or types of violence. One of the overarching general principles of the Family Law Act 1996 is:

> that any risk to one of the parties to a marriage, and to any children, of violence from the other party should, so far as reasonably practicable, be removed or diminished. (Family Law Act 1996, s.1(d))

The Family Law Act 1996 requires, in particular, that in publicly-funded mediation, the mediator complies with a code of practice that includes 'arrangements designed to ensure – (a) that parties participate in mediation only if willing and not influenced by fear of violence or other harm; (b) that cases where either party may be influenced by fear of violence or other harm are identified as soon as possible' (ss.27(6) and 27(7)).

Review by mediation

There should be an opportunity to return to mediation to review or renegotiate an agreement if it is thought to be unfair or does not work out in practice. Changes of circumstance may make revision necessary, and in some cases an agreement may only be acceptable to the parties if it is provisional, to be reviewed subject to a trial implementation of limited duration.

Co-working

Recent research indicates that co-working can increase the risks of mediators exerting unacceptable pressure, for example by underlining each other's interventions rather than counteracting bias or omission (Dingwall, 1988). No gender implications of co-working are explored in this research. Consumer research (Davis and Roberts, 1988) has found that the use of co-workers of each sex did help prevent any one gender outlook predominating. The presence of a male mediator was found to be reassuring to some women who feared intimidation by their former spouses. Co-workers can monitor each other, limiting bias or omission (see above, Chapter 5, pp.96–97).

Independent legal review

Another check on unfairness arising in mediation is that afforded by independent legal advice and review. Both parties should know what their legal rights are, including the fact that resort to mediation jeopardizes none of these rights. Where anyone is not legally represented, they should be urged to consult a solicitor. The availability of advice under the Green Form Scheme and of Legal Aid should be explained to them. If agreements are reached in mediation which may be legally binding – for example, where any financial or property issues form part of an agreement over residence or contact – the parties should submit these to their respective solicitors for review. It is important that the full tax and legal implications of any agreement are clearly understood by the parties, that nothing important has been omitted, and that the agreement is expressed in terms that are faithful to the parties' understanding and meaning. The parties must still 'own' their agreement, but with the reassurance of partisan confirmation.

Training

The mediator's own potential to abuse his/her role has to be recognized explicitly in the training of mediators (Roberts, 1988). Findings have identified inadequate training as responsible for failures of practice – for the mediator's failure both to recognize the problem and to do anything about it (Cobb and Rifkin, 1990).

Training needs to include anti-discriminatory practice and study of the impact of culture on disputes, because of the likelihood of increasing numbers of intercultural mediations, either where the disputants come from different cultures or where the mediator is culturally different from the party or parties (see Chapter 6 for further discussion on different approaches to this issue).

Professional regulation

The movement to mediation represents, on the one hand, the reassertion of *party* control over decision-making in place of *professional* control. But despite the modest ambition of mediation to support party decision-making, it remains an expert intervention requiring the normal safeguards of professional regulation. These safeguards assume even greater significance in the light of the privacy and informality inherent in the practice of mediation (see page 153).

Prior to the launch in 1996 of the UK College of Family Mediators, family mediation providers (NFM in particular) have created their own extensive and stringent quality control mechanisms for establishing appropriate national standards for practitioners, for evaluating practice against these standards, and for meeting and raising them. National Family Mediation, as the non-profitmaking provider of family mediation, has set out to achieve these goals expressly through its national professional and organizational framework, consisting of affiliation criteria for services, a code of practice for regulating ethical and professional standards of practice, its equal opportunities policy and equal opportunities monitoring, and national procedures for selection, training, supervised practice and accreditation of mediators on the basis of competence.[4] In addition to this regulatory framework, further monitoring of standards of provision takes place by means of the publication of annual statistics, reports and guidelines; external monitoring of developments through research and consultancy; links with institutions of higher education and European bodies, and built-in evaluation and reviewing procedures (for further discussion,[5] see Roberts, 1994).

The main objective of the UK College of Family Mediators is to provide a regulatory framework for all practitioners, whatever sector they work in – non-profitmaking, statutory or private sector – in order to protect the public. The objects for which the college has been established are:

- to advance the education of the public in the skills and practice of family mediation;
- to set, promote, improve and maintain the highest standards of professional conduct and training for those practising in the field of family mediation;
- to make available the details of registered mediators qualified to provide family mediation. (UK College of Family Mediators, 1996, p.3)

The college also has a responsibility to ensure that mediation is accessible to all members of the community regardless of their cultural, religious or ethnic background. The establishment of the college marks the arrival of family mediation as a new profession. All the hallmarks of a profession are now present:

- It has its own recognized body of knowledge.
- There are mechanisms for the transmission of this body of knowledge.
- There are mechanisms for self-regulation and evaluation – the college has set up a Disciplinary Committee and a Complaints Committee.

The Family Law Act 1996 introduces additional quality assurance requirements for publicly-funded family mediation provision. There is a statutory requirement that any contract entered into by the Legal Aid Board for the provision of mediation 'must require the mediator to comply with a code of practice' (s.27(6)). Such a code requires the mediator to have 'arrangements designed to ensure', among other things, pre-mediation screening for domestic violence, as well as the consultation of children in mediation (ss.27(7) and 27(8)).

Research

More research is needed into the process and practice of family mediation – research that does justice to its complex, difficult and, at times, ambivalent demands, as well as the socio-cultural context in which it takes place. More knowledge is needed if the inherent limitations in the process are to be offset and failures in practice are to be avoided. Research should explore the impact of cultural difference and its implications for recruiting and training mediators, and should include consumer evaluation, with a focus on the perspectives and meanings of the parties (for a discussion of these issues, see Roberts, 1992b; Dingwall and Greatbatch, 1993; Roberts, 1994; Dingwall and Greatbatch, 1995). The pilot studies to be introduced prior to the implementation of the Family Law Act 1996 will yield valuable research data on family mediation provision.

This raises the larger question as to whether and to what extent it is possible or desirable for there to be a productive exchange between researchers and practitioners (Roberts, 1994). While the interests of researchers and practitioners do not necessarily coincide, common understanding would seem to be important if practice is to be informed by reputable research and there is to be the co-operation and confidence on the part of practitioners necessary for research to take place in the field.

Two questions are posed in an article entitled, interestingly, 'The *practitioner's* dilemma' (Rifkin, 1994; emphasis added):

- Do innovative theoretical perspectives frustrate mediation practitioners?
- How can research and theory have a meaningful impact on practice?

The large body of research in North America on dispute-resolution (and mediation in particular) encompasses a range of perspectives and conclusions, some of which raise serious concerns about the political implications of informal justice (see Chapter 1) and about power, neutrality and coercion. As Rifkin notes (1994, p.204), these are concerns that 'mediators themselves debate and worry over'. Notwithstanding this mutual concern, a lack of interaction has characterized relations between researchers and practitioners in North America, with the result that research and theory have had little impact on practice. A number of reasons for this have been suggested:

- the absence of explicit theories of practice underpinning mediation training programmes, which are unable, as a consequence, to incorporate innovative theoretical perspectives;
- the problem of practitioners continuing to be shaped by the professional training of their professions of origin;
- the lack of consensus among practitioners and their professional organizations as to what constitutes 'good practice';
- the failure of scholars, few of whom offer recommendations for the transformation of practice; this, they argue, goes beyond the boundaries of their aims;
- the lack of opportunities for researchers and practitioners to collaborate in exploring the practical implications of research studies.

Fortunately, the situation in the UK is more encouraging. A number of practitioners involved in mediation policy and practice in the UK are already engaged in productive exchange with a number of researchers in the field expressly focused on identifying models of good mediation practice, informed both by research findings and practice experience. This covers research work on mediation in relation to children and divorce (Simpson,

1989), all-issues mediation (Walker et al., 1994) and domestic violence (Hester and Pearson, 1993; Kaganas and Piper, 1993), and more generally, in relation to child abduction, child maintenance and child protection.

There is, however, no room for complacency. Notwithstanding the best practice standards of NFM and the objectives of the nascent UK College of Family Mediators, mediation practice has a long way to go before high standards are provided throughout the UK to all who choose to use mediation. The consolidation of family mediation for the future requires reputable research, critical debate, constant monitoring and analysis of practice by the profession and, above all, consumer evaluation.

Notes

1   Emery (1994) has highlighted how, despite the clarity and consistency of these findings, they have nevertheless been misrepresented as indicating that mediation is 'bad' for women. The results, across a range of items, showed high average levels of satisfaction for mothers who mediated, mothers who litigated, and fathers who mediated. However, across those same items, fathers who litigated reported a notably lower level of satisfaction.

2   Judges have no formal power to order mediation, although the Family Law Act 1996 gives judges the power to require the parties to attend a meeting for the purpose of receiving an explanation about facilities available for mediation and of providing an opportunity for each party to agree to take advantage of those facilities (ss.13.1(a) and 13.1(b)).

3   For a useful presentation of the debate on fairness in mediation in the USA, with arguments in favour of 'lawyer participation' as representatives in mandatory mediation to ensure fairness, see McEwen et al., 1995.

4   In so far as NFM's national professional framework recognizes the necessity of all its components – personal aptitude for mediation, training, supervised practice *and* performance evaluation based on competence – it meets the major challenges that have been raised about the North American *Interim Guidelines for Selecting Mediators*, published by the National Institute for Dispute Resolution (NIDR, 1993) (see, for example, Kolb and Kolb, 1993; Baruch Bush, 1993; Menkel-Meadow, 1993b; McEwen, 1993).

5   NFM is a signatory to the European Charter on Training and has collaborated in the preparation of the English-language version.

Epilogue

... I think the beauty of it was they [the mediators] let you make your own decisions. They weren't forcing their opinions on you. They were just giving you another side of an argument perhaps. They were exposing the whole thing so you could look at it logically. *Mother with residence*

We were fair to each other ... there was a fairness and the [mediator] represented a certain kind of fairness, exuded a sort of reasonableness. *Non-resident father*

By the time we came back the second time, really the problems had been solved at that first meeting, simply by saying 'Well, OK, you know this is the agreement.' And from then on it was much smoother too – it sounds almost miraculous — but emotionally it became much less fraught. We'd solved the problem over access and a lot of other things at the same time ... *Non-resident father*

Her dad and I, oh, we have our ups and downs still, we have our little ... I feel sometimes I could say something, I think, no we've got to keep the peace for the children. I never ever pull her dad down and hope he hasn't ... [since] mediation we've been able to communicate more, which I think has helped Linda [daughter] tremendously. *Non-resident mother*

We came to an amicable agreement [at the mediation session] my wife and I, over it [access] ... We was [sic] trying to both be very sensible about it and not let our feelings get in the way of trying to do what was best for the children, which was the whole point, I think. I tried to make sure that the children weren't hurt if it could be helped. It's bad enough for them without having their mother there, without causing arguments in front of them. *Father with residence, subsequently reconciled*

Unless we went there we'd most likely end up in court. And ... they [the mediators] felt the sort of service that they were doing and the sort of service they were offering was keeping people out of court – keeping decisions between the partners and not involving all the legal machinery. And I would actually agree with that, as far as we're concerned anyway. And it seems so simple, what they were doing in fact. I mean, it's like anything. It was really simple. *Mother with residence*

173

Useful organizations

Family mediation organizations

National Family Mediation (NFM)   Tel: 0171 383 5993
9 Tavistock Place   Fax: 0171 383 5994
London
WC1H 9SN

An association of nearly seventy services throughout England, Wales and Northern Ireland, providing mediation to all regardless of ability to pay and with a main focus on children.

Family Mediators Association (FMA)   Tel/fax: 01273 747750
PO Box 20/28
Hove
East Sussex
BN3 3HU

A private sector association of individual mediators.

Family Mediation Scotland (FMS)   Tel: 0131 220 1610
127 Rose Street   Fax: 0131 220 6895
South Lane
Edinburgh
EH2 5BB

An association of services in Scotland providing mediation to all regardless of ability to pay.

UK College of Family Mediators
PO Box 3067
London
WC1H 9SP

Professional body for family mediators in England, Wales, Northern Ireland and Scotland.

Post Adoption Centre   Tel: 0171 284 0555
5 Torriano Mews
Torriano Avenue
London
NW5 2RZ

Offers mediation on contact and other matters in open adoptions.

Alone in London   Tel: 0171 278 4486
3rd Floor, 188 Kings Cross Road   Fax: 0171 837 7943
London
WC1X 9DE

Offers mediation for the homeless young to re-establish family contact.

Other mediation bodies

Mediation UK   Tel: 0117 924 1234
82a Gloucester Road
Bishopston
Bristol
BS7 8BN

An umbrella body for community mediation centres.

Centre for Dispute Resolution (CEDR)   Tel: 0171 430 1852
100 Fetter Lane
London
EC4A 1DD

Non-profitmaking providers of civil and commercial mediation.

Alternative Dispute Resolution (ADR Group)   Tel: 0117 925 2090
Equity & Law Building   Fax: 0117 929 4429
36–38 Baldwin Street
Bristol
BS1 1NR

Civil and commercial private sector mediation providers in association with
IDR Europe Ltd.

Jams Endispute Europe   Tel: 0171 533 2421
222 Grays Inn Road   Fax: 0171 533 2000
London
WC1X 8HB

Providers of ADR in the transnational corporate sphere.

Advisory, Conciliation and Arbitration Service (ACAS) Tel: 0171 210 3000
Brandon House   Fax: 0171 210 3708
180 Borough High Street
London
SE1 1LW

State funded but independent advisory, arbitration, conciliation and
mediation service for industrial disputes.

Environmental Resolve   Tel: 0171 824 8411
The Environmental Council   Fax: 0171 730 9941
21 Elizabeth Street
London
SW1W 9RP

Consensus-building and mediation service in the environmental field.

Mediators Institute Ireland (MII)   Tel: 00 353 12845277
c/o 13 Royal Terrace West   Fax: 00 353 12800259
Dun Laoghaire
Co. Dublin
Ireland

The umbrella body for mediators working in different fields in Ireland.

Counselling services

Relate   Tel: 01788 573241
Herbert Gray College   Fax: 01788 535007
Little Church Street
Rugby
CV21 3AP

Counselling provider in relation to marriage and relationship matters.

Marriage Care   Tel: 0171 371 1341
(Formerly Catholic Marriage Guidance)
Clitheroe House
1 Blythe Mews
Blythe Road
London
W14 0NW

For those with relationship difficulties.

Jewish Marriage Council   Tel: 0181 203 6314 (*Get* Advisory Service)
23 Ravenshurst Avenue   0181 203 6211 (Helpline)
London   0345 581999 (Crisis Helpline)
NW4 4EE

Provides a counselling service for the single, married, divorced, separated or widowed.

Asian Family Counselling Service   Tel: 0181 997 5749
74 The Avenue
London
WC13 8LB

Parent groups

Stepfamily   Tel: 0171 209 2460
Chapel House   0171 209 2464 (Helpline)
18 Hatton Place
London
EC1N 8RU

Provides advice, support and information to stepfamilies, including a confidential telephone counselling service, newsletters and local support groups.

National Council for One Parent Families   Tel: 0171 267 1361
255 Kentish Town Road
London
NW5 2LX

Works to help parents who are looking after children on their own, and produces a range of books, reports, pamphlets and leaflets on issues that a lone parent may have to deal with, including taxation, housing, social security, benefits, divorce, children and employment.

Gingerbread   Tel: 0171 336 8184 (Helpline)
16–17 Clerkenwell Close
London
EC1R 0AA

A support organization for lone parents and their families, with over 275 groups in England and Wales. Also publishes advice and information leaflets.

Family Rights Group   Tel: 0171 923 2628
The Print House
18 Ashwin Street
London
E8 3DL

Advises families with children in public care and child protection procedures or receiving family support services.

Families Need Fathers   Tel: 0171 613 5060
                               0181 886 0970 (Helpline)
Postal address:
BM Families
London
WC1N 3XX

Office:
134 Curtain Road
London
EC2A 3AR

Advice, support and representation to parents (particularly non-resident parents) following separation and divorce.

Reunite   Tel: 0171 404 8356
(National Council for Abducted Children)
PO Box 4
London
WC1X 3DX

A self-help network for parents whose children have been abducted.

Advice agencies

Citizens' Advice Bureaux (CAB)   Tel: See your local telephone directory

Over a hundred bureaux in the country offer advice and practical assistance.

Independent Representation For   Tel: 0151 342 7852
Children In Need (IRCHIN)
1 Downham Road South
Heswall
Wirral
Merseyside
L60 5RG

Legal advice

Children's Legal Centre   Tel: 01206 872466 (Office)
University of Essex   01206 873820 (Helpline)
Wivenhoe Park
Colchester
Essex
CO4 3SQ

Gives free and confidential information and advice by letter and phone on all aspects of law and policy affecting children and young people.

Solicitors Family Law Association (SFLA)   Tel: 01689 850227
PO Box 302
Keston
Kent
BR2 6EZ

Will supply a list of members in particular areas. Aims to provide a conciliatory approach to dealing with family disputes.

Rights of Women   Tel: 0171 251 6577
52–54 Featherstone Street
London
EC4Y 8RT

Provides free legal advice to women.

Domestic violence

Women's Aid Federation   Tel: 0117 963 3542 (National Helpline)
PO Box 391   0345 023 468 (England)
Bristol   0171 251 6537 (London)
BS99 7WS   0161 839 8574 (Manchester)

Provides support and advice for any woman worried by violence, whether physical or mental. Finds temporary refuge for women and their children.

Northern Ireland Women's Aid   Tel: 01232 249041
129 University Street
Belfast
BT7 1HP

Scottish Women's Aid   Tel: 0131 221 0401
13/19 North Bank Street
The Mound
Edinburgh
EH1 2LP

Welsh Women's Aid   Tel: 01222 390874
38–48 Cruwys Road
Cardiff
CF2 4NN

Southall Black Sisters   Tel: 0181 571 9595
52 Norwood Road
Southall
UB2 4DW

Provide counselling and advice for Asian and black women experiencing domestic violence. Their advice also covers immigration, housing and matrimonial issues.

Domestic Violence Intervention   Tel/fax: 0181 563 7983
Project (DVIP)
PO Box 2838
London
W6 9ZE

Bibliography

Abel, R.L. (1982), 'The contradictions of informal justice', in Abel, R.L. (ed.), *The Politics of Informal Justice*, Vol.1, New York: Academic Press.

Acland, A.F. (1995), *Resolving Disputes Without Going to Court*, London: Random Century Books.

Advisory, Conciliation and Arbitration Service (ACAS) (no date), *The ACAS Role in Conciliation, Arbitration and Mediation*, London: ACAS Reports and Publications.

Amundson, J.K. and Fong, L. (1993), 'She prefers her aesthetics. He prefers his pragmatics: A response to Roberts and Haynes', *Mediation Quarterly*, Vol.11, No.2.

Astor, H. (1994), 'Violence and family mediation policy', *Australian Journal of Family Law*, Vol.8, No.1.

Auerbach, J.S. (1983), *Justice Without Law?*, New York: Oxford University Press.

Bainham, A. (1990), 'The privatisation of the public interest in children', *Modern Law Review*, Vol.53, No.2, p.207.

Baruch Bush, R.A. (1993), 'Mixed messages in the interim guidelines', *Negotiation Journal*, Vol.9, No.4.

Benians, R.C. (1976), 'Marital breakdown and its consequences for children', address to the Medico-Legal Society, Royal Society of Medicine, London, 14 October.

Benians, R.C. (1980), 'Impact of marital breakdown on children', *Journal of Maternal and Child Health*, Parts I and II, October and November.

Benjamin, M. and Irving, H.H. (1995), 'Research in family mediation: review and implications', *Mediation Quarterly*, Vol.13, No.1.

Berger, B. and Berger, P.L. (1983), *The War Over the Family: Capturing the Middle Ground*, London: Hutchinson.

Bernard, J. (1971), 'No news but new ideas', in Bohannan, P. (ed.), *Divorce and After*, New York: Doubleday.

Bernard, J. (1973), *The Future of Marriage*, New York: Bantam.

Bohannan, P. (ed.) (1971), *Divorce and After*, New York: Doubleday.

Bohmer, C. and Ray, M.L. (1994), 'Effects of different disputes resolution methods on women and children after divorce', *Family Law Quarterly*, Vol.28, No.2.

Booth Committee (1985), *Report of the Committee on Matrimonial Causes*, London: HMSO.

Bordow, S. and Gibson, J. (1994), *Evaluation of the Family Court Mediation Service*, Research Report No.12, Melbourne: Family Court of Australia.

Bottomley, A. (1984), 'Resolving family disputes: A critical view', in Freeman, M.D.A. (ed.), *State, Law and the Family*, London: Tavistock.

Bottomley, A. (1985), 'What is happening to family law? A feminist critique of conciliation', in Brophy, J. and Smart, C. (eds), *Women in Law*, London: Routledge and Kegan Paul.

Bottomley, A. and Olley, S. (1983), 'Conciliation in the USA', *LAG Bulletin*, January.

Bromley, P. M. and Lowe, N.V. (1992), *Family Law*, 8th edn, London: Butterworths.

Brophy, J. and Smart, C. (eds) (1984), *Women in Law*, London: Routledge and Kegan Paul.

Brown, H. (1991), *Alternative Dispute Resolution: Report*, prepared by Henry Brown for the Courts and Legal Services Committee, London: Law Society, Legal Practice Directorate.

Burgoyne, J. (1984), *Breaking Even: Divorce, Your Children and You*, Harmondsworth: Penguin.

Campbell, D., Draper, R. and Huffington, C. (1989), *Second Thoughts on the Theory and Practice of the Milan Approach to Family Therapy*, London: D.C. Associates.

Campbell, D., Reder, P., Draper, R. and Pollard, D. (no date), *Working with the Milan Method: Twenty Questions*, Occasional Papers on Family Therapy No.1, London: Institute of Family Therapy.

Caplan, G. (1986), 'Preventing psychological problems in children of divorce: General practitioner's role', *British Medical Journal*, Vol.292, May.

Caplan, L. (1995), 'The milieu of dispute: Managing quarrels in E. Nepal', in Caplan, P. (ed.), *Understanding Disputes: The Politics of Argument*, Oxford: Berg.

Caplan, P. (1995), 'Anthropology and the study of disputes', in Caplan, P. (ed.), *Understanding Disputes: The Politics of Argument*, Oxford: Berg.

Christie, N. (1977), 'Conflicts as property', *Bristol Journal of Criminology*, Vol.17, No.1.

Clulow, C. (ed.) (1995), *Women, Men and Marriage*, London: Sheldon Press.

Cobb, S. and Rifkin, J. (1990), 'Rethinking neutrality: Implications for mediation practice', unpublished.

Cobb, S. and Rifkin, J. (1991), 'Practice and paradox: Deconstructing neutrality in mediation', *Law and Social Inquiry*, Vol.16, No.1.

Cockett, M. and Tripp, J. (1994), *The Exeter Family Study: Family Breakdown and its Impact on Children*, Exeter: University of Exeter Press.

Collinson, J. and Gardner, K. (1990), 'Conciliation and children', in Fisher, T. (ed.), *Family Conciliation Within the UK: Policy and Practice*, Bristol: Jordan and Sons.

Conciliation Project Unit (1989), *Report to the Lord Chancellor on the Costs and Effectiveness of Conciliation in England and Wales*, London: Lord Chancellor's Department.

Consultation Paper (1993), *Looking to the Future: Mediation and the Ground for Divorce*, Cm 2424, London: HMSO.

Coogler, O.J. (1978), *Structured Mediation in Divorce Settlement*, Lexington, MA: Lexington Books/D.C. Heath.

Cormick, G.W. (1977), 'The ethics of mediation: Some unexplored territory', unpublished paper presented to the Society of Professionals in Dispute Resolution Fifth Annual Meeting, Washington, DC, October.

Cormick, G.W. (1981), 'Environmental mediation in the US: Experience and future directions I', unpublished paper presented to the American Association for Advancement of Science Annual Meeting, Toronto, Canada.

Cormick, G.W. (1982), 'Intervention and self-determination in environmental disputes: A mediator's perspective', *Resolve*, Winter, pp.260–5.

Cretney, S.M. and Masson, J.M. (1990), *Principles of Family Law*, 5th edn, London: Sweet and Maxwell.

Cretney, S.M. and Masson, J.M. (1997), *Principles of Family Law*, 6th edn, London: Sweet and Maxwell.

Cross, R. (1985), *Cross on Evidence*, 6th edn, London: Butterworths.

Cross, R. and Wilkins, N. (1975), *An Outline of the Law of Evidence*, 4th edn, London: Butterworths.

Davis, A.M. (1984), 'Comment', in Vermont Law School Dispute Resolution Project, *A Study of Barriers to the Use of Alternative Methods of Dispute Resolution*, South Royalton, VT: VLSDRP.

Davis, A.M. and Gadlin, H. (1988), 'Mediators gain trust, the old fashioned way – We earn it!', *Negotiation Journal*, January.

Davis, G. (1981), 'Report of a research to monitor the work of the Bristol Courts Family Conciliation Service in its first year of operation', *30th Legal Aid Annual Reports, 1979–80*, London: HMSO.

Davis, G. (1983), 'Conciliation and the professions', *Family Law*, Vol.13, No.1.

Davis, G. (1985), 'The theft of conciliation', *Probation Journal*, Vol.32, No.1, March.

Davis, G. (1988), *Partisans and Mediators: The Resolution of Divorce Disputes*, Oxford: Oxford University Press.

Davis, G. and Bader, K. (1985), 'In-court mediation: The consumer view', Parts I and II, *Family Law*, Vol.15, No.3.

Davis, G., Cretney, S.M. and Collins, J. (1994), *Simple Quarrels*, Oxford: Clarendon Press.

Davis, G., MacLeod, A. and Murch, M. (1983), 'Divorce: Who supports the family?', *Family Law*, Vol.13, No.7, p.217.

Davis, G. and Roberts, M. (1988), *Access to Agreement: A Consumer Study of Mediation in Family Disputes*, Milton Keynes: Open University Press.

Davis, G. and Roberts, M. (1989a), 'Mediation in disputes over children: learning from experience', *Children and Society*, Vol.3, No.3, pp.275–9.

Davis, G. and Roberts, M. (1989b), 'Mediation and the battle of the sexes', *Family Law*, Vol.19, August, p.305.

Deech, R. (1995), 'Divorced from reality', *The Spectator*, 4 November.

Department of Health (1989), *Rights of the Subject: The Access to Personal Files (Social Services/Regulations No.206)*, London: HMSO.

Deutsch, M. (1973), *The Resolution of Conflict: Constructive and Destructive Processes*, New Haven, CT: Yale University Press.

Dingwall, R. (1986), 'Some observations on divorce mediation in Britain and the United States', *Mediation Quarterly*, No.11, pp.5–24.

Dingwall, R. (1988), 'Empowerment or enforcement? Some questions about power and control in divorce mediation', in Dingwall, R. and Eekelaar, J. (eds), *Divorce Mediation and the Legal Process*, Oxford: Oxford University Press.

Dingwall, R. and Eekelaar, J. (1986), 'Judgments of Solomon: Psychology and family law', in Richards, M. and Light, P. (eds), *Children of Social Worlds: Development in a Social Context*, Cambridge: Polity.

Dingwall, R. and Eekelaar, J. (eds) (1988), *Divorce Mediation and the Legal Process*, Oxford: Oxford University Press.

Dingwall, R. and Greatbatch, D. (1993), 'Who is in charge? Rhetoric and evidence in the study of mediation', *Journal of Social Welfare and Family Law*, pp.367–87.

Dingwall, R. and Greatbatch, D. (1995), 'Family mediation researchers and practitioners in the shadow of the Green Paper: A rejoinder to Marian Roberts', *Journal of Social Welfare and Family Law*, Vol.17, No.2.

Eckhoff, T. (1969), 'The mediator and the judge', in Aubert, V. (ed.), *Sociology of Law*, Harmondsworth: Penguin.

Eekelaar, J. (1978), *Family Law and Social Policy*, London: Weidenfeld and Nicolson.

Eekelaar, J. and Maclean, M. (1986), *Maintenance After Divorce*, Oxford: Oxford University Press.

Eekelaar, J., Clive, E., Clarke, K. and Raikes, S. (1977), *Custody After Divorce*, Oxford: Centre for Socio-Legal Studies and Social Science Research Council.

Effron, J. (1989), 'Alternatives to litigation: Factors in choosing', *Modern Law Review*, Vol.52, No.4.

Emery, R.E. (1994), *Renegotiating Family Relationships: Divorce, Child Custody and Mediation*, New York: Guilford Press.

Emery, R.E., Matthews, S. and Wyer, M. (1991), 'Child custody mediation and litigation: Further evidence on the differing views of mothers and fathers', *Journal of Consulting and Clinical Psychology*, Vol.59, No.3, pp.410–18.

Epstein, E.S. and Loos, V.E. (1989), 'Some irreverent thoughts on the limits of family therapy: Toward a language-based explanation of human systems', *Journal of Family Psychology*, Vol.2, No.4, pp.405–21.

Falk Moore, S. (1995), 'Imperfect communications', in Caplan, P. (ed.), *Understanding Disputes: The Politics of Argument*, Oxford: Berg.

Family Policy Studies Centre (1987), *One Parent Families*, fact sheet, London: FPSC.

Family Policy Studies Centre (1996), *The Family Law Bill*, Family Briefing Paper No.1, London: FPSC, March.

Felstiner, W.L.F. and Sarat, A. (1992), 'Enactments of power: Negotiating reality and responsibility in lawyer–client interactions', *Cornell Law Review*, Vol.77, No.6.

Felstiner, W.L.F. and Williams, L. (1985), 'Community mediation in Dorchester, Mass.', in Goldberg, S.B., Green, E.D. and Sander, F.E.A. (eds), *Dispute Resolution*, Boston and Toronto: Little, Brown.

Felstiner, W.L.F., Abel, R.L. and Sarat, A. (1980), 'The emergence and transformation of disputes: Naming, blaming, claiming...', *Law and Society Review*, Vol.15, No.3.

Finer Report (1974), *Report of the Committee on One Parent Families*, Cmnd 5629, London: HMSO.

Fisher, R. and Ury, W. (1981), *Getting to Yes*, Boston: Houghton-Mifflin.

Fisher, T. (1986), 'Family and industrial conciliation: Identifying common practice', unpublished.

Folberg, J. (1983), 'Divorce mediation – Promises and problems', paper prepared for midwinter meeting of American Bar Association Section on Family Law, St Thomas.

Folberg, J. (1984), 'Divorce mediation – The emerging American model', in Eekelaar, J.M. and Katz, S.N. (eds), *The Resolution of Family Conflict: Comparative Legal Perspectives*, Toronto: Butterworths.

Folberg J. and Milne, A. (eds) (1988), *Divorce Mediation: Theory and Practice*, New York: Guilford Press.

Folberg, J. and Taylor, A. (1984), *Mediation: A Comprehensive Guide to Resolving Conflicts Without Litigation*, San Francisco: Jossey-Bass.

Forster, J. (1982), *Divorce Conciliation: A Study of Services in England and Abroad with Implications for Scotland*, Edinburgh: Scottish Council for Single Parents.

Freeman, M.D.A. (1983), *The Rights and Wrongs of Children*, London: Frances Pinter.

Freeman, M.D.A. (1984), 'Questioning the delegalization movement in family law: Do we really want a Family Court?', in Eekelaar, J.M. and Katz, S.N. (eds), *The Resolution of Family Conflict: Comparative Legal Perspectives*, Toronto: Butterworths.

Fuller, L.L. (1971), 'Mediation – Its forms and functions', *Southern California Law Review*, Vol.44, pp.305–39.

Galanter, M. (1984), 'What else is new? The emergence of the judge as mediator in civil cases 1930–1980', working paper, Disputes Processing Research Programme, Madison: University of Wisconsin.

Gale, D. (1994), 'The impact of culture on the work of family mediators', *Family Mediation*, Vol.4, No.2.

Garwood, F. (1989), *Children in Conciliation: A Study of the Involvement of Children in Conciliation by the Lothian Family Conciliation Service*, Edinburgh: Scottish Association of Family Conciliation Services.

Gilligan, C. (1982), *In a Different Voice*, Cambridge, MA: Harvard University Press.

Glasser, C. (1994), 'Solving the litigation crisis', *The Litigator*, Vol.1, p.14.

Goldstein, J., Freud, A. and Solnit, A.J. (1973), *Beyond the Best Interests of the Child*, New York: Free Press.

Goldstein, S. (1986), *Cultural Issues in Mediation: A Literature Review*, PCR Working Paper, Honolulu: University of Hawaii.

Goolishian, H. and Anderson, H. (1992), 'Strategy and intervention versus non-intervention: A matter of theory?', *Journal of Marital and Family Therapy*, Vol.18, pp.5–15.

Grant, B. (1981), *Conciliation and Divorce: A Father's Letters to his Daughter*, Chichester and London: Barry Rose.

Green Paper (1993), *Looking to the Future: Mediation and the Ground for Divorce*, Cm 2424, London: HMSO.

Green Paper (1995), *Legal Aid: Targeting Need*, Cm 2854, London: HMSO.

Grillo, T. (1991), 'The mediation alternative: Process dangers for women', *Yale Law Journal*, Vol.100, No.6.

Gulliver, P.H. (1971), *Neighbours and Networks*, Berkeley: University of California Press.

Gulliver, P.H. (1977), 'On mediators', in Hamnett, I. (ed.), *Social Anthropology and Law*, London: Academic Press.

Gulliver, P.H. (1979), *Disputes and Negotiations: A Cross-cultural Perspective*, New York: Academic Press.

Haley, J. and Hoffman, L. (1967), *Techniques of Family Therapy*, New York: Basic Books.

Hamnett, I. (ed.) (1977), *Social Anthropology and Law*, London: Academic Press.

Haynes, J.M. (1980), 'Managing conflict: The role of the mediator', *Conciliation Courts Review*, Vol.18, No.2.

Haynes, J.M. (1981a), *Divorce Mediation: A Practical Guide for Therapists and Counsellors*, New York: Springer.

Haynes, J.M. (1981b), *Divorce Mediation*, New York: Springer.

Haynes, J.M. (1982), 'A conceptual model of the process of family mediation: Implications for training', *American Journal of Family Therapy*, Vol.10, No.4.

Haynes, J.M. (1983), 'The process of negotiations', *Mediation Quarterly*, No.1, pp.75–92.

Haynes, J.M. (1985), 'Matching readiness and willingness to the mediator's strategies', *Negotiation Journal*, January, pp.79–92.

Haynes, J.M. (1992), 'Mediation and therapy: An alternative view', *Mediation Quarterly*, Vol.10, No.1.

Haynes, J.M. (1993), *The Fundamentals of Family Mediation*, London: Old Bailey Press.

Hester, M. and Pearson, C. (1993), 'Domestic violence, mediation and child contact arrangements', *Family Mediation*, Vol.3, No.2.

Hester, M. and Radford, L. (1992), 'Domestic violence and access arrangements for children in Denmark and Britain', *Journal of Social Welfare and Family Law*, No.1, pp.57–70.

Hester, M. and Radford, L. (1996), *Domestic Violence and Child Contact Arrangements in England and Denmark*, Bristol: Policy Press.

Home Office (1994), *National Standards for Probation Service Family Court Welfare Work*.

Howard, J. and Shepherd, G. (1982), 'Conciliation – New beginnings?', *Probation Journal*, Vol.29, No.3.

Howard, J. and Shepherd, G. (1987), *Conciliation, Children and Divorce: A Family Systems Approach*, London: B.T. Batsford.

Ingleby, R. (1992), *Solicitors and Divorce*, Oxford: Clarendon Press.

Ingleby, R. (1994), 'The legal process in family disputes and the alternatives', in Eekelaar, J. and Maclean, M. (eds), *A Reader on Family Law*, Oxford: Oxford University Press.

James, A.L. (1988), ' "Civil work" in the Probation Service', in Dingwall, R. and Eekelaar, J. (eds), *Divorce Mediation and the Legal Process*, Oxford: Clarendon Press.

James, A.L. and Hay, W. (1993), *Court Welfare in Action: Practice and Theory*, Hemel Hempstead: Harvester Wheatsheaf.

James, A.L. and Wilson, K. (1984), 'Towards a natural history of access arrangements in broken marriages', in Eekelaar, J.M. and Katz, S.N. (eds), *The Resolution of Family Conflict*, Toronto: Butterworths.

James, A.L. and Wilson, K. (1986), *Couples, Conflict and Change: Social Work with Marital Relationships*, London: Tavistock.

Johnston, J. (1993), 'Gender, violent conflict and mediation', *Family Mediation*, Vol.3, No.2.

Joseph Rowntree Foundation (1996a), *The Impact of the Child Support Act on*

Lone Mothers and their Children, Social Policy Research 92, March, York: JRF.

Joseph Rowntree Foundation (1996b), *Lone Mothers and Work*, Social Policy Research 96, May, York: JRF.

Kaganas, F. and Piper, C. (1993), 'Towards a definition of abuse', *Family Mediation*, Vol.3, No.2.

Kelly, J.B. (1995), 'Power imbalances in divorce and interpersonal mediation assessment and intervention', *Mediation Quarterly*, Vol.13, No.2.

Kelly, J.B. and Duryee, M.A. (1992), 'Women's and men's views of mediation in voluntary and mandatory mediation settings', *Family and Conciliation Courts Review*, Vol.30, No.1.

King, M. (1987), 'Playing the symbols: Custody and the Law Commission', *Family Law*, Vol.17, p.186.

King, M. and Trowell, J. (1992), *Children's Welfare and the Law: The Limits of Legal Intervention*, London: Sage.

Kolb, D.M. (1985), *The Mediators*, Cambridge, MA: MIT Press.

Kolb, D.M. and Kolb, J.E. (1993), 'All the mediators in the garden', *Negotiation Journal*, Vol.9, No.4.

Kressel, K. (1985), *The Process of Divorce*, New York: Basic Books.

Kressel, K. and Pruitt, D.G. (1985), 'Themes in the mediation of social conflict', *Journal of Social Issues*, Vol.41, No.2.

Labour Party (1995), *Access to Justice: A Consultation Paper on Labour's Proposals for Improving the Justice System*, London: Labour Party.

Landsberger, H.A. (1956), 'Final report on a research project in mediation', *Labour Law Journal*, Vol.7, pp.501–10, August.

Lansdown, G. (1995), *Taking Part: Children's Participation in Decision-making*, London: Institute of Public Policy Research.

Larner, G. (1995), 'The real as illusion: Deconstructing power in family therapy', *Journal of Family Therapy*, Vol.17, pp.191–217.

Law Commission (1988), *Facing the Future – A Discussion Paper on the Ground for Divorce*, Law Com. No.170. London: HMSO.

Law Commission (1990), *Family Law: The Ground for Divorce*, Law Com. No.192, London: HMSO.

Law Society (1993), *Guide to the Professional Conduct of Solicitors*, London: Law Society.

Legal Aid Board (LAB) (1996), *Family Mediation Pilot Project Proposals: A Proposed Approach to the Piloting of Publicly Funded Family Mediation Services within the Framework of the Family Law Act 1996*, London: LAB.

Lemmon, J.A. (1985), *Family Mediation Practice*, Free Press.

Lord Chancellor (1995), House of Lords, *Hansard*, Vol.567, No.10, 30 November, p.704.

Lord Chancellor's Department (1995), *Notes to Accompany Draft New Rules*, Ancillary Relief Working Party, Rules Committee Working Party, London: Lord Chancellor's Department.

Lukes, S. (1973), *Individualism*, Oxford: Basil Blackwell.

Lukes, S. (1974), *Power: A Radical View*, Basingstoke: Macmillan Education.

Lund, M. (1984), 'Research on divorce and children', *Family Law*, Vol.14, pp.198–201.

Maccoby, E.A. and Mnookin, R.H. (1992), *Dividing the Child: Social and Legal Dilemmas of Custody*, Cambridge, MA: Harvard University Press.

Maclean, M. (1991), *Surviving Divorce: Women's Resource After Separation*, London: Macmillan.

Maclean, M. and Eekelaar, J. (1984), 'The economic consequences of divorce for families with children', in Eekelaar, J.M. and Katz, S.N. (eds), *The Resolution of Family Conflict*, Toronto: Butterworths.

Maidment, S. (1977), 'Access and family adoptions', *Modern Law Review*, Vol.40, No.3.

Maidment, S. (1984), *Child Custody and Divorce*, Beckenham: Croom Helm.

Mather, L. and Yngvesson, B. (1981), 'Language, audience and the transformation of disputes', *Law and Society Review*, Vol.15, pp.775–821.

Mather, L., Maiman, R.J. and McEwen, C.A. (1995), 'The passenger decides on the destination and I decide on the route: Are divorce lawyers expensive cab drivers?', *International Journal of Law and the Family*, Vol.9, pp.286–310.

Matthews, R. (ed.) (1988), *Informal Justice?*, London: Sage.

Mayer, B. (1989), 'Mediation in child protection cases: The impact of third party intervention on parental compliance attitudes', *Mediation Quarterly*, No.24.

Mayer, J.E. and Timms, N. (1970), *The Client Speaks: Working Class Impressions of Casework*, London: Routledge and Kegan Paul.

McCarthy, P. and Walker, J. (1996a), 'Involvement of lawyers in the mediation process', *Family Law*, Vol.26, pp.154–8.

McCarthy, P. and Walker, J. (1996b), *Evaluating the Longer Term Impact of Family Mediation: Report to the Joseph Rowntree Foundation*, Newcastle upon Tyne: Relate Centre of Family Studies, University of Newcastle upon Tyne.

McCrory, J.P. (1981), 'Environmental mediation – Another piece for the puzzle', *Vermont Law Review*, Vol.6, No.1.

McCrory, J.P. (1985), 'The mediation process', paper delivered at the Bromley Conference, organized by S.E. London Family Mediation Bureau, April.

McCrory, J.P. (1988), 'Confidentiality in mediation of matrimonial disputes', *Modern Law Review*, Vol.51, No.4.

McDermott, F.E. (1975), 'Against the persuasive definition of self-determination', in McDermott, F.E. (ed.), *Self-determination in Social Work*, London: Routledge and Kegan Paul.

McEwen, C.A. (1993), 'Competence and quality', *Negotiation Journal*, Vol.9, No.4.

McEwen, C.A., Rogers, N.H. and Maiman, R.J. (1995), 'Bring in the lawyers:

Challenging the dominant approaches to ensuring fairness in divorce mediation', *Minnesota Law Review*, Vol.79, No.6, June.

Menkel-Meadow, C. (1985), 'Portia in a different voice: Speculation on a women's lawyering process', *Berkeley Women's Law Journal*, Vol.1, No.39, p.50.

Menkel-Meadow, C. (1993a), 'Lawyer negotiations: Theories and realities – What we learn from mediation', *Modern Law Review* (special issue: *Dispute Resolution: Civil Justice and Its Alternatives*), Vol.56, No.3.

Menkel-Meadow, C. (1993b), 'Measuring both the art and science of mediation', *Negotiation Journal*, Vol.9, No.4.

Merry, S. and Rocheleau, A.M. (1985), *Mediation in Families: A Study of the Children's Hearing Project*, Cambridge, MA: Cambridge Family and Children's Service.

Meunch, G.A. (1960), 'A clinical psychologist's treatment of labour management conflicts', *Journal of Humanistic Psychology*, 3.

Meyer, A.S. (1960), 'Functions of the mediator in collective bargaining', *Industrial and Labor Relations Review*, 13.

Milne, A. and Folberg, J. (1988), 'The theory and practice of divorce mediation: An overview', in Folberg, J. and Milne, A. (eds), *Divorce Mediation – Theory and Practice*, New York: The Guilford Press.

Minuchin, S. (1974), *Families and Family Therapy*, London: Tavistock.

Mitchell, A. (1985), *Children in the Middle: Living Through Divorce*, London: Tavistock.

Mnookin, R.H. (1984), 'Divorce bargaining: The limits on private ordering' in Eekelaar, J.M. and Katz, S.N. (eds), *The Resolution of Family Conflict: Comparative Legal Perspectives*, Toronto: Butterworths.

Mnookin, R.H. and Kornhauser, L. (1979), 'Bargaining in the shadow of the law: The case of divorce', *Yale Law Journal*, Vol.88, p.950.

Murch, M. (1980), *Justice and Welfare in Divorce*, London: Sweet and Maxwell.

National Family Conciliation Council (NFCC) (1985a), *Annual Report*, Swindon: NFCC.

National Family Conciliation Council (NFCC) (1985b), 'NFCC Code of Practice', *Family Law*, Vol.15, pp.274–6.

National Family Conciliation Council (NFCC) (1986), *Guidelines on Confidentiality*, Swindon: NFCC, October.

National Family Mediation (NFM) and Family Mediators Association (FMA) (1993), *Joint Code of Practice*, London: NFM and FMA.

National Family Mediation (NFM) (1994a), *Giving Children a Voice in Mediation*, London: NFM.

National Family Mediation (NFM) (1994b), *Statistical Report, January to December 1993*, London: NFM.

National Family Mediation (NFM) (1996a), *Policy on Domestic Violence*, London: NFM.

National Family Mediation (NFM) (1996b), *Child Protection: Guidance and Procedure*, London: NFM.

National Institute for Dispute Resolution (NIDR) (1993), *Interim Guidelines for Selecting Mediators*, Washington, DC: NIDR.

Nichols, M.P. (1989), 'Some irreverent comments', *Journal of Family Psychology*, Vol.2, No.4, pp.422–5.

Office of Population Censuses and Surveys (1995), *1993 Marriage and Divorce Statistics*, London: HMSO.

Ogus, A., McCarthy, P. and Wray, S. (1989), 'Court-annexed mediation programmes in England and Wales', in Vermont Law School Dispute Resolution Project, *The Role of Mediation in Divorce Proceedings: A Comparative Perspective*, South Royalton, VT: VLSDRP.

Pagelow, M. (1990), 'Effects of domestic violence on children and their consequences for custody and visitation agreements', *Mediation Quarterly*, Vol.7, No.4.

Parker, D. and Parkinson, L. (1985), 'Solicitors and family conciliation services – A basis for professional cooperation', *Family Law*, Vol.15, p.270.

Parkinson, L. (1983), 'Conciliation: Pros and cons', *Family Law*, Vol.13, Parts I and II.

Parkinson, L. (1986), *Conciliation in Separation and Divorce: Finding Common Ground*, Beckenham: Croom Helm.

Parliamentary Working Party on Child Abduction (PWPCA) (1993), *Home and Away: Child Abduction in the Nineties*, London: Reunite.

Pearson, J. (1993), 'Ten myths about family law', *Family Law Quarterly*, Vol.27, No.2.

Pearson, J. and Thoennes, N. (1989), 'Divorce mediation: Reflections on a decade of research', in Kressel, K. et al., *Mediation Research: The Process and Effectiveness of Third Party Intervention*, San Francisco: Jossey-Bass.

Post Adoption Centre (1995), *Interim Report*, Mediation Service, London: Post Adoption Centre.

Poulter, S. (1982), 'Child custody – Recent developments', *Family Law*, Vol.12, No.1, p.5.

Pound, R. (1964), 'The place of the Family Court in the judicial system', *Crime and Delinquency*, Vol.10, No.4.

Power, M. (1994), *The Audit Explosion*, London: Demos.

Pruitt, D.G. (1981), *Negotiation Behaviour*, New York: Academic Press.

Pruitt, D.G. and Carnevale, P.J. (1993), *Negotiation in Social Conflict*, Buckingham: Open University Press.

Pugsley, J. and Wilkinson, M. (1984), 'The Court Welfare Officer's role: Taking it seriously?', *Probation Journal*, Vol.31, No.3.

Raiffa, H. (1982), *The Art and Science of Negotiation*, Cambridge, MA: Belknap, Harvard University Press.

Richards, M. (1981), 'Children and the divorce courts', *One Parent Times*, No.7.

Richards, M. (1994a), 'Divorcing children: Roles for parents and the state', reprinted in Eekelaar, J.M. and Maclean, M. (eds), *A Reader on Family Law*, Oxford: Oxford University Press.

Richards, M. (1994b), 'Giving a voice or addressing needs? A comment on the report "Giving Children a Voice in Mediation"', *Family Mediation*, Vol.4, No.3.

Rifkin, J. (1994), 'The practitioner's dilemma', in Folger, J.P. and Jones, T.S. (eds), *New Directions in Mediation*, London: Sage.

Riskin, L.L. (1984), 'Towards new standards for the neutral lawyer in mediation', *Arizona Law Review*, Vol.26.

Roberts, M. (1988), *Mediation in Family Disputes: A Guide to Practice*, 1st edn, Aldershot: Wildwood House.

Roberts, M. (1992a), 'Systems or selves? Some ethical issues in family mediation', *Mediation Quarterly*, Vol.10, No.1.

Roberts, M. (1992b), 'Who is in charge? Reflections on recent research on the role of the mediator', *Journal of Social Welfare and Family Law*, No.5, pp.372–87.

Roberts, M. (1994), 'Who is in charge? Effecting a productive exchange between researchers and practitioners in the field of family mediation', *Journal of Social Welfare and Family Law*, No.4, pp.439–54.

Roberts, M. (1996), 'Family mediation and the interests of women – Facts and fears', *Family Law*, Vol.26, April, pp.239–41.

Roberts, S. (1979), *Order and Dispute: An Introduction to Legal Anthropology*, Harmondsworth: Penguin.

Roberts, S. (1983a), 'Mediation in family disputes', *Modern Law Review*, Vol.46, No.5.

Roberts, S. (1983b), 'The study of dispute: Anthropological perspectives', in Bossy, J.A. (ed.), *Disputes and Settlements: Law and Human Relations in the West*, Cambridge: Cambridge University Press.

Roberts, S. (1986), 'Towards a minimal form of alternative intervention', *Mediation Quarterly*, Vol.11.

Roberts, S. (1992), 'Mediation in the lawyers' embrace', *Modern Law Review*, Vol.55, No.3.

Roberts, S. (1993a), 'Mediation and "The Family Justice System"', *Family Mediation*, Vol.3, No.1.

Roberts, S. (1993b), 'Alternative dispute resolution and civil justice: An unresolved relationship', *Modern Law Review*, Vol.56, No.3.

Roberts, S. (1995a), 'Litigation and settlement', in Zuckermann, A.A.S. and Cranston, R. (eds), *Reform of Civil Procedure: Essays on Access to Justice*, Oxford: Clarendon Press.

Roberts, S. (1995b), 'Decision making for life apart', *Modern Law Review*, Vol.58, No.5.

Robinson, M. (1991), *Family Transformation through Divorce and Remarriage: A Systemic Approach*, London: Routledge.

Robinson, M. and Parkinson, L. (1985), 'A family systems approach to conciliation in separation and divorce', *Journal of Family Therapy*, Vol.7, pp.357–77.

Rose, P. (1985), *Parallel Lives*, Harmondsworth: King Penguin.

Ross, J. (1986), 'The Scottish scene: A summary of recent developments in conciliation throughout Scotland', *Mediation Quarterly*, No.11.

Rubin, J.Z. and Brown, B.R. (1975), *The Social Psychology of Bargaining and Negotiation*, New York: Academic Press.

Rwezaura, B. (1984), 'Some aspects of mediation and conciliation in the settlement of matrimonial disputes in Tanzania', in Eekelaar, J.M. and Katz, S.N. (eds), *The Resolution of Family Conflict: Comparative Legal Perspectives*, Toronto: Butterworths.

Ryan, J.P. (1986), 'The lawyer as mediator: A new role for lawyers in the practice of nonadversarial divorce', *Canadian Family Law Quarterly*, Vol.1, No.1.

Sander, F.E.A. (1984), 'Towards a functional analysis of family process', in Eekelaar, J.M. and Katz, S.N. (eds), *The Resolution of Family Conflict: Comparative Legal Perspectives*, Toronto: Butterworths.

Saposnek, D.T. (1983), *Mediating Child Custody Disputes*, San Francisco: Jossey-Bass.

Sarat, A. (1994), 'Patrick Phear: Control, commitment, and minor miracles in family and divorce mediation', in Kolb, D.M. (ed.), *When Talk Works: Profiles of Mediators*, San Francisco: Jossey-Bass.

Sarat, A. and Felstiner, W.L.F. (1995), *Divorce Lawyers and Their Clients: Power and Meaning in the Legal Process*, Oxford: Oxford University Press.

Schelling, T.C. (1960), *The Strategy of Conflict*, Cambridge, MA: Harvard University Press.

Seidenberg, R. (1973), *Marriage Between Equals: Studies from Life and Literature*, New York: Doubleday Anchor Press.

Selvini Palazzoli, M., Boscolo, L., Cecchin, G. and Prata, G. (1978), *Paradox and Counterparadox: A New Model in the Therapy of the Family in Schizophrenic Transaction*, New York: Jason Aronson.

Shah-Kazemi, S. (1996) 'Family mediation and the dynamics of culture', *Family Mediation*, Vol.6, No.3.

Shapiro, M. (1981), 'Judging and mediating in Imperial China', in *Courts: A Comparative and Political Analysis*, Chicago: University of Chicago Press.

Shepherd, G. and Howard, J. (1985), 'Theft of conciliation? The thieves reply', *Probation Journal*, Vol.32, No.2.

Shepherd, G., Howard, J. and Tonkinson, J. (1984), 'Conciliation: Taking it seriously?', *Probation Journal*, Vol.31, No.1.

Silbey, S.S. and Merry, S.E. (1986), 'Mediator settlement strategies', *Law and Policy*, Vol.8, No.1.

Simpson, B. (1989), 'Giving children a voice in divorce: The role of family conciliation', *Children and Society*, Vol.3, No.3.

Simpson, B. (1994), 'Bringing the "unclear" family into focus: Divorce and remarriage in contemporary Britain', *Man*, (The Journal of the Royal Anthropological Institute), New Series, Vol.29, No.4.

Smart, C. (1982), 'Justice and divorce: The way forward?', *Family Law*, Vol.12, No.5, p.135.

Smart, C. (1984), *The Ties That Bind*, London: Routledge and Kegan Paul.

Society of Professionals in Dispute Resolution (SPIDR) Commission (1989), *Qualifying Neutrals: The Basic Principles*, Washington, DC: National Institute for Dispute Resolution.

Stevens, C.M. (1963), *Strategy and Collective Bargaining Negotiation*, New York: McGraw-Hill.

Stulberg, J. (1981), 'The theory and practice of mediation: A reply to Professor Susskind', reprinted in Goldberg, S.B., Green, E.D. and Sander, F.E.A. (eds), *Dispute Resolution*, Boston and Toronto: Little, Brown.

Sutton, A. (1981), 'Science in court', in King, M. (ed.), *Childhood, Welfare and Justice*, London: B.T. Batsford.

Thoennes, N.A. and Pearson, J. (1985), 'Predicting outcomes in divorce mediation: The influence of people and process', *Journal of Social Issues*, Vol.41, No.2, pp.115–26.

Timms, J. (1995), 'Safeguarding the interests of children in divorce', in *Representing Children*, Vol.8, No.4.

UK College of Family Mediators (1996), *The Policies and Standards Document*, London: UK College of Family Mediators.

Updike, J. (1965), *Of the Farm*, London: Penguin.

Utting, D. (1995), *Family and Parenthood: Supporting Families, Preventing Breakdown*, York: Joseph Rowntree Foundation.

Vermont Law School Dispute Resolution Project (1984), *A Study of Barriers to the Use of Alternative Methods of Dispute Resolution*, South Royalton VT: VLSDRP.

Walczak, Y. with Burns, S. (1984), *Divorce: The Child's Point of View*, London: Harper and Row.

Walker, J.A. (1986), 'Assessment in divorce conciliation: Issues and practice', *Mediation Quarterly*, No.11.

Walker, J.A. (1987), 'Divorce mediation – An overview from Great Britain', in Vermont Law School Dispute Resolution Project, *The Role of Mediation in Divorce Proceedings: A Comparative Perspective*, South Royalton, VT: VLSDRP.

Walker, J., McCarthy, P. and Timms, N. (1994), *Mediation: The Making and Remaking of Cooperative Relationship: An Evaluation of the Effectiveness of Comprehensive Mediation*, Newcastle-upon-Tyne: Relate Centre for Family Studies.

Walker, J. and Robinson, M. (1992), 'Conciliation and family therapy', in Fisher, T. (ed), *Family Conciliation Within the UK: Policy and Practice*, Bristol: Jordan and Sons Ltd.

Wallerstein, J. and Kelly, J.R. (1980), *Surviving the Break Up*, London: Grant McIntyre.

Walrond-Skinner, S. (1976), *Family Therapy: The Treatment of Natural Systems*, London: Routledge and Kegan Paul.

Walrond-Skinner, S. (1987), 'Introduction', in Walrond-Skinner, S. and Watson, D. (eds), *Ethical Issues of Family Therapy*, London: Routledge and Kegan Paul.

Watson, D. (1987), 'Family therapy, attachment theory and general systems theory: Separation may be no loss', in Walrond-Skinner, S. and Watson, D. (eds), *Ethical Issues of Family Therapy*, London: Routledge and Kegan Paul.

Wegelin, M.M. (1984), 'The policing of motherhood and fatherhood after divorce in the Netherlands', paper given at the Second International Interdisciplinary Congress on Women, University of Amsterdam.

Weingarten, H.R. (1986), 'Strategic planning for divorce mediation', *Social Work*, Vol.31, No.3.

White Paper (1995), *Looking to the Future: Mediation and the Ground for Divorce*, Cm 2799, London: HMSO.

White Paper (1996), *Striking the Balance: The Future of Legal Aid in England and Wales*, Cm 3303, London: HMSO.

Wilkinson, M. (1981), *Children and Divorce*, Oxford: Basil Blackwell.

Williams, J.C. (1989), 'Deconstructing gender', *Michigan Law*, Vol.87, p.797.

Wishik, H. (1984), 'Family disputes: Problems arising from the regulation of the legal practice', in Vermont Law School Dispute Resolution Project, *A Study of Barriers to the Use of Alternative Methods of Dispute Resolution*, South Royalton, VT: VLSDRP.

Woolf Report (1995) *Interim Report to the Lord Chancellor on the Civil Justice System in England and Wales: Access to Justice*, London: HMSO.

Index

دوسر ں آ یم
دوری ے اسلام دیکھنا نا یکھر
د ر و طا صا دین